MW01598400

Life Skills Instruction

GEORGIAN COLLEGE LIBRARY 2502

#49.90

Life Skills Instruction

A Practical Guide for Integrating Real-Life
Content into the Curriculum at the Elementary
and Secondary Levels for Students with
Special Needs or Who Are Placed at Risk

Second Edition

250201

Mary E. Cronin

James R. Patton

Susan J. Wood

Library Commons
Georgian College
825 Memorial Avenue
Box 2316
Orillia, ON L3V 6S2

pro·ed
An International Publisher

8700 Shoal Creek Boulevard
Austin, Texas 78757-6897
800/897-3202   Fax 800/397-7633
www.proedinc.com

HV888.5 .C757 2007
0134110332381
Cronin, Mary E.

Life skills instruction
: a practical guide for
c2007.

2007 11 07

© 1993, 2007 by PRO-ED, Inc.
8700 Shoal Creek Boulevard
Austin, Texas 78757-6897
800/897-3202   Fax 800/397-7633
www.proedinc.com

All rights reserved. No part of the material protected by this copyright notice may be reproduced or used in any form or by any means, electronic or mechanical, including photocopying, recording, or by any information storage and retrieval system, without prior written permission of the copyright owner.

Library of Congress Cataloging-in-Publication Data

Cronin, Mary E.
    Life skills instruction : a practical guide for integrating real-life content into the curriculum at the elementary and secondary levels for students with special needs or who are placed at risk / Mary E. Cronin, James R. Patton, Susan J. Wood.—2nd ed.
       p. cm.
    Includes bibliographical references.
    ISBN-13: 978-1-4164-0142-1
    ISBN-10: 1-4164-0142-3
    1. Children with disabilities—United States—Life skills guides.
2. Life skills—Study and teaching—United States.   I. Patton, James R. II. Wood, Susan J.   III. Title.
HV888.5.C76   2007
371.9—dc22

                    2006012492

Art Director: Jason Crosier
Designer: Sandy Salinas
This book is designed in Fairfield LH and Lucida Sans.

Printed in the United States of America

1 2 3 4 5 6 7 8 9 10   10 09 08 07 06

Dedication

To Stuart, Joy, Kimi, and Joseph

The authors of this book live in different parts of the United States yet all have strong connections to New Orleans, Louisiana, and the overall Gulf Coast region. We have worked closely with students, parents, teachers, administrators, and others throughout the area. Hence, we would like also to dedicate this book to those individuals and their exemplary demonstration of life skills in the wake of Hurricane Katrina and the subsequent flooding. The power and force of nature leads us all to reflect on the abilities and fortitude of the human spirit not only to persevere in the wake of extreme devastation but to continuously adapt and apply life skill knowledge and understanding to overcome and move forward.

CONTENTS

PREFACE—SECOND EDITION

As we experience adulthood, we come to recognize the complexities of dealing successfully with the demanding responsibilities that befall us. Much of the time, we deal with these demands in appropriate ways; too often, we fail miserably. However, we continue to learn all of the time, as the mastering of life skills challenges is a lifelong endeavor!

The importance of being prepared for various adult challenges was made clear to us when the first child of one of the authors was born. Such an event presents many opportunities to demonstrate competence in a range of areas. For example, within 4 days of the child's birth, it was necessary to administer a suppository to her. It is difficult to imagine that one would have to do this at all—much less to such a small creature. It became apparent that this skill as well as a whole set of other specific life skills for dealing with a newborn infant were never taught formally and, unfortunately, were never learned incidentally either. Suffice it to say that the cognitive study of life skills does not necessarily prepare one for performing any of them successfully.

We consider ourselves educated folks and know, for the most part, how to exercise good common sense. We often wonder how others, many of whom do not have the resources or supports that we have, cope with the demands of daily living. Having been special education teachers, we especially wonder how students who have an array of special needs along with limited support systems, and who have not shown a great ability in picking things up incidentally from their environments, deal with the challenges as well as the pleasures of life.

This guide was inspired by many different motivations. Personal reasons aside, our combined teaching experiences and reflections on the frustrations we felt in preparing students for what happened to them upon exiting school were significant factors. First-hand experience in developing and implementing a life skills curriculum in pilot classrooms in Louisiana's Jefferson and St. Bernard Parishes, discussions with many classroom teachers throughout the country and other countries, and the work of our colleagues, convinced us that teachers needed a practical guide to help them cover life skills topics.

We feel strongly that *all* students—whether or not they have special needs—must be presented opportunities to acquire requisite life skills. Because we have seen many students prosper from being taught these skills, we decided to develop a guide that would provide anyone interested in teaching life skills with (a) a general procedure for doing so; (b) specific suggestions for making the task more successful, including information on assessing life skills and ways to teach these skills; and (c) lists of resources for making the endeavor less time intensive.

The second edition of this book includes the following features:

- An appendix with completely updated instructional resources, organized by domains and subdomains
- Complete updating of all chapters

- An expanded chapter on assessment
- An entire chapter dedicated to family considerations
- More in-depth coverage of how to infuse real-life topics into existing content
- Suggestions on how to align real-life topics with standards
- More detailed coverage of community-based instruction

We hope you will find this material user friendly. We have tried to organize it in such a manner that users can find information and topics easily. We like to think that this book is worth adding to one's professional library under the "practical resource" category.

We do not claim that this is the definitive work on life skills—it is only a guide to developing locally referenced and culturally responsive programs. In our opinion, quality life skills programs are not found in books like this; professionals who are keenly aware of their students' interests, preferences, and needs develop them at the local level. We hope that we can be of some assistance to those who feel as strongly as we do that students need to be prepared for the "real world."

Over the years we have been fortunate to get to know professionals such as Gary Clark, Don Brolin, Robert Loyd, Gene Edgar, Pat Sitlington, Diane Bassett, and their colleagues who have had a major impact on our thinking and motivated us to continue the struggle. For years, these folks have been championing the need to teach functional skills and offer innovative curricular options—now in a standards-based culture. Their professional contributions (writings and curricular materials), as well as the work of others to whom we apologize for failing to mention by name, have directly or indirectly benefited many students with special needs. We only hope that we can do the same.

Personnel of school systems in Louisiana, Texas, and Iowa need to be recognized for their willingness to try something innovative and for their ongoing support of our efforts. In the early years, Barbara Turner, Mary Carlton, Barbara Speigal, Dan Webre, and Marla Seelig of Jefferson Parish; Janice Campagna, Michelle Crosby, Ronnie Palmisano, Deborah Lord, Kathy Wendling, Michele Burmaster, and Lena Blaise of St. Bernard Parish; and Nancy Hicks of the Special Education Department of the State of Louisiana were all significant players in addressing the life skills needs of many students. Donald Moeker and Nola Hamlin of Temple Texas Independent School District and Lynn Helmke of Dubuque Community School District (Iowa) were extremely helpful to us, as they implemented draft forms of our life skills model in various ways.

We would like to thank colleagues at the Rhode Island Department of Education and the Rhode Island Technical Assistance Project for their support and encouragement. Special thanks and appreciation is given to Kenneth Swanson, Thomas DiPaola, Jane Keane, Paula Achin, Sally Arsenault, Barbara Burgess, Emily Klein, David Sienko, and Ina Woolman.

We would be negligent if we did not recognize the Adult Performance Level (APL) Project of The University of Texas at Austin for the initial work in the 1970s that led to an adaptation of the APL model for students with mild disabilities. Ann LaQuey spearheaded the adaptation and modification project, and her work and that of her colleagues greatly influenced many of our early conceptualizations of life skills instruction.

We want to acknowledge some other people to whom we owe a great deal of thanks. We want to thank Cindy Bechtel for her many hours of assistance in making this guide a reality. We also want to thank Randy Scott, Joan Clum, Sonya Yates, Cindy Andress, Rebecca Fletcher, Gwenn Long, Celine Velosa, Mary Rita Ducote, Ryan Mire, Myra Timberlake, Fonali Zutshi, and Jen Staley for their involvement in various aspects of this project. We also want to give special thanks to Chris Anne Worsham, without whose help this second edition would not exist. We are grateful to the production folks at PRO-ED [first edition: Alan Grimes, Lori Kopp, and Adrienne Booth; second edition: Darinda LaFlash, Laura Balch, and Sandy Salinas] for their expertise in guiding this work through the hoops and for making the final product look so good. We want to thank Nancy Meredith, who diligently copyedited the manuscript.

Our friends Dr. Don Moecker, Dr. Sandy Meents, Janet Persyn, and Elaine Diaz from Northside Independent School District in San Antonio, Texas, assisted us in moving to the next level in the second edition of this book. We will be forever grateful to them.

We also want to express our gratitude to our spouses, Stuart Dixon, Joy Kataoka, and Joseph Phillips, for putting up with all of the meetings needed to pull this off. The initial work on this project necessitated much travel and time away from family; we are acutely aware of how invaluable support systems are. Susan J. Wood would like to thank her husband, Joseph Phillips, for his continuous love, support, wonderful sense of humor, and fabulous culinary skills. She is also very grateful to her mother Jean and brother John. All of us are also very grateful to all of our family members for their endless love and encouragement.

■ *M. E. C.*
■ *J. R. P.*
■ *S. J. W.*

BASIC CONCEPTS OF LIFE SKILLS INSTRUCTION

The schooling experience is designed to prepare individuals for adulthood, essentially to create a competent citizenry. In the early school years, students are taught basic skills that they will use in applied ways in subsequent school endeavors and ultimately in life. The mastery of the scholastic skills of reading, writing, speaking, and performing mathematical tasks is the *sine qua non* for a literate society. Their relevance in terms of career options and personal fulfillment is extremely important, resulting in these skills being the foundation upon which one's early schooling experience is based.

Many other skills and areas of knowledge are extremely valuable but are not fundamental academic skills or the type of content knowledge covered in the traditional general education curriculum. Many skills needed to get by in today's world do not involve knowledge of the periodic table or the use of various trigonometric functions; instead, they involve the ability to handle the events that occur on a day-to-day basis at home, at work, and in the community. Later in this chapter we identify 146 major demands of adulthood for which we all must develop a level of competence. For the most part, many students—those with special needs or placed at risk as well as students without barriers in their lives—leave school unprepared to deal effectively with the array of day-to-day challenges that most of us face as adults.

This guide provides recommended procedures and suggestions of useful resources for covering life skills topics in which students with or without special needs must display competence to successfully deal with adulthood. The conceptual framework of the guide derives from a realistic appraisal of likely subsequent environments for students and application of a top-down process to effect curricular coverage of important topics. In other words, the scope and sequence of what should be taught to students must be predicated on a thorough examination of the demands of adulthood that these students are likely to face. In a bottom-up approach to life skills instruction, curricular content is arbitrarily selected with the expectation that it will benefit students in their future living and work environments.

While we believe that this guide is appropriate for all students, regardless of any identifiable specific need, we use the term *students with special needs* throughout the guide. We are referring to individuals who are placed at risk either for not doing well in school-related tasks or for having difficulty dealing with the demands of daily living. This might include individuals who have disabilities, are low-achieving, require alternative learning conditions, or come from environments that create other barriers to their opportunities for success.

Terminology and Definition

As seen in the title of this book, we have decided to use the term *life skills* as our operative term to describe key skills needed for life. As Cronin (1996b) noted in her review of the use of life skills–related terminology, a range of terms has been used to convey the concept of life skills. Table 1.1 highlights some of the major terms that have been used and provides brief descriptions of the terms as used in the professional literature.

The important point that needs to be made is that a myriad of terms is used to describe the skills needed for living. At times, the meaning associated with the terms is interchangeable; however, at other times, differences in meaning are apparent. For instance, the term *applied academics* suggests skills that are clearly different from self-care skills of toileting and grooming that are associated with *daily living skills.*

As indicated, we have chosen to use *life skills* as the generic term in this book. Following is our definition of *life skills,* along with an explanation of key features of the definition.

LIFE SKILLS | Specific competencies (i.e., knowledge, skills, and their application) of local and cultural relevance needed to perform everyday activities across a variety of settings.

- *Knowledge acquisition, skill performance (or procedural knowledge), and the application of the knowledge and skills:* Three elements of competence are essential for successful functioning. *Knowledge acquisition* refers to the need to learn basic factual information that will be important for accomplishing a specific life skill (e.g., in taking a person's temperature, the knowledge component would involve identification of appropriate equipment and understanding of normal body temperature). *Skill performance* implies that one can execute a series of specific actions related to the life skill (e.g., appropriate use of a traditional or digital thermometer). Neither of these components alone is sufficient to demonstrate competency in most situations. One still needs to display the *appropriate application* of the knowledge and skills. This element relates closely to the concept of *everyday intelligence* (practical and social intelligence), as promoted by Greenspan, Switzky, and Granfield (1996; see also Table 1.1). In essence, this element implies that an individual can reason well enough to make key decisions on when to use the knowledge and skills (i.e., problem solving) and how to use the resulting information (e.g., to call the doctor if the temperature is above a certain level).

- *Local relevance:* This part of the definition imparts the idea that the specific life skills needed in one's life milieu are very much a function of the specific demands of their settings (i.e., context) and accordingly vary from one location to another. For instance, the major life demand of "using pubic transportation," although generic to a certain extent (schedules are posted, signage is present), requires specific life skills that vary from one city to another because the details of each system are different. As a result, the specific life skills that a person must possess must be validated at the local level.

Table 1.1
Select Terminology Related to Life Skills

Activities of daily living
- activities such as cleaning, shopping, cooking, taking public transportation, paying bills, maintaining a residence, caring appropriately for one's grooming and hygiene, using telephones and directories, and using a post office (Reschly, Myers, & Hartel, 2002, p. 175)
- term used in the field of occupational therapy to describe daily living occupations that consist of self-care activities (Hinojosa & Blount, 2000, p. 8)

Applied academics
- those skills and bodies of knowledge typically associated with core academic content areas that are applied to real-life contexts and situations (Patton & Trainor, 2002, pp. 56–57)

Career education
- a curriculum designed to teach individuals the skills and knowledge necessary to have a career (Smith & Luckasson, 1995, p. 434)

Daily living skills
- those skills that individuals use in their personal self-care and occasionally in their interactions with others (Reynolds & Fletcher-Janse, 1990, p. 296)

Everyday intelligence/competence
- a function of practical and social intelligence (Greenspan & Driscoll, 1997, p. 133)

Functional academics
- practical skills rather than academic learning (Hallahan & Kauffman, 1994)
- basic academic skills taught in the context of real-life activities. A curricular emphasis on academic skills that are meaningful and useful for daily living (Hunt & Marshall, 1994, p. 162)

Functional curriculum
- a way of delivering instructional content that focuses on the concepts and skills needed by all students with disabilities in the areas of personal–social, daily living, and occupational adjustment (Clark, 1994, p. 36)

Functional literacy
- ability to read (decode and comprehend) materials needed to perform everyday vocational tasks (Miller, 1973, p. 7)
- rudimentary social literacy—that is, those skills required by a prospective employer or institution that a student is deemed likely to encounter in adult life (Buchanan, 1975, p. 73)

Functional skills
- the skills that are useful in accomplishing some activity in important environments (Wolery & Haring, 1994, p. 279)
- those skills required to operate in normal daily life (Bigge, 1988, p. 2)

Independent living skills
- preparation to function independently as adults; must include more than just attaining a particular vocational or occupational skill (Meese, 1994, p. 385)

Life skills
- those skills that are relevant to independent, day-to-day living (Mastropieri & Scruggs, 1994, p. 320)
- those skills used to manage a home, cook, shop, and organize personal living environments (Smith & Luckasson, 1995, p. 421)

Survival skills
- everyday coping skills needed in adulthood (McClure, Cook, & Thompson, 1977, p. 26)
- skills necessary to function effectively in an environment (Bullock, 1992, p. 552)

Note. Adapted from "Life Skills Curricula for Students with Learning Disabilities: A Review of the Literature," by M. E. Cronin, in *Transition and Students with Learning Disabilities* (p. 88), edited by J. R. Patton & G. Blalock, 1996, Austin, TX: PRO-ED. Copyright 1996 by PRO-ED. Adapted with permission.

- *Cultural relevance:* Many life skills are tied to family and/or cultural values. As a result, sensitivity to these values and mores is imperative when developing curriculum and planning instruction. For instance, for the major life demand of "planning a nutritional diet," certain life skills like identifying meals that are healthy will be influenced by one's family and/or cultural situation. What is considered a nutritious breakfast for a family of Latino heritage in South Texas is likely to look very different from the breakfast offerings of a family living on the island of Kauai.

- *Performs:* This aspect of the definition refers to the intelligent and reasonable application of the skill in the appropriate setting(s).

- *Everyday activities:* Life skills are those skills that a person must use in whatever setting he or she functions. Most life skills are general and apply to most people; however, some life skills may be specific to one's geographic location (e.g., treating a jellyfish sting) or working situation (e.g., handling dangerous materials at the workplace).

- *Across a variety of settings:* It is important to understand that many life skills are not situation specific. For instance, the life skills associated with the major life demand of "getting along with others" cuts across a host of situations that a person may encounter (e.g., at work or on the softball field).

Rationale for Teaching Life Skills

Concern for what happens to students when formal schooling ends has increased over the years. The amount of attention given to the transition needs and the post-school outcomes of students has been evident in the professional literature and has been underscored in the Individuals with Disabilities Education Improvement Act (IDEA) of 2004. IDEA now defines the transition process from school to adult living as a "results-oriented" process.

The adult status of many individuals has been a driving force behind the need for transition services. In a related sense, the fact that special education had been mandated for all students with disabilities since 1975 promulgated the need to examine what impact this special education was ultimately having on students when they departed formal schooling. Follow-up studies conducted in various parts of the country in the 1980s and early 1990s pointed to a less than positive scenario of unemployment and underemployment, restricted living options, and few social interactions and activities (Hasazi, Gordon, & Roe, 1985; Mithaug, Horiuchi, & Fanning, 1985; Sitlington, Frank, & Carson, 1993).

The most comprehensive study conducted in the late 1980s and published in the early 1990s was the National Longitudinal Transition Study (M. Wagner, Blackorby, Cameto, Hebbeler, & Newman, 1993). The overall results of this study corroborated the findings of other studies. Currently, a second study—the National Longitudinal Transition Study–2 (NLTS–2)—is being conducted and the results are being released incrementally. Go to http://www.nlts2.org to see the results that have been made available.

A source of data on adult outcomes is the U.S. Census Bureau (http://www.census.gov/main/www/cen2000.html). The following statistics, based on the 2000 census, provide additional information in regard to the outcomes of persons with disability. The following figures are available online from the U.S. Census Bureau:

- number of people age 5 and over in the civilian, noninstitutionalized population with at least one disability: 49.7 million
- percentage of people with disabilities who report more than one disability: 46%
- percentage of working-age men with disabilities who are employed: 60% [10.4 million]
- percentage of working-age women with disabilities who are employed: 51% [8.2 million]
- median 1999 earnings of the 12 million year-round, full-time workers (in six disability areas): $28,803 [Median income of nondisabled workers: $33,970]
- percentage of individuals with disabilities ages 18 to 34 of all individuals enrolled in school: 12% [1.9 million individuals]

The published studies, as well as others conducted locally by school districts throughout the country, have had a significant impact on current thinking and professional discussion. However, for a number of reasons they provide only a partial picture of the lives and resultant problems facing many adults. First, most of the research, the NLTS–2 not included, provides a "snapshot" (i.e., at one point in time) of the lives (i.e., outcomes) of young adults. As a result, little information exists on the impact that their special needs have over time and on the quality of their lives. This is due to the simple fact that this type of research can be methodologically problematic, expensive, and effort intensive. Yet, the need to obtain a longitudinal sense of how these adults cope with the demands of adulthood remains an important and relatively untapped area for research activity (Gajar, 1992). Current discussion of conceptualizing the transition process as a results-oriented process will increase the need to document the "results" of transition efforts.

Second, most studies conducted to date examine a restricted range of outcome measures, typically focusing on employment and other general demographic dimensions (e.g., marital status). Omitted are measures of performance on day-to-day facets of adulthood such as managing money, getting along with one's spouse, or utilizing community services. Perhaps even more important, little information has been collected on various qualitative aspects of adulthood such as one's values, happiness, well-being, and goals. These omissions—similar to those made for the lack of longitudinal studies—result from the fact that gathering this type of information is difficult, expensive, and time consuming.

Curricular Considerations and Standards-Based Education

Upon inspection of school curricula, it is possible to draw some conclusions that tend to represent the nature of the content that is being taught in schools today. This section highlights the curricular features of elementary and secondary curriculum and offers some salient arguments for curricular innovation.

Grade-Level Distinctions

In general, the focus of the curriculum for all students at the *elementary level* is the development and mastery of basic skills. As students progress through the upper elementary grades, emphasis is put on using these skills in more applied ways. In essence, these skills are being refined so that students can handle the growing amount of content knowledge being introduced and deal effectively with increasingly more complex demands associated with secondary-level coursework. For some students who are in special education, more time is likely to be devoted to remediation of the basic skills that have not been acquired.

Although providing career education at this level is warranted and advocated strongly (Clark, Carlson, Fisher, Cook, & D'Alonzo, 1991), in reality, little instruction in this area occurs (Moore, Agran, & McSweyn, 1990). Covering career education with elementary-age students provides a valuable linkage with transitional activities that must occur at the secondary levels. Such instruction can cover topics that are precursors to life skills that can be taught at a later time. Clark and colleagues offer the following principles:

- Education for career development and transition is for individuals with disabilities at all ages.
- Career development is a process begun at birth that continues throughout life.
- Early career development is essential for making satisfactory choices later.
- Significant gaps or periods of neglect in any area of basic human development affects career development and the transition from one stage of life to another.
- Career development is responsive to intervention and programming when the programming involves direct instruction for individual needs.

Teaching career education obviously has direct relevance to the development of life skills. As Chapter 3 discusses, a comprehensive conceptualization of life skills instruction extends the preparation for adulthood down to the elementary level.

Curricular focus at the *secondary level,* particularly for students with special needs, can be more clearly specified. However, clarity of focus does not correlate highly with sensitivity to individual student needs. Much of the literature suggests three general orientations, each of which contains more specific curricular models: support within the general education classroom, academic and social skill development or remediation, and specialized functional programming. Due to confusion associated with these terms and in consort with what is occurring in schools, Polloway, Patton, and Serna (2005) presented an overview of program options for students with special needs at the secondary level (see Table 1.2).

Table 1.2
Program Options at the Secondary Level

Program option	Content
General education curriculum without supports or accommodations	
General education curriculum with supports and accommodations	Cooperative teaching Tutorial assistance Paraeducators Natural supports Accommodations to content, materials, and instruction Learning strategies Study skills
Special education curriculum with a focus on academic and social skill development and remediation	Basic skills Social skills
Special curriculum with focus on adult outcomes	Life skills Vocational training Apprenticeship

Relationship of Life Skills to Standards-Based Education

The emphasis on standards and the testing of whether students are meeting these standards has become a major theme in general education in recent years. Students with special needs have been affected by this standards-based movement because of the heavy emphasis in the reauthorization of IDEA in 1997 given to making sure that these students have access to the general education curriculum.

At first glance, it seems that life skills instruction and content and performance standards are not a good match. However, real-life topics can fit well within a standards-based world. In a review of standards taken from a variety of states, Patton and Trainor (2002) concluded that most standards do relate to real-life topics, and life skills coverage could be worked into lessons that meet state standards. Some examples of standards that have "direct," "indirect," or even "distant" functional relevance are provided in Table 1.3. The critical dimension for ensuring that functional content is addressed, however, is that teachers must make the effort to relate course content that has to be covered (i.e., explicit curriculum) to life skills–related topics. Chapter 3 of this book presents some practical ways of integrating real-life topics into the curriculum.

Table 1.3
Examples of Standards Related to Functional Outcomes

Degree of relationship	Source of standard	Standard/student expectations	Performance outcomes
Direct	Texas: Mathematics / Middle School / Grade 6	Underlying processes and mathematical tools: The student applies Grade 6 mathematics to solve problems connected to everyday experiences, disciplines, and activities in and outside of school.	Determine amount of paint needed to paint a room, as a part of a house improvement project.
	North Carolina: Technology / English / Grades 9–12	Use electronic resources for research.	Use Internet browser to locate several types of sources on a topic of choice.
	New Jersey: Mathematics Core Curriculum Standards / Grades 9–12	Use measurement appropriately in other subject areas and career-based contexts.	Maintain a portfolio of occupations that require extensive use of measurement skills; include interviews with professionals.
	New Jersey: Science Core Curriculum Standards / Grades 9–12	Use computer spreadsheet, graphing, and database programs to assist in quantitative analysis.	Collect and organize data from school sports teams in terms of wins and losses. Analyze according to sport, team membership, and location of event.
	North Carolina: Social Studies / World Cultures / Grade 10	Engage in cross-cultural comparisons of such phenomena as religion, education, and language.	Create a "World Atlas" of countries and cultures represented by the family histories of class members. Interview members of each group and include a visitor's guide of "Do's and Don'ts."
Indirect	Texas: English, Language Arts, Reading / High School / English I	Reading / word identification / vocabulary development: The student uses a variety of strategies to read unfamiliar words and to build vocabulary.	Introduce occupational vocabulary that is essential in the job acquisition process.
	Texas: Science / Grade 8	Science concepts: The student knows that substances have chemical and physical properties.	Change a solid to a liquid during a cooking activity.
	North Carolina: Algebra / High School	Use matrices to display and interpret data.	Create and maintain a matrix of grades received on homework assignments, tests, and projects.

(continues)

Table 1.3 (*Continued*)

Degree of relationship	Source of standard	Standard/student expectations	Performance outcomes
	Hawaii: Language Arts / Grade Cluster 9–12	Use reading strategies appropriate to text and purpose (e.g., annotating, quoting, alluding to text, rethinking initial responses).	Write a persuasive essay or engage in formal debate regarding the importance of the First Amendment and the need to protect citizens from acts of terrorism.
Distant	Texas: Social Studies / High School / United States History Studies Since Reconstruction	Government: The student understands the changing relationships among the three branches of the federal government.	Find out which representatives from home area hold offices in the three branches of government.
	North Carolina: English I / Grade 12	The learner will deepen understanding of British literature through exploration and extended engagement.	Identify themes commonly found in Shakespeare's dramas in contemporary film.
	Hawaii: Science / Grade Cluster 9–12	Describe and explain properties of elements and their relationship in the periodic table.	Analyze the elements contained in common substances such as salt and water.
	New Jersey: Language Arts Core Curriculum Standards Grades 9–12	Understand the range of literary forms and content that elicit aesthetic response.	Keep a journal of movies, books, and songs that illustrate literary forms; provide a personal response or critique for each entry.
	North Carolina: Geometry / High School	Identify, name, and draw sets of point, such as line, ray, segment, and plane.	Create a "Geometry Dictionary" and post on line as a reference tool for fellow students.

Note. From "Using Applied Academics to Enhance Curricular Reform in Secondary Education," by J. R. Patton and A. Trainor, in *Aligning Transition and Standards-Based Education* (pp. 55–75), by C. Kochhar-Bryant and D. S. Bassett, 2002, Arlington, VA: Council for Exceptional Children. Copyright 2002 by the Council for Exceptional Children. Reprinted with permission.

Need for Curricular Innovation

The appropriateness of the various program options described in Table 1.3 depends on a number of variables that must be considered (see Polloway, Patton, Smith, & Roderique, 1991). Nevertheless, we propose that all students, whether or not they have been identified as having special needs, should be provided instruction on dealing with the day-to-day demands of adulthood (i.e., life skills). For students with special needs, it is imperative that their current and future needs be considered in designing programs.

With the movement to provide the educational programs of as many students with special needs as possible in general education settings, creative ways to deliver life skills instruction are needed. Doing so poses some special challenges, as the importance of covering real-life topics must be recognized, understood, and acted on by general education teachers, as well as by special education personnel. Interestingly, providing this type of instruction within the general education setting offers great benefits to teachers (i.e., makes the content more meaningful) and to *all* students, as there are many students in these settings who are at risk for unsuccessfully dealing with adulthood.

Relationship of Life Skills to the IEP and the Transition Planning Process

Life skills instruction is often closely woven with the Individualized Education Program (IEP) and definitely relates to the whole notion of transition planning. Figure 1.1 depicts an overview of addressing the real-life needs of students. As can be seen at the far left of the figure, proactive transition education provides the basis for curricular attention throughout the schooling process. *Transition education* is defined as all education-related activities, particularly in the areas of curriculum and instruction, that correspond with and prepare students for the demands of adulthood. The very topics that should be addressed throughout the school process become the focus of attention when transition planning occurs. Starting with the assessment of transition needs and leading to the generation of instructional (aca-

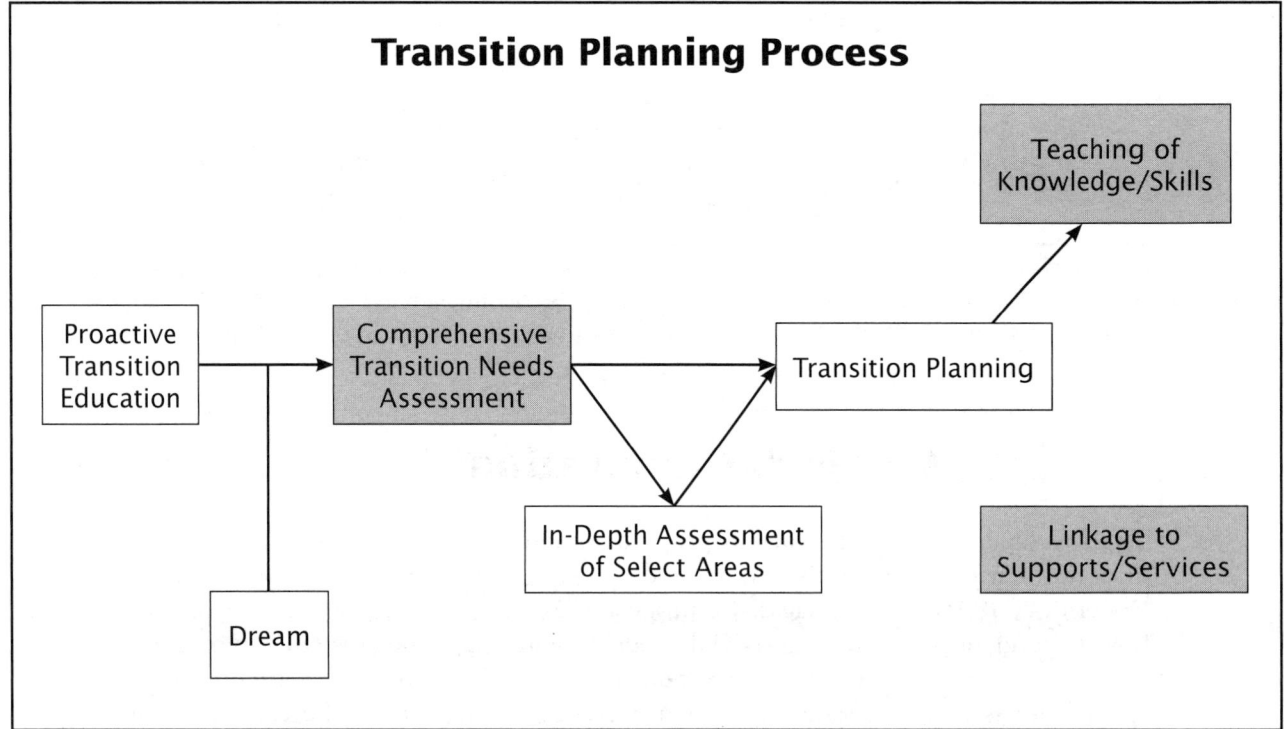

FIGURE 1.1. Transition planning process. *Note.* Adapted from *Transition Planning Inventory* (p. 26), by G. M. Clark and J. R. Patton, 1997, Austin, TX: PRO-ED. Copyright 1997 by PRO-ED. Adapted with permission.

demic, behavioral, social) goals as well as linkage goals (i.e., connecting the student and his or her family with supports and services that will be needed when the student is no longer in school). The "Dream" box refers to the notion that a student should have opportunities to think about and explore various adult outcome topics such as careers or where he or she wants to live. Each student should be encouraged to "dream" and then to see if those dreams can happen.

Individualized Education Program

The IEP serves as the "management tool that is used to ensure that each student is provided special education and related services appropriate to address identified learning needs" (Strickland & Turnbull, 1990, p. 13). Many life skills can be included as academic or behavioral goals or objectives on students' IEPs. For instance, an annual goal in math focusing on measurement can easily be related to a life skill need. The inclusion of life skills goals and objectives in IEPs helps ensure that students are taught these important topics. Unfortunately, far too often the IEPs for students who are in general education settings contain very few goals and corresponding objectives related to career development and life skills.

Transition Planning

The Individuals with Disabilities Education Act (IDEA) of 2004 requires that the IEP include a "statement of needed transition services" by age 16. The law defines transition services [§ 300.29(a)] as

> a coordinated set of activities for a student with a disability that—
>
> (1) is designed within a results-oriented process, that promotes movement from school to post-school activities including postsecondary education, vocational training, integrated employment (including supported employment), continuing and adult education, adult services, independent living or community participation;
>
> (2) is based on the individual student's needs, taking into account the student's preferences and interests; and
>
> (3) includes—(i) instruction; (ii) related services; (iii) community experiences; (iv) the development of employment and other post-school adult living objectives; and (v) if appropriate, acquisition of daily living skills and functional vocational evaluation.

Although this requirement is extremely important, it is possible that many important areas of adult functioning may still be overlooked. For this reason, comprehensive transition plans are essential. Clearly, the elements described above relate very closely to the main substantive features of life skills instruction.

Comprehensive transition planning should address the major life skills areas for which students need to be prepared prior to leaving school. Frequently, this involves the direct instruction in specific skills that students will need in their subsequent environments as well as the establishment of linkages with post-school services, as indicated in Figure 1.1. As emphasized earlier in this chapter, the actual goals and objectives to be included as part of a student's transition plan will be determined after assessing needs. Once transition needs have been established, goals can be developed. One possible way to do this is to consult the list of major life demands presented in the next section of this chapter (see Table 1.5). We feel that these demands can usually serve as goal statements, and the short-term objectives can be generated from a careful analysis of the specific life skills associated with each major life demand.

Implications

Based on the preceding discussion, we can conclude that

- many individuals with special needs are not being prepared for the multidimensional demands of adulthood;
- a large percentage of students who have special needs are not finding the school experience to be valuable and are dropping out;
- the educational programs of many students are not meeting their current and future needs;
- opportunities for continuing-education options (i.e., recruitment, ongoing support, specialized training, and follow-up services) for adults with special needs are needed; and
- a pressing need exists to reexamine school curriculum at both elementary and secondary levels and to develop innovative ways to address the functional needs of students within the context of the general education curriculum and standards-based education.

The Nature of Life Skills Instruction

All students need to acquire those life skills necessary for successfully dealing with everyday living (i.e., productive adulthood). Unfortunately, few functional life skills are actually addressed in the traditional curricula found in most schools, and those that are covered typically are taught in classrooms rather than in applied community settings (Halpern, Benz, & Lindstrom, 1992). Although many individuals do learn specific life skills on their own in informal ways or from family and friends, many others do not. The stakes are too high to leave this area of learning to chance.

In light of the realities highlighted in the previous section, efforts are warranted to find ways to teach important life skills to students at risk for failing or dropping out of school as well as to students who will stay in school but need the competencies to deal with their future worlds. This section discusses the nature of life skills instruction that can contribute to addressing the needs of students.

Although it is easy to make a case for teaching life skills, we note that they are not taught often enough. This guide helps professionals address that very concern. The first part of this section presents a brief look at previous initiatives supporting the development of programs that prepare students for adulthood. The next part provides a framework on which life skills instruction can be based.

Historical Perspective on Teaching Functional Skills

Interest in teaching functional skills is not a new phenomenon, as many dedicated people have argued for such instruction for a long time. As Kolstoe (1976) pointed out, the goals of the National Education Association as specified in a 1938 document suggest a strong interest in functional outcomes. The goals focus on economic efficiency, worthy home membership, worthy citizenship, and self-realization.

Many programs of the 1950s and 1960s for students with mental retardation were designed with adult outcomes in mind. Programs heavily emphasized functional skills, particularly related to vocational training and employment. Typically, school districts developed curriculum guides with functional themes that were used extensively with students in special education.

During the 1980s, the dramatic realization that disappointing adult outcomes existed for many former students gave rise to more formal study of the transition from school to adult life. This realization was particularly painful, considering that many of these former students had received extensive special education services during their school careers. Even though the transition movement has focused more on linking students to adult services and enhancing the mechanisms that facilitate these linkages, some attention was given to the curricular implications of this process (Patton, 1986).

In a more contemporary context, as discussed previously, some confusion exists today concerning how to address the need for life skills preparation in light of the demands of the general education curriculum and standards-based education movement, whereby many students are receiving academically oriented educational programs within regular education classes. As suggested, this should not be a problem, but tactics for covering life skills in such settings are not obvious. Chapter 3 shows some examples of how life skills instruction can be provided to students in inclusive settings.

Given the realities of current restructuring in special education, innovative curricular options emphasizing the skills needed to be successful adults should be available to students. The future challenge is to balance the need for students to be in integrated, academically oriented settings with the need to provide instruction on life skills topics that they will most certainly need in their foreseeable futures.

Top-Down Approach to Curriculum Development

The model used in this guide for identifying specific life skills relies on a top-down approach to content or curriculum development. This model, depicted in Figure 1.2, emphasizes the need to consider likely subsequent environments of students and basing curriculum development on working "down" from consideration of anticipated outcomes. The various major life demands required for success in different postschool environments can be organized into general domains. Ultimately, this process leads to the identification of specific life skills that can be taught to students.

The top-down process to curricular development is a powerful approach to determining the content being taught in today's schools. The top-down process, also

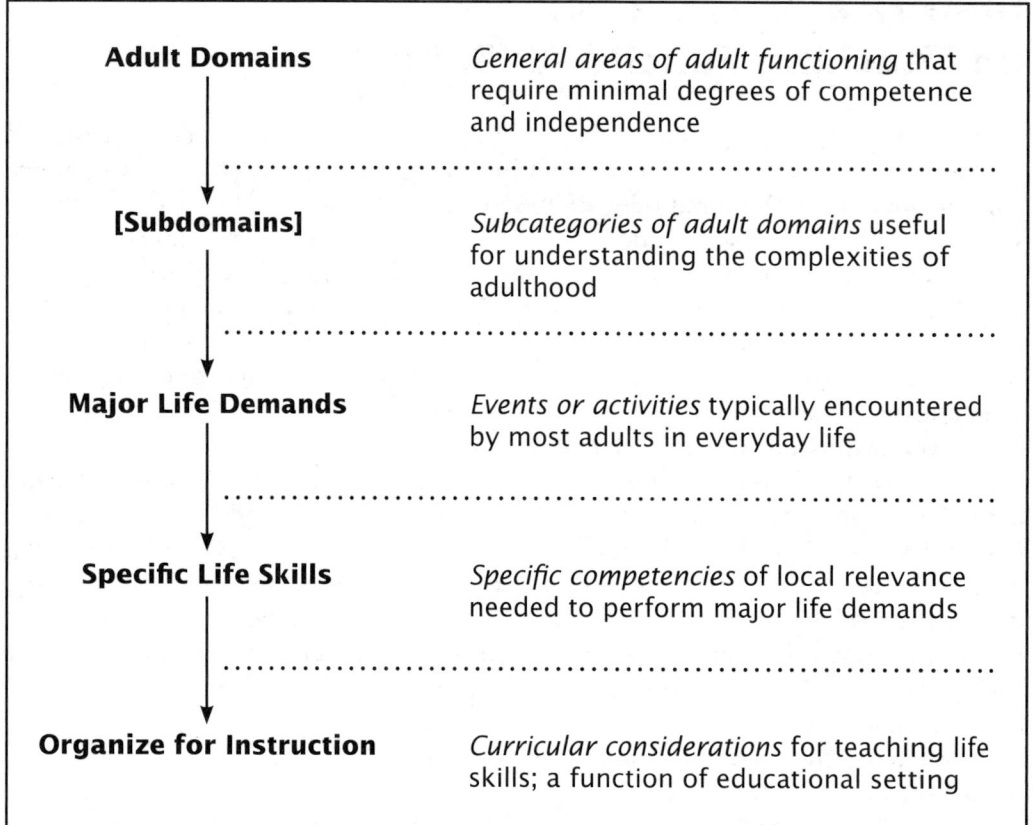

Adult Domains	*General areas of adult functioning* that require minimal degrees of competence and independence
[Subdomains]	*Subcategories of adult domains* useful for understanding the complexities of adulthood
Major Life Demands	*Events or activities* typically encountered by most adults in everyday life
Specific Life Skills	*Specific competencies* of local relevance needed to perform major life demands
Organize for Instruction	*Curricular considerations* for teaching life skills; a function of educational setting

FIGURE 1.2. Top-down approach to curriculum development.

referred to as the outcome-based approach (Champlin, 1991; Friedland, 1992; King & Evans, 1991; Spady, 1986; Spady & Marshall, 1991), identifies the objectives or competencies based on a student's desired outcomes. The top-down process is used extensively in many fields, including vocational technical programs, NASA training for space flight, and professional degree programs (e.g., doctors, lawyers, teachers, nurses).

The question asked when developing a top-down curriculum in any area is, "What are the competencies these individuals need to know in order to competently perform the adult tasks?" The outcomes of each job are examined first to provide the foundation for building the curriculum. Outcomes are examined to determine the competencies needed to perform the tasks of the job. Those identified competencies or objectives are then organized into a curriculum or program of study. If any of the aforementioned fields and occupations did not develop curriculum from the top down, many of our professionals would be haphazardly trained. The need to use a top-down approach for any adult outcome–oriented curriculum is imperative, even more so in preparing all students with special needs for the basic everyday demands of adulthood.

The generation of life skills developed from the top-down process needs to begin at the local level. Local needs should drive the focus of the competencies of the curriculum. There are "generic" or general competencies or life demands that all adults face, such as transportation, shopping, banking, and driving, which should be addressed in every life skills curriculum. The local generation of life skills competencies in the curriculum will reflect the differences in many locales—urban, rural, small community, big city, regional, and sometimes even within states. The differences reflected in locally generated life skills topics include vocabulary (e.g., use of the term *neutral ground* for the median on a street or boulevard), transportation (subway, ferry, bus, streetcar), culture (type of music, such as country, pop, soul, jazz), shopping practices (bagging vs. not bagging your own groceries), and driving ordinances (e.g., right turn on red, U-turns). The identification of specific life skills by local school personnel when developing a life skills curriculum must reflect the competencies needed to be successful in that particular community.

Major Life Demands

This section provides an organizational framework for the various day-to-day demands of living. This framework is the centerpiece of planning life skills coverage. The focal component is the set of "major life demands"—events or activities that most individuals will have to face in everyday life.

Domains of Adult Life. Adult domains, as defined in Figure 1.2, are categories depicting very general areas of adult functioning that require minimal degrees of competence and independence. A number of sources exist where one can find formats for organizing skills deemed necessary for adult living. Table 1.4 summarizes a select list of such sources. Although all use different descriptors to refer to functional areas, they share common themes. All of these models have merit and are worth further examination.

The conceptualization of adult domains used in this guide was developed out of the Hawaii Transition Project (1987). One of the early efforts of the project focused on the development of a frame of reference for looking at the transitional needs of students. Initially, nine areas of transition were identified; however, over time these nine areas were reduced to six, as indicated in Table 1.4. These six domains fell under one of two overriding areas: life domains and support domains. Patton and Browder (1988) explained the distinction between the two areas:

> The designation of life domains is simple—the domains represent how most individuals explicitly or implicitly organize their lives. The selection of support domains is likewise simple—the need to provide financially for one's food, shelter, clothing, and physical and emotional health must be met before individuals can take on adult responsibilities and activities beyond themselves. (p. 296)

The life and support domains used in the Hawaii Transition Project were modified over time into a new set of general adult domains. One source that contributed to our thinking was Knowles's (1990) categorization of the adult problems of young adults. Figure 1.3 shows the domains used in this guide. We feel that all of the activities we do as adults can fall into one of the six domains, which are closely related to the way we organize our lives and the transition planning domains typically used in schools.

The major domains of adult functioning identified in Figure 1.3 provide the format or structure from which to identify workable classifications called subdomains to generate the major life demands. The subdomains organize the adult domains

Table 1.4
Select Conceptualizations of Adulthood Dimensions

Source	Major functional areas
Life Centered Career Education (LCCE) (Brolin, 1993)	22 competencies divided across three domains: • Daily Living • Personal–Social • Occupational Guidance and Preparation
Community-Referenced Curriculum (M. A. Smith & Schloss, 1988)	Major areas: • Work • Leisure and Play • Consumer • Education and Rehabilitation • Transportation
Community Living Skills Taxonomy (Dever, 1988)	Major areas: • Personal Maintenance and Development • Homemaking and Community Life • Vocational • Leisure • Travel
Life Problems of U.S. Adults (Knowles, 1990)	Major areas: • Vocation and Career • Home and Family Living • Enjoyment of Leisure • Community Living • Health • Personal Development
Hawaii Transition Project (1987)	Four life domains: • Vocation/Education • Home and Family • Recreation/Leisure • Community/Citizenship (Guardianship/Advocacy) Two support domains: • Financial Support • Emotional/Physical Health

into workable categories for long-range goal planning. The domains and their key subdomains are listed below.

Employment/Education
• General Job Skills
• General Education/Training Considerations

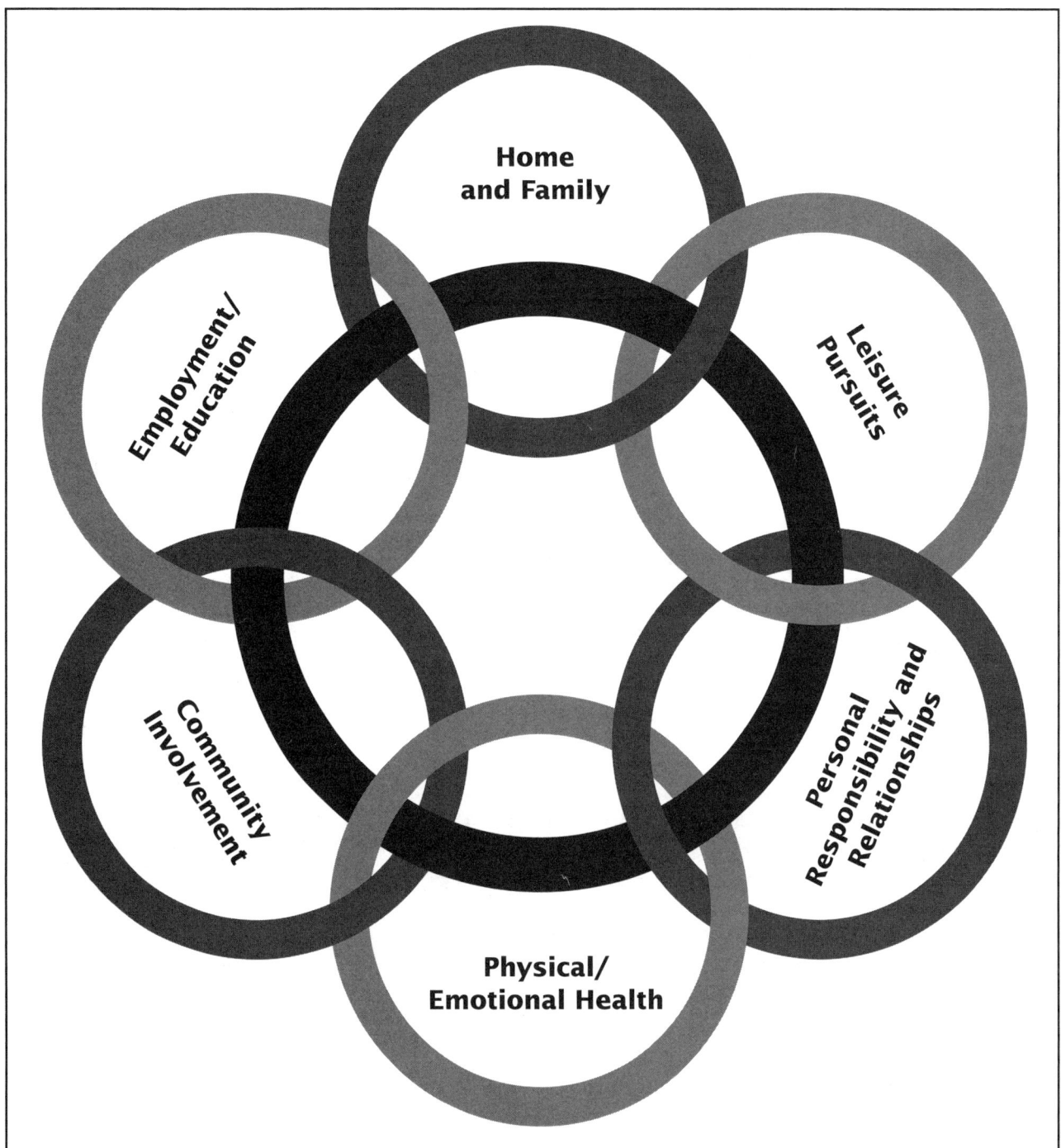

FIGURE 1.3. Domains of adulthood.

- Employment Setting
- Career Refinement and Reevaluation

Home and Family
- Home Management
- Financial Management

- Family Life
- Child Rearing

Leisure Pursuits
- Indoor Activities
- Outdoor Activities
- Community/Neighborhood Activities
- Travel
- Entertainment

Community Involvement
- Citizenship
- Community Awareness
- Services/Resources

Physical/Emotional Health
- Physical Health
- Emotional Health

Personal Responsibility and Relationships
- Personal Confidence/Understanding
- Goal Setting
- Self-Improvement
- Relationships
- Personal Expression

With a top-down perspective of life skills identification, it is useful to begin with general dimensions for organizing the events and activities associated with adulthood (i.e., adult domains and subdomains). However, as indicated at the beginning of this section, the most important component of the model shown in Figure 1.2 is the listing of the major life demands.

Identification of Major Life Demands. The identification of critical life skills should be based on the behaviors that individuals will need in their specific community environments. The major life demands provide the foundation for local school systems to generate, develop, and identify life skills for competency and course development.

The identification of the major life demands for this guide drew upon the authors' teaching experiences, the experiences of school-based personnel and other professionals interested in life skills instruction, personal schooling, consultation with colleagues, study of relevant literature, and observation of students, parents, teachers, siblings, friends, and strangers. Table 1.5 provides a list of these major life demands and represents a core from which life skills curricula, competencies, instructional objectives, courses, and activities can emerge. Additional life demands, created by school-based personnel, should reflect those demands and tasks deemed necessary in the specific community in which the students live and, therefore, need to know in order to function successfully in that environment. Identification of these community- or individual-specific life demands is necessary in order to realize the most complete and efficient transition program for each student during his or her middle and high school years.

(text continues on p. 22)

Table 1.5
Major Life Demands

Domain	Subdomain	Life demands
Employment/ Education	General Job Skills	seeking and securing a job learning job skills maintaining one's job understanding fundamental and legal issues
	General Education/ Training Considerations	knowing about education/training options gaining entry to postsecondary education/training settings (higher education, adult education, community education, trade/technical schools, military service) finding financial support utilizing academic and system survival skills (e.g., study skills, organizational skills, and time management) requesting employment services when needed (e.g., vocational rehabilitation, unemployment) accessing support services of training setting
	Employment Setting	recognizing job duties and responsibilities exhibiting appropriate work habits/behavior getting along with employer and coworkers understanding company policies (e.g., fringe benefits, wages, sick/personal leave, advancement procedures) understanding take-home pay/deductions managing employment-related expenses (travel, clothes, dues) understanding OSHA [Occupational Safety and Health Administration] regulations
	Career Refinement and Reevaluation	revitalizing career choice exploring alternative career options pursuing career change
Home and Family	Home Management	setting up household operations (e.g., initiating utilities) arranging furniture and equipment identifying and implementing security provisions and safety procedures cleaning dwelling maintaining and landscaping a yard laundering and maintaining clothes and household items performing/contracting for home repairs/improvements and regular maintenance storing household items maintaining automobile(s) and equipment, appliances, etc. reacting to environmental dangers (e.g., pollution, extreme weather conditions)
	Financial Management	creating a general financial plan (e.g., savings, investments, retirement) maintaining a budget using banking services paying bills establishing a good credit rating purchasing day-to-day items (clothes, food, etc.) renting an apartment selecting and buying a house (building new/purchasing existing) making major purchases (e.g., auto) determining payment options for major purchases (cash, credit, layaway, debit card, finance plan, etc.) preparing and paying taxes buying insurance

(continues)

Table 1.5 (*Continued*)

Domain	Subdomain	Life demands
Home and Family (*cont.*)	Financial Management (*cont.*)	purchasing specialty items throughout the year (e.g., birthday gifts, Christmas gifts) planning for long-term financial needs (e.g., major purchases, children's education) obtaining government assistance when needed (e.g., Medicare, food stamps, student loans)
	Family Life	preparing for marriage, family maintaining physical/emotional health of family members maintaining family harmony scheduling and managing daily, weekly, monthly, yearly family events (e.g., appointments, social events, leisure/recreational pursuits) planning and preparing meals (menu, buying food, ordering take-out food, dining out) arranging for/providing day care (children or older relatives) managing incoming/outgoing mail
	Child Rearing	acquiring realistic information about raising children preparing for pregnancy and childbirth understanding childhood development (physical, emotional, cognitive, language) managing children's behavior preparing for out-of-home experiences (e.g., day care, school) helping children with school-related needs hiring and training in-home babysitter
Leisure Pursuits	Indoor Activities	playing table or electronic games (e.g., cards, board games, puzzles, video games, arcades) performing individual physical activities (e.g., weight training, aerobics, dance, swimming, martial arts) participating in group physical activities (e.g., racquetball, basketball) engaging in individual hobbies and crafts (e.g., reading, handicrafts, sewing, collecting)
	Outdoor Activities	performing individual physical activities (e.g., jogging, golf, bicycling, swimming, hiking, backpacking, fishing) participating in group physical activities (e.g., softball, football, basketball, tennis) engaging in general recreational activities (e.g., camping, sightseeing, picnicking)
	Community/ Neighborhood Activities	going to various ongoing neighborhood events (e.g., garage sales, block parties, barbecues) attending special events (e.g., fairs, trade shows, carnivals, parades, festivals)
	Travel	preparing to go on a trip (e.g., destination, transportation arrangements, hotel/motel arrangements, packing, preparations for leaving home) dealing with the realities of travel via air, ground, or water
	Entertainment	engaging in in-home activities (e.g., TV, videos, music) attending out-of-home events (e.g., theaters, spectator sports, concerts, performances, art shows) going to socially oriented events (e.g., restaurants, parties, nightclubs) and other social events
Community Involvement	Citizenship	understanding legal rights exhibiting civic responsibility voting in elections understanding tax obligations obeying laws and ordinances

(*continues*)

Table 1.5 (*Continued*)

Domain	Subdomain	Life demands
Community Involvement (*cont.*)	Citizenship (*cont.*)	serving on a jury understanding judicial procedures (e.g., due process, criminal/civil courts, legal documents) attending public hearings creating change in the community (e.g., petition drives)
	Community Awareness	being aware of social issues affecting community knowing major events at the local, regional, national, world levels using mass media (TV, radio, newspapers, Internet) understanding all sides of public opinion on community issues recognizing and acting on fraudulent practices
	Services/ Resources	knowing about the wide range of services available in a specific community using all levels of government agencies (tax office, drivers license [Department of Motor Vehicles], permits, consumer agencies [Better Business Bureau]) accessing public transportation (trains, buses, subways, ferries, etc.) accessing private services (humane society, cable services, utilities [phone, water, electric, sewage, garbage, Internet provider, cell phones]) accessing emergency services/resources (police, emergency medical service, hospital, fire, civil defense) accessing agencies that provide special services (advocacy centers) securing legal representation (e.g., lawyer referral)
Physical/ Emotional Health	Physical Health	living a healthy lifestyle planning a nutritional diet exercising regularly as part of lifestyle having regular physical/dental checkups understanding illnesses and medical/dental needs across age levels using proper dental hygiene/dental care preventing illness and accidents recognizing health risks recognizing signs of medical/dental problems reacting to medical emergencies administering simple first aid using medications providing treatment for chronic health problems recognizing and accommodating physical changes associated with aging recognizing and dealing with substance use/abuse
	Emotional Health	understanding emotional needs across age levels recognizing signs of emotional needs managing life changes managing stress dealing with adversity and depression dealing with anxiety coping with separation/death of family members and friends understanding emotional dimensions of sexuality seeking personal counseling

(*continues*)

Table 1.5 (*Continued*)

Domain	Subdomain	Life demands
Personal Responsibility and Relationships	Personal Confidence/ Understanding	recognizing one's strengths and weaknesses appreciating one's accomplishments identifying ways to maintain or achieve a positive self-concept reacting appropriately to the positive or negative feedback of others using appropriate communication skills following one's religious beliefs
	Goal Setting	evaluating one's values identifying and achieving personal goals and aspirations exercising problem-solving/decision-making skills becoming independent and self-directed
	Self-Improvement	pursuing personal interests conducting self-evaluation seeking continuing education improving scholastic abilities displaying appropriate personal interaction skills maintaining personal appearance
	Relationships	getting along with others establishing and maintaining friendships developing intimate relations deciding upon potential spouse or partner being sensitive to the needs of others communicating praise or criticism to others being socially perceptive (e.g., recognizing contextual clues) dealing with conflict nurturing healthy child/parent interactions solving marital problems
	Personal Expression	sharing personal feelings, experiences, concerns, desires with other people writing personal correspondence (e.g., letters, e-mails, notes, greeting cards)

Table 1.5 lists the six adult domains, 23 subdomains, and 146 major life demands. The major life demands represent the events or activities typically encountered by most adults in everyday life. It is from these demands that specific life skills, or the competencies needed to perform major life demands, will be generated to develop instructional objectives to meet students' real-life needs.

Examples of Specific Life Skills Identification

Figure 1.2 describes the actual sequence suggested for identifying specific life skills. Table 1.6 contains top-down examples for the six domains of adulthood. It is important to note that these examples provide only a sampling of possible specific life

Table 1.6
Examples of Specific Life Skills Identification

Adult domain	Specific subdomain	Major life demand	Specific life skills
Employment/ Education	General Job Skills	seeking and securing a job	• identify marketable job skills and interests • identify sources of job possibilities • use all sources of available jobs to identify appropriate jobs for the skills you possess • send e-mail or letters of inquiry or make calls of inquiry regarding the job, its availability, and application procedures • locate the site of the prospective job on the map • determine transportation needs for prospective jobs • obtain and fill out a job application • call for an interview appointment • record time, place, location, and name of person interviewing for future reference • determine appropriate dress for interview • practice interview skills • generate list of questions to ask about the job • compute weekly or monthly income • calculate mileage to work • ask about subsequent evaluations of job performance • identify appropriate dress for the job
Home and Family	Financial Management	purchasing day-to-day items (e.g., clothes)	• know where to shop • compare prices • understand cleaning and care instructions • be aware of available money in checking account
Leisure Pursuits	Entertainment	engaging in in-home activities (e.g., renting videos/DVDs)	• compare prices at various multimedia stores • determine costs and amount of available cash • identify multimedia store and location • understand terms of video/DVD rental • agree on movie selection with others • know how to use video/DVD player
Community Involvement	Citizenship	voting in elections	• register to vote • identify appropriate polling place and its location • obtain information on offices and candidates • determine distance from home to polling place • schedule time to vote
Physical/ Emotional Health	Physical Health	recognizing signs of medical/dental problems	• know symptoms of common illnesses (e.g., flu) • determine the temperature of your body • know when to call or go to the doctor • describe symptoms over the phone to health care worker • understand the roles of doctor, nurse, pharmacist

(continues)

Table 1.6 (*Continued*)

Adult domain	Specific subdomain	Major life demand	Specific life skills
Personal Responsibility and Relationships	Self-Improvement	maintaining personal appearance	• buy appropriate clothes for work • understand directions for cleaning work clothes • wear appropriate clothes for weather • style hair when needed • brush/floss teeth regularly

skills associated with a given major life demand and are by no means exhaustive of the specific life skills competencies necessary for dealing with the selected major life demands.

The generation of a list of life skills, as mentioned earlier in this section, depends on local needs and expectations for success in each community. The importance of this local input cannot be overstated. The success of programs is reflected in the ability of students to perform adult tasks within their own community, and coverage of life skills topics must reflect those adult tasks.

Guiding Principles for This Book

In light of the preceding discussion on the challenges facing us, professionals concerned about the adult outcomes of youth in today's schools must identify a philosophy that guides policy, decisions, and actions. We want to share the principles that guide how we conceptualize service delivery:

- *Utilize the notion of "subsequent environment as attitude."* The concept described by Polloway et al. (1991) implies that everything we do with students should be considered in the context of where they will likely be in the near future.
- *Treat each instructional day as if it were the last day in a student's scholastic life.* This idea emphasizes the importance of making every moment count. As many teachers know, there are students who may at any time drop out of school and never return.
- *Reevaluate what we are doing with students on a regular basis.* It is extremely important that we continually strive to be innovative in terms of curricular design and instructional methodology.
- *Take advantage of opportunities to cover real-life topics within the context of existing standards, curricula, and materials.* In today's classrooms, it is important to balance the need to be always mindful of the critical standards that guide curricula, to work effectively with the set curricula and the materials associated with it, and to address the real-life needs of students.

These four principles should apply to all educational decisions related to youth with special needs or placed at risk. These principles certainly apply to the themes discussed in the remainder of this book.

LIFE SKILLS AND TRANSITION ASSESSMENT

Audrey McCray Sorrells
James R. Patton

To plan and provide appropriate programs for students with special needs, teachers need to determine students' levels of functioning in all programming areas, deliver effective instruction, and monitor progress over time. In addition to the usual skill and subject areas to which students are exposed, attention should focus on key additional areas that include functional academics, vocational aptitude and interest, social skills, study skills, and life skills competence. Each of these areas is important to the students' success in many settings in which they will find themselves upon leaving high school. In addition, appropriate assessment, instruction, and action are essential in planning transition programs that prepare students for life after school. As indicated above, many variables contribute to the success of any student's program. One of these components—the assessment of life skills and transition needs—is covered in this chapter.

The Nature of Life Skills Assessment

Assessing the life skills competencies of students is an important component in planning programs at all levels of schooling. Understanding the role that assessment plays in life skills and transition programming requires an understanding of what assessment is, the different purposes for conducting assessment, and the different types of assessment instruments that are available. In addition, some guiding principles need to be acknowledged and followed during the assessment process.

Meaning of Assessment

The term *assessment* can be used to convey an array of different ideas. Often, conflicting meanings are associated with the term. For the purpose of this book, *assessment* refers to the process of gathering relevant information to use in making decisions about students (Salvia & Ysseldyke, 2000). This is a broad conceptualization; however, this perspective aptly captures the essence of what we suggest in this book—the acquisition of useful information for skill development and planning purposes. A number of general approaches can be used to gather information. Some of the most common techniques are presented in Table 2.1.

Purposes of Assessment in Life Skills Programming and Transition Planning

Assessment can serve many purposes in life skills programming and transition planning. However, four key reasons stand out. These rationales are listed below and then discussed briefly in the subsequent paragraphs:

- to determine a student's present levels of educational performance for the purpose of program planning for life skills instruction;
- to monitor and evaluate a student's progress in the acquisition and maintenance of life skills;

Table 2.1
Methods of Assessment

Type	Method
Formal testing	Standardized, norm-referenced instruments
	Standardized instruments (without norms)
Informal techniques	Observation
	Recollection methods
	Interviewing
	Checklists
	Rating scales
	Work sample analysis
	Error analysis
	Curriculum-based assessment
	Task analysis
	Response journals/learning logs
	Think-aloud techniques
	Questionnaires
	Self-evaluation
	Peer evaluation
	Rubric scoring
	Holistic
	Analytical
Performance assessment	Authentic assessment
	Portfolio assessment

Note. From *Classroom Assessment for Students with Special Needs in Inclusive Settings,* by C. G. Spinelli, 2002, Upper Saddle River, NJ: Prentice Hall. Copyright 2002 by Prentice Hall.

- to identify a student's interests and preferences on which to base programming and planning, including occupational interests; and
- to establish a student's current levels of competence in a variety of transition domains (i.e., transition needs; see Figure 2.1), including occupational aptitude and vocational skill levels.

Determining Present Levels of Educational Performance. Determining the level of any skill is imperative for three reasons: (a) to identify the instructional level at which a student is performing; (b) to have an index on which appropriate goals are generated; and (c) to know where to begin instruction. In addition, within the transition planning process, the assessment of life skills should be done with every student receiving special education services. Life skills assessment should begin during the early grades and continue throughout the secondary years, as life skills preparation for transition to life after high school is an ongoing process.

Present levels of educational performance are mandated by the Individuals with Disabilities Education Act (IDEA) as a critical part of the Individualized Education Program (IEP). Well-written levels of performance serve as the starting point for writing appropriate goals and are characterized as possessing the following elements (Gibb & Dyches, 2000):

- statement of how the disability affects the student's involvement and progress in the general education curriculum;
- description of the student's performance levels in the skill areas affected by the disability; and
- logical cues for writing the accompanying goals for improvement.

Monitoring and Evaluating Performance. A range of assessment techniques is needed to monitor student progress during the course of intervention and to determine the nature of ongoing and future interventions. Techniques that allow for the ongoing measurement of progress provide a way for teachers to know whether the students are learning what is being taught. Recommended practice suggests that data be collected on a regular basis and charted for visual inspection so that sound educational decisions can be made.

Identifying Interests and Preferences. One of the primary elements of the transition provisions of IDEA is that transition plans should be based on a

Employment	Health
Further Education or Training	Self-Determination
Daily Living	Communication
Leisure Activities	Interpersonal Relationships
Community Participation	

FIGURE 2.1. Transition planning inventory.

student's interests, preferences, and needs. Far too often, school-based personnel and parents are the ones who make the decisions about a young person's life without consulting him or her about various life-changing topics.

As a result of the above-referenced realities along with the notion that certain rights come to students when they attain the "age of majority"—and are capable of making prudent decisions about their lives—IDEA 2004 continues to emphasize that planning for the future must involve and be based on a student's wishes. Therefore, mechanisms must be identified, developed, and implemented for fulfilling this requirement.

Establishing Current Transition Needs. To develop useful and meaningful transition plans for students with disabilities, teachers need to conduct assessments that provide information about a student's transition needs and strengths. The reasons for performing these activities are (a) to identify adult-referenced areas for which instructional goals should be developed and (b) to identify services and supports that the individual needs now or in the future to deal competently with the demands of adulthood.

Types of Assessment Instruments

We can distinguish the different types of assessment instruments and techniques that are available in a number of ways. Often, various terms are used without concern for what they really mean. As a result, confusion and misunderstanding are introduced. In this book, we use two systems for identifying assessment techniques. The first system distinguishes whether an instrument is commercially available (formal instrument) or has not been published formally. The other system separates standardized from nonstandardized assessments.

The distinction between formal and informal instruments can be blurred because commercial availability is not exact. With the advent of small, home-based publishing, it is now possible to obtain materials that in the past would have been considered informal instruments. The bottom line suggests that the difference between formal and informal really does not matter much, as long as the instrument under consideration does what is needed and possesses requisite technical features.

Typically, standardized instruments are norm-referenced and available from commercial publishers due in great part to the time, effort, and expense of developing such devices. However, not all standardized instruments are norm-referenced. Technically, as Hammill (1987) pointed out, "a well-standardized technique will have clear rules governing its use and will require uniform skills in administering the test and interpreting its results" (p. 30).

The instruments and techniques that will be most useful in the area of life skills programming and transition planning are most frequently those that do not include norms. Some of these instruments, such as the *Transition Planning Inventory* (Clark & Patton, 2006), are standardized but do not have norms.

Guiding Principles for Conducting Assessments

Good assessment practice demands that certain procedures be followed to guarantee that information that is gathered is valid and reliable. The following guidelines provide a few important points in regard to the gathering of information from students with special needs, their families, teachers, and other school-based and agency personnel. The following list is not an exhaustive one, and readers are encouraged to consult other resources (e.g., J. A. McLaughlin & Lewis, 2005; Salvia & Ysseldyke, 2000; Sattler, 2002; R. Taylor, 2003) for a more thorough discussion of assessment practices.

- All assessment must be sensitive to culture and family values.
- Life skills and transition competence assessment should be comprehensive—that is, it should cover a breadth of adult-referenced domains.
- The assessment of life skills and transition competence, while certainly evaluating areas in which planning and programming will be needed, should also focus on strengths.
- Assessment information should lead easily to programming and planning activities.
- Different sources of information are desirable (e.g., student himself or herself, parents, teachers, related service personnel).
- Administration procedures of standardized, norm-referenced instruments must be followed exactly for the derived scores to be valid.
- Assessment techniques should be selected on their appropriateness and efficiency (i.e., minimum of time needed to administer, not complicated to use).

Commercially Available Instruments

A surprising number of commercially available (i.e., formal) instruments, used for various reasons in education, may provide information that can contribute to a better understanding of a student's life skill competence or level of transition need or strength in a given area. For instance, achievement or language measures that are used for a variety of purposes with students can be helpful to those who are charged with assisting students in planning for their futures.

We focus on four areas that provide useful information related to life skills and transition needs. Each of the areas—adaptive behavior measures, life skills instruments, transition instruments, and occupational measures—is discussed briefly and accompanied by a reference table listing features of selected instruments from the area. Sample pages from some commercially available instruments are provided in Appendix 2.A.

Adaptive Behavior Measures

A definition of *adaptive behavior* first presented by Heber in 1961 is still appropriate today: Adaptive behavior is the manner in which individuals cope with the natural and social demands of their environment. Adaptive behavior can also be conceptualized as the ability to cope with the demands of everyday life. It is a measure of typical behavior, not of the best behavior possible. Consideration of age and cultural context is an essential component of this type of assessment.

Most adaptive behavior measures use a structured-interview format whereby information is obtained through the reports of others about the performance of the student being assessed. In other words, adaptive behavior measures do not use direct observation to generate data; the information is generated indirectly through interviews with persons who have observed and are familiar with the individual. The informant, therefore, should have a good idea of typical performance on a range of domains.

More than any other measure used in schools—excluding specific transition instruments—adaptive behavior measures provide the most extensive set of information about real-world functioning. Adaptive behavior instruments typically examine the following areas: self-care and daily living skills, home living skills, social behavior, communication skills, leisure skills, community use skills, health and safety skills, functional academic skills, self-direction, and occupational skills. As can be seen easily, these areas relate closely to the life skills domains discussed in Chapter 1. Some of the more widely used instruments are listed in Table 2.2.

Life Skills Instruments

A number of instruments focus specifically on life skills. At times, the areas of focus are similar to those covered by adaptive behavior measures. The difference between life skills and adaptive behavior measures tends to be in how the instruments are administered. As noted earlier, adaptive behavior measures rely on the information provided by a person who knows the student. Life skills measures typically involve the student in some observable activity—answering questions (knowledge related) or performing activities (skill related). Some of the more widely used life skills instruments are listed in Table 2.3.

Transition Instruments

Until the 1990 amendments of IDEA when planning for transition services was first introduced as a requirement in the law, few instruments existed that focused primarily on assessing transition needs. Transition instruments, while related in some ways to adaptive behavior and life skills measures, focus on the perceived competence levels of students. Most instruments seek the perspective of different parties—student, family, and school personnel.

The main intent of these types of instruments is ultimately to guide programming and contribute to transition planning. Clark and Patton (2006), as introduced in Figure 1.1, emphasized that two types of outcomes should evolve from the use of transition planning techniques: (1) the generation of instructional goals and (2) the development of linkage goals (i.e., identification of services and supports that will be needed). Some of the more widely used transition-related instruments are listed in Table 2.4.

Occupational Measures

We want to recognize the place and importance of commercially available instruments. The information gained from the administration of these types of measures,

(text continues on p. 34)

Table 2.2
Adaptive Behavior Measures

Instrument	Age range	Adaptive skill domains/subtests	Features
Vineland–II Adaptive Behavior Scales– Second Edition (Sparrow, Cicchetti, & Balla, 2005)	Birth to 90 (Survey Interview, Parent/Caregiver Expanded Interview Forms) 3 to 21-11 (Teacher Rating Form)	• Communication • Daily living • Socialization • Motor • Maladaptive behaviors	• Four forms: —Survey Interview Form —Parent/Caregiver Rating Form —Expanded Interview Form —Teacher Rating Form • Scoring software
Adaptive Behavior Assessment System– Second Edition (ABAS–II) (Harrison & Oakland, 2003)	Birth to 89	• Communication • Community use • Functional academics • Home/school living • Health and safety • Leisure • Self-care • Self-direction • Social • Work	• Five forms: —Parent Form, birth to 5 —Parent Form, 5 to 21 —Teacher/Day Care Form, 2 to 5 —Teacher Form, 5 to 21 —Adult Form, 16 to 89 • Scoring software
AAMR Adaptive Behavior Scales— School: Second Edition (ABS–S:2) (Lambert, Nihira, & Leland, 1993)	3 to 21	Part One: Adaptive Behaviors • Independent functioning • Physical development • Economic activity • Language development • Numbers and time • Domestic activity • Prevocational/vocational activity • Self-direction • Responsibility • Socialization Part Two: Maladaptive Behaviors • Social behavior • Conformity • Trustworthiness • Stereotyped and hyperactive behavior • Self-abusive behavior • Social engagement • Disturbing interpersonal behavior	• One form, two parts: —Part One: Adaptive behavior skills —Part Two: Maladaptive behaviors • Factor scores: —Personal self-sufficiency —Personal–social responsibility —Community self-sufficiency —Social adjustment —Personal adjustment

(continues)

Table 2.2 (*Continued*)

Instrument	Age range	Adaptive skill domains/subtests	Features
AAMR Adaptive Behavior Scales— Residential and Community: Second Edition (ABS–RC:2) (Nihira, Leland, & Lambert, 1993)	18 to 60+	[see ABS–S:2]	[see ABS–S:2]
Adaptive Behavior Evaluation Scale–Revised (McCarney, 1995)	5 to 18	• Communication skills • Self-care • Home living • Social • Community use • Self-direction • Health and safety • Functional academics • Leisure • Work	• Two forms: —School Version Rating Form —Home Version Rating Form
Scales of Independent Behavior–Revised (SIB–R) (Bruininks, Woodcock, Weatherman, & Hill, 1996)	Infancy to 80+	• Motor —Gross motor skills —Fine motor skills • Social interaction and communication —Social interaction —Language comprehension —Language expression • Personal living o Eating and meal preparation o Toileting o Dressing o Personal self-care o Domestic skills • Community living o Time and punctuality o Money and value o Work skills o Home and community orientation	• Four cluster areas, 14 subscales • Three forms: —Full-scale form —Short form —Early development form • Maladaptive behavior assessed by looking at areas of problem behavior • Short form of the scale is called Inventory for Client and Agency Planning

Note. Adapted from *Mental Retardation: An Introduction to Intellectual Disabilities*, by M. Beirne-Smith, J. R. Patton, and S. Kim, 2006, Upper Saddle River, NJ: Prentice Hall. Copyright 2006 by Prentice Hall. Adapted with permission.

Table 2.3
Life Skills Instruments

Instrument	Publisher	Target groups	Features
Life Centered Career Education Knowledge Battery (Brolin, 1992)	Council for Exceptional Children	mild cognitive disabilities; mild to severe learning disabilities, behavior disorders	• 20 competency areas; 200 multiple choice items • relates to LCCE curriculum
Life Centered Career Education Performance Battery (Brolin, 1992)	Council for Exceptional Children	mild cognitive disabilities; mild to severe learning disabilities, behavior disorders	• criterion referenced skill assessment • 3–4 hours
Life Skills Inventory (Brigance, 1995)	Curriculum Associates	most disability populations; reading grade levels 2–8	• criterion referenced, performance based • 10 subscales
Quality of Student Life Questionnaire (Keith & Schalock, 1995)	IDS Publishing	all disabilities; mild to severe	• 4 subscales • interview or rating, 15 minutes
Tests for Everyday Living (Halpern, Irvin, & Landman, 1979)	CTB/McGraw-Hill	all junior high school students and average to low functioning senior high school students	• 7 subtests, 245 items • orally administered; some reading • 20–30 minutes

Table 2.4
Transition Instruments

Instrument	Publisher	Target groups	Features
Enderle–Severson Transition Rating Scale-J–Revised (Enderle & Severson, 2003a)	ETRS	mild	• 5 subscales • ratings—teacher and parent or caregiver
Enderle–Severson Transition Rating Scale–III (Enderle & Severson, 2003b)	ETRS	severe	• 5 subscales • ratings—teacher and parent or caregiver
Transition Behavior Scales–Second Edition (McCarney & Anderson, 2000)	Hawthorne Educational Services	any disability group; mild to severe	• 3 subscales • 15 minutes • ratings—3 persons
Transition Planning Inventory–Updated Version (Clark & Patton, 2006)	PRO-ED	all disabilities; mild to severe	• 3 levels, 9 planning areas, 46 items • ratings by student, family, and school

some of which are norm-referenced instruments, helps determine the long-term and transitional programs for students with special needs. The value and use of these types of instruments has already been discussed; however, many of these instruments will not have an impact on daily instruction. For the purpose of evaluating student progress and building more effective programs for individual students, other techniques may be needed (Deno, 1985; Wood, 1992). The next section describes and gives examples of how informal techniques can be utilized in a life skills program and for transition planning purposes.

Informal Assessment Techniques

Many of the approaches listed in Table 2.1 are informal techniques for gathering information. Informal measures are attractive to school-based personnel for any number of reasons, including the following: (a) they can and should tie closely into the existing curriculum, (b) they are likely to be less expensive to use, and (c) they can be developed by school-based personnel.

Clark (1996) developed a list of examples of informal techniques that illustrates the range of possibilities that exist for assessing life skills and transition-related competencies (see Table 2.5). As can be seen, the table provides sample items for each of the informal procedures.

The following discussion of informal techniques for gathering information borrows from ideas introduced by Salvia and Ysseldyke (2000). They identified four general approaches to gathering information: observation, recollection (via interview and rating scales), record or portfolio review, and testing. We have modified their schema by adding the categories of curriculum-based measures and person-centered planning. We have also omitted the testing area in this discussion, as this topic was covered in a previous section.

Observational Techniques

With observational techniques, a student is observed in one or a variety of situations about which the assessors have interest. Such techniques provide a picture of how a student behaves or performs in actual classroom, community, or home situations. These techniques are particularly valuable for determining whether an individual can perform a specific skill or sequence of skills associated with a particular life skill. Typically, the person conducting the observation will use a predesigned form for collecting data. Data collection requires the use of one of many types of data collection techniques (e.g., frequency, duration, latency).

Recollection Techniques

Recollection techniques require the involvement of other parties who provide useful information about a student. As indicated previously, the two most common techniques are interviewing and the completion of various types of scales. With interviewing, it is essential that the person being interviewed is informed. In other words, the interviewee needs to be very familiar with the student about whom questions are

Table 2.5
Types of Nonstandardized Assessment Instruments
or Procedures, with Sample Items

Instrument/Procedure	Sample items/Information
Learning styles inventories	How do you learn a list of words for a test? Do you like studying with a partner?
Observational learning styles assessments	Student always goes to a quiet place to read. Student remembers things she sees.
Curriculum-based assessments (course specific)	Name the three branches of the federal government. What are two examples of toxic waste in your home?
Observational reports	J. C. complained of a headache twice today. M. N. needs help with grooming. O. P. makes no eye contact with girls.
Structured situational assessments	M. C. has been absent 10 days in 6 weeks. P. M. has been on time for work all month. J. P. completed every task assigned today.
Environmental assessments of student's situational placements or future placement options	M. C. is expected to prepare evening meals for five people every evening at home. N. L. will be expected, in algebra class, to compute probability problems. J. S. will be working in a work setting that is extremely high pressure and fast paced.
Person-centered planning or futures planning procedures	What is your dream in life? What is your greatest fear of the future? Who are your best supports?
Structured interviews with students	What do you like to do with your free time? What are three occupations that interest you at this time?
Structured interviews with parents/guardians	What would you like to see M. C. doing after she leaves school next year? Where and with whom would you like P. M. to live when he leaves home?
Adaptive, behavioral, or functional skills assessments	Does P. M. manage his own money? Does M. C. use the bus to get to work? Does G. G. purchase her own clothes?
Social histories	M. C. has shown a consistent pattern of relating well to male authority figures. Since P. M.'s family moved and he went to live with his grandmother, he has run away from home six times.
Rating scales (employability, independent living, personal–social skills, etc.)	M. C. follows directions without prompts. P. M. relates well to coworkers. L. P. cleans room and makes bed regularly.
Applied technology/vocational education prerequisite skills assessments	Can _____ perform metric linear measurements? Can _____ demonstrate safety procedures on a drill press, band saw, and jointer?
Self-determination checklists (Yes or No)	I can describe why I am in a special education program. I can explain my disability to a teacher/peer/employer/supervisor.

Note. From "Transition Planning Assessment for Secondary-Level Students with Learning Disabilities," by G. M. Clark, 1996, *Journal of Learning Disabilities,* 29(1), pp. 79–92. Copyright 1996 by *Journal of Learning Disabilities.* Adapted with permission.

being asked. We recommend that a set of questions be generated prior to the interview and used to format the session.

Recollection techniques also include the use of checklists and rating scales. The key difference between the two is that a checklist requires a simple "yes" or "no" response. A rating scale, on the other hand, provides a more qualitative response in that such a scale usually has a range of choices. For instance, a rating scale related to life skills might have choices ranging from "does not perform the skills at all" to "performs the skills whenever needed."

All of the recollection techniques described above have merit and can provide very useful information on knowledge attainment and skill acquisition. However, we advise that information come from a variety of sources. Interview and checklist or rating scale data should be obtained from more than one source, and at least one source should be from the student's cultural group. This latter point protects for the reality that the proficiency of some life skills varies across cultural settings.

Curriculum-Based Measures

Measures of students' performance in the context of the curriculum requirements of their classroom settings has been documented as the most useful way to assess student needs and progress (Durkin, 1984; Samuels, 1984). Curriculum-based assessment (CBA) has emerged to fill this need for an assessment process based on a student's progress through an individual curriculum (Wood, 1992).

The nature of life skills instruction lends itself effectively to this type of assessment technique. A number of informal techniques used in CBA can be implemented to determine students' abilities to perform a host of life skills competencies. The steps to develop a CBA are described elsewhere (Blankenship, 1985; Wood, 1992). When using CBA for the first time, start slowly developing the CBA with one life skill at a time. This can be done as individual students are working on specific life skills. As you develop life skill CBAs, exchange CBAs with other teachers of life skills to help build your life skill CBA files in many areas for future use.

Table 2.6 provides examples of how CBA can be used in the context of selected life skills within each of the major adult domains, as introduced in the previous chapter. The selected life skills used in Table 2.6 are common everyday skills in which most individuals will need to demonstrate competence. The sample goal, related test item pool, and measurement procedure relate to the life skill under each adult domain.

Portfolios

An area that has received increasing attention recently is the use of portfolios to generate useful life skills and transition-related information. In terms of transition planning, the use of portfolios is beneficial because it allows students to engage in authentic, adult-referenced topics at an earlier age. As a result, students are more familiar with the topics about which they will be asked when the more formal transition process commences and they are asked about their interests and preferences.

Table 2.6
Curriculum-Based Measurement Procedures by Adult Domains

Life skill domain	Simple goal	Related test item materials	Measurement procedure
Employment/ Education	Given a local newspaper's classified ads, the student will locate 3 entry-level jobs appropriate for his or her skill level and interest with 100% accuracy.	local newspaper classified ads	Provide the classified section of the local newspaper. Direct the student to locate 3 job openings appropriate to his or her skills and interest; score performance if student locates 3 job openings of appropriate skill and interest level.
Home and Family	Given $20 and 7 items selected at a grocery store for purchase, the student will total the cost of all items and determine whether $20 will cover the cost with 100% accuracy.	7 grocery store items	Randomly select items from grocery store shelves. Present the student with items and a small hand calculator; provide directions; score performance if student correctly determines that $20 will cover the cost of all 7 items.
Leisure Pursuits	Given a local weather broadcast on radio or TV, the student will determine whether an outdoor activity is appropriate with 100% accuracy.	radio or TV	Provide the student a radio or TV to listen for a weather broadcast; direct student to listen for the weather forecast to see if he or she should plan an outdoor activity; score performance if student makes an appropriate decision based on outdoor activity and current weather conditions.
Community Involvement	Given a pencil and blank local voter registration card, the student will complete the form with 100% accuracy.	local voter registration form	Provide the student with a blank voter registration form; direct student to fill out form completely; score performance if student fills in all blanks correctly.
Physical/ Emotional Health	Given a local phone book and the direction to find the phone number of the poison control center, the student will locate and write down the number and tape it to the phone with 100% accuracy.	phone book, tape, pencil, paper, telephone	Provide the student with a local phone book with the directions to find the number of the poison control center, write it down, and tape on phone; score performance if student finds either the local poison control number or the national 800 number, correctly writes the number on paper, and tapes it to phone.
Personal Responsibility and Relationships	Given stationery, envelope, pen, and a stamp, the student will write an appropriate thank-you note, including address, for a gift with 100% accuracy.	stationery, envelope, pen, stamp	Provide student with stationery, envelope, pen, and stamp; direct student to write an appropriate thank-you note, including addressing envelope, for a gift he or she has received; score performance if student writes an appropriate note, including all essential elements such as date, salutation, mention of gift, appreciation for gift, closing, student's name, and envelope addressed correctly.

Person-Centered Planning

A final area that has gained attention is the application of person-centered planning (Clark, 1998). Clark defines person-centered planning as a group of approaches or procedures that propose an informal, but structured, way of planning for an individual with a disability. The strengths and preferences of the person are the central focus in a plan that uses a variety of formal or informal support systems to achieve the person's dreams. The major principles embedded in person-centered planning include (a) a focus on the student's strengths, interests, and preferences; (b) a focus on capacities and opportunities, informed by a vision; (c) a process that is flexible, dynamic, and informal; (d) a collaborative team effort with commitment to action; and (e) an effective facilitator.

The person-centered planning process is effective only to the extent to which the focus person is involved and can communicate what his or her interests and preferences are. In addition, the planning process is enhanced further when the focus person's cultural and ethnic background and family and community ethos are natural components of decision making, possibilities, and opportunities. The apparent strength of this process, according to Clark (1998), is that it

> brings together the focus person with a variety of stakeholders in that person's life and future and helps loosen the constraints of school and service agency approaches to working with students with disabilities. The process results in a plan of action that is based on preferences and strengths of the individual and is developed so specifically that IEP goals, objectives, and action statements are easily completed. (p. 52)

Relationship of Assessment to Planning and Instruction

Planning programs for students with special needs based on appropriate assessment is an integral part of special education service delivery. To effectively plan for students, teachers need information about the students' level of functioning in all program areas, including academics, vocational aptitude and interest, social skills, study skills, and life skills competence and transition. Moreover, effective planning requires teachers to understand assessment, what it is, why it is necessary, and how to conduct assessment that will yield useful information for programming and the monitoring of progress. This chapter addressed formal and informal assessments, including traditional and alternative assessments, and components of programming that can lead to providing students with real-life learning and life skills for successful transition. Emphasized throughout the chapter is the idea that assessment is key to effectively planning for and delivering instruction to students with special needs, and that teachers must be familiar with, and skilled in, conducting assessments using a variety of instruments and techniques.

APPENDIX
SAMPLE PAGES FROM COMMERCIALLY AVAILABLE INSTRUMENTS

Self-Care Skills Scale

> The ABI self-care skills scale includes a list of 30 items. Some of these phrases will describe the student you are rating very well and some will not. You will indicate the extent to which the student has mastered these skills. When a student has mastered a task, circle the 3 preceding the item. When a student usually performs a task, but does not do so consistently, circle the 2. A 1 indicates that the student is beginning to perform the task. A 0 indicates that the student does not perform the task described in an item.

Student does not perform skill	Student is beginning to perform skill	Student performs skill most of time	Student has mastered skill	
0	1	2	3	1. Moves independently from one area to another at school/work.
0	1	2	3	2. Performs personal grooming and hygiene tasks independently.
0	1	2	3	3. Exhibits acceptable table manners.
0	1	2	3	4. Knows the meaning of signs that appear in public (e.g., "Restrooms," "Exit," "Stop").
0	1	2	3	5. Takes care of own belongings.
0	1	2	3	6. Knows own address, house number, street, city, and state (e.g., 1800 Ridge Road, Columbia, Missouri).
0	1	2	3	7. Knows the names and values of bills.
0	1	2	3	8. Knows own birth date, month, and year (e.g., March 13, 1978).
0	1	2	3	9. Makes local telephone calls without assistance.
0	1	2	3	10. Seeks appropriate help in an emergency.
0	1	2	3	11. Operates small household appliances (e.g., toaster, blender, carpet sweeper).
0	1	2	3	12. Tells time using traditional or digital watch or clock.
0	1	2	3	13. Organizes own leisure activities (e.g., hobbies, reading, seeing a movie, listening to music).
0	1	2	3	14. Performs basic household chores (e.g., washing dishes, sweeping).
0	1	2	3	15. Orders meals in public.
0	1	2	3	16. Prepares simple meals.
0	1	2	3	17. Writes personal letters.
0	1	2	3	18. Seeks medical assistance when signs of illness are present.
0	1	2	3	19. Consults written references (e.g., dictionary, telephone book, encyclopedia) for information.
0	1	2	3	20. Knows approximate cost of common items.
0	1	2	3	21. Buys stamps, mails letters at post office.
0	1	2	3	22. Knows basic first aid.
0	1	2	3	23. Takes prescribed medication without supervision.
0	1	2	3	24. Makes long distance telephone calls without assistance.
0	1	2	3	25. Arranges own transportation to school/work.
0	1	2	3	26. Launders and mends own clothing.
0	1	2	3	27. Buys groceries.
0	1	2	3	28. Uses public transportation (e.g., bus, taxi, train, airplane).
0	1	2	3	29. Plans balanced daily/weekly menus.
0	1	2	3	30. Is aware of basic social service agencies (e.g., employment commission, community counseling services, planned parenthood clinic).

Ceiling Item _____

Basal Item _____ × 3 = _____

Points Earned from Basal to Ceiling = + _____

Raw Score = _____

See Table A (Normal Intelligence Sample) or Table B (Mentally Retarded Sample) to convert the Raw Score to a Standard Score or Percentile Rank. The Standard Error of Measurement is reported in Tables 8 and 9. These figures should be entered in Section II on the front of the ABI Profile & Response Sheet.

Note. From *Adaptive Behavior Inventory* (p. 2), by L. Brown and J. E. Leigh, 1986, Austin, TX: PRO-ED. Copyright 1986 by L. Brown and J. E. Leigh. Reprinted with permission.

PART ONE
DOMAIN I.

Independent Functioning

A. Eating
ITEM 1   **Use of Table Utensils**
                                                              (Circle highest level)
Uses table knife for cutting or spreading 6
Feeds self neatly with spoon and fork
(or appropriate alternate utensil, e.g., chopsticks) 5
Feeds self causing considerable spilling with spoon and
fork (or appropriate alternate utensil, e.g., chopsticks) 4
Feeds self with spoon—neatly 3
Feeds self with spoon—considerable spilling 2
Feeds self with fingers 1
Does not feed self or must be fed 0

ITEM 2   **Eating in Public**
                                                              (Circle highest level)
Orders complete meals in restaurants 3
Orders simple meals like hamburgers or hot dogs 2
Orders single items, e.g., soft drinks, ice cream,
donuts, etc. at soda fountain or canteen 1
Does not order in public eating places 0

ITEM 3   **Drinking**
                                                              (Circle highest level)
Drinks without spilling, holding glass in one hand 3
Drinks from cup or glass unassisted—neatly 2
Drinks from cup or glass
unassisted—considerable spilling 1
Does not drink from cup or glass unassisted 0

ITEM 4   **Table Manners**
                                                              (Circle all answers)
If these items do not apply to the individual,
e.g., because he or she is bedfast and/or has
liquid food only, place a check in the blank and
mark "Yes" for all statements. _____

	Yes	No
Throws food	0	1
Swallows food without chewing	0	1
Chews food with mouth open	0	1
Drops food on table or floor	0	1
Does not use napkin	0	1
Talks with mouth full	0	1
Takes food off others' plates	0	1
Eats too fast or too slow	0	1
Plays in food with fingers	0	1

B. Toilet Use
ITEM 5   **Toilet Training**
                                                              (Circle highest level)
Never has toilet accidents 4
Has toilet accidents only at night 3
Occasionally has toilet accidents during the day 2
Frequently has toilet accidents during the day 1
Is not toiled trained at all 0

ITEM 6   **Self-Care at Toilet**
                                                              (Circle all answers)

	Yes	No
Lowers pants at the toilet without help	1	0
Sits on toilet seat without help	1	0
Uses toilet tissue appropriately	1	0
Flushes toilet after use	1	0
Puts on clothes without help	1	0
Washes hands without help	1	0

C. Cleanliness
ITEM 7   **Washing Hands and Face**
                                                              (Circle all answers)

	Yes	No
Washes hands and face with soap and water without prompting	1	0
Washes hands with soap	1	0
Washes face with soap	1	0
Washes hands and face with water	1	0
Dries hands and face	1	0

ITEM 8   **Bathing**
                                                              (Circle highest level)
Prepares and completes bathing unaided 6
Washes and dries self completely
without prompting or helping 5
Washes and dries self reasonably well with prompting 4
Washes and dries self with help 3
Attempts to soap and wash self 2
Cooperates when being washed and dried by others 1
Makes no attempt to wash or dry self 0

ITEM 9   **Personal Hygiene**
                                                              (Circle all answers)
If these items do not apply to the individual,
e.g., because he or she is completely dependent
on others, place a check in the blank and
mark "Yes" for all statements. _____

	Yes	No
Has strong underarm odor	0	1
Does not change underwear regularly by self	0	1
Skin is often dirty if not assisted	0	1
Does not keep nails clean by self	0	1

ITEM 10   **Toothbrushing**
                                                              (Circle highest level)
Cleans dentures appropriately 5
Applies toothpaste and brushes teeth
with up and down motion 5
Applies toothpaste and brushes teeth
with sideways motion 4
Brushes teeth without help, but cannot apply toothpaste 3
Brushes teeth with supervision 2
Cooperates in having teeth brushed 1
Makes no attempt to brush teeth 0
Does not clean dentures 0

D. Appearance
ITEM 11   **Posture**
                                                              (Circle all answers)
If these items do not apply to the individual,
e.g., because he or she is bedfast or
non-ambulatory, place check in the blank
and mark "Yes" for all statements. _____

	Yes	No
Mouth hangs open	0	1
Head hangs down	0	1
Stomach sticks out because of posture	0	1
Shoulders slumped forward and bent back	0	1
Walks with toes out or toes in	0	1
Walks with feet far apart	0	1
Shuffles, drags, or stamps feet when walking	0	1
Walks on tiptoe	0	1

Note. From *AAMR Adaptive Behavior Scale—School, Second Edition* (p. 4), by N. Lambert, K. Nihira, and H. Leland, 1993, Austin, TX: PRO-ED. Copyright 1993 by the American Association on Mental Retardation. Reprinted with permission.

Planning Areas	Not Appropriate	Strongly Disagree 0	1	2	3	4	Strongly Agree 5	Don't Know
FURTHER EDUCATION/TRAINING								

Not all of the statements in this section (Items 6–10) may apply to you. They depend on where you are likely to be after high school. For those that do *not* apply, circle "NA." For those that *do* apply, circle the appropriate number for each statement.

	Not Appropriate	0	1	2	3	4	5	Don't Know
6. I know how to get into a community employment training program that meets my needs.	NA	0	1	2	3	4	5	DK
7. I know how to get into a General Education Development (GED) program.	NA	0	1	2	3	4	5	DK
8. I know how to get into a vocational/technical school that meets my needs.	NA	0	1	2	3	4	5	DK
9. I know how to get into a college or university that meets my needs.	NA	0	1	2	3	4	5	DK
10. I can do well in a program after high school that meets my needs.	NA	0	1	2	3	4	5	DK
DAILY LIVING								
11. I can do my own personal grooming and hygiene.	NA	0	1	2	3	4	5	DK
12. I can find a place to live.	NA	0	1	2	3	4	5	DK
13. I know how to move in and set up a place to live.	NA	0	1	2	3	4	5	DK
14. I can do everyday household tasks.	NA	0	1	2	3	4	5	DK
15. I can take care of my own money.	NA	0	1	2	3	4	5	DK
16. I can use local transportation systems when I need to.	NA	0	1	2	3	4	5	DK
LEISURE ACTIVITIES								
17. I can do different kinds of indoor leisure activities.	NA	0	1	2	3	4	5	DK
18. I can do different kinds of outdoor leisure activities.	NA	0	1	2	3	4	5	DK
19. I go to different places for entertainment.	NA	0	1	2	3	4	5	DK
COMMUNITY PARTICIPATION								
20. I know my basic legal rights	NA	0	1	2	3	4	5	DK
21. I am an active citizen.	NA	0	1	2	3	4	5	DK
22. I can make legal decisions affecting my life.	NA	0	1	2	3	4	5	DK
23. I can find community services and resources I need.	NA	0	1	2	3	4	5	DK
24. I know how to use a variety of services and resources successfully.	NA	0	1	2	3	4	5	DK
25. I know how to get help from programs to pay for the costs of day-to-day living.	NA	0	1	2	3	4	5	DK

Note. From *Transition Planning Inventory–Updated Version,* by G. M. Clark and J. R. Patton, 2006, Austin, TX: PRO-ED. Copyright 2006 by PRO-ED, Inc. Reprinted with permission.

Transition Skills Inventory (*Continued*)

U—USUALLY S—SOMETIMES H—HARDLY EVER NA—NOT APPLICABLE		
Living On Your Own	**Ratings**	
MONEY MANAGEMENT	**Teacher**	**Support Person**
61. How often does the student pay for things in stores without making mistakes? Some examples are (a) knowing if he or she has enough money to buy what he or she wants, and (b) knowing if he or she has received the correct change?		
62. How often does the student shop carefully and get things for good prices?		
63. How often does the student use a checking or savings account to manage his or her money?		
64. How often does the student budget his or her money well enough to pay for the things the student wants and needs?		
HOME MANAGEMENT		
65. How often does the student use basic tools, such as a hammer, pliers, or a screwdriver, to fix things around the home?		
66. How often does the student help out with chores, such as washing dishes and cleaning up his or her room?		
67. How often does the student help prepare meals?		
68. How often does the student help do the laundry?		
COMMUNITY AND LEISURE ACTIVITIES		
69. How often does the student use the telephone to get information about things he or she needs, such as finding out when a movie starts or making a doctor's appointment?		
70. How often does the student use some form of transportation, such as a bus, a bicycle, or a car to get around independently?		
71. How often does the student volunteer to do something that helps other people? Some examples are (a) getting food for hungry people, (b) collecting money for a charity, and (c) doing things for a volunteer group, such as the Red Cross or Special Olympics.		
72. Even if the student can't vote, how often is the student aware of the people who are running for office, and how often does he or she think about who should win?		
PERSONAL SAFETY		
73. How often does the student provide first aid for minor cuts, burns, bruises, or sprains?		
74. How often does the student use a seat belt in a car, or a helmet with a bicycle, motorcycle, or roller blades?		
75. If a person asks the student to do something that is dangerous, such as hitchhiking, how often does the student say "no"?		
76. If the student needs emergency help for a serious sickness or injury, how often does he or she know how to get the help?		

Note. From *NEXT S.T.E.P.–Second Edition: Student Transition and Educational Planning* (p. 274), by A. S. Halpern, C. M. Herr, B. Doren, and N. K. Wolf, 2000, Austin, TX: PRO-ED. Copyright 2000 by PRO-ED, Inc. Reprinted with permission.

CLASSROOM-BASED INSTRUCTION
INTEGRATION INTO EXISTING CONTENT AND COURSEWORK

In program development, certain instructional components can make the difference in successfully implementing a life skills curriculum. Considerations such as where the instruction takes place, the method or technique used, and the materials used during the instructional process are integral to student success in the program. This chapter will discuss instructional considerations for classroom-based instruction.

Instructional Considerations

Recent years have produced a plethora of federal (No Child Left Behind Act of 2001; Individuals with Disabilities Education Improvement Act of 2004) and state mandates designed to ensure that all students have access to quality education that leads to improved outcomes for all learners. The alignment of these mandates to research-based best practices has also been on the forefront of recent educational reform initiatives. Teachers need to review and consider an array of research-based best practices when planning a life skills program for their students. Billingsley and Albertson (1999), Brinckerhoff, McGuire, and Shaw (2002), Browder and Grasso (1999), Collins (2003), M. W. McLaughlin (2001), Neubert and Moon (2000), Raskind, Goldberg, Higgins, and Herman (2002), and others have suggested many factors that contribute to students' exiting high school prepared for a successful adult experience. The literature (P. Brown, 2000; Clark, 1998; Garland, 1999; Kohler & Hood, 2000; Norris & Schumacker, 2000) overwhelmingly supports including the following considerations in planning instruction for a life skills program: teaching for the improvement of the student's overall quality of life, teaching adult outcomes tasks, teaching those relevant adult tasks in the natural (community) environment, and teaching tasks related to the students' probable subsequent experiences and environment (student outcomes). This section discusses the variables of classroom-based and community-based instruction against the backdrop of accountability.

District and School Improvement Planning

Improvement planning and life skills instruction bear an important point of convergence: improving outcomes for students. In the era of increased accountability, instructional planning occurs not only on an individual teacher level but also on a district and school level. District improvement planning presents an overall framework outlining the main focal areas toward which a district is directing its energy and resources. Each school's improvement plan typically is aligned with the district's plan although allowing for variables particular to the individual school. With all improvement planning the focus should be on improving outcomes for students. A life skills curriculum paves the road for improving outcomes for students by utilizing both classroom-based and community-based instruction. Teachers should be aware of both their district and school improvement plans and how a life skills curriculum can interface with the overall improvement vision.

Teaching and Learning

Research-based best practices are universally viewed as a must-have foundation for all instructional practices. The National Center on Accessing the General Curriculum (2003) defined research to practice as "implementing research-proven instructional and assessment practices identified through scientifically based research. The purpose is to advance the quality of education, make teaching more effective and efficient, thus enhance learning outcomes for all students" (p. 1). The continued national emphasis on quality teaching and learning has focused on a myriad of instructional approaches to teaching and learning.

As individual educators and school improvement teams examine data to inform instruction and to close any equity gaps of performance, research-based best practices such as universal design of learning (UDL) and differentiated instruction (DI) are getting significant attention (Pettig, 2000; Pisha & Coyne, 2001; Rose, 2001; Tomlinson, 2000). These philosophies are designed to engage a community of diverse learners. While there are numerous articles and books devoted to each of these topical areas, our focus is on understanding their relationship to teaching a life skills curriculum.

Universal design for learning framework originated from the design movement in architecture. It is based on the belief that educators should design the curriculum to anticipate and meet the learners' needs right from the start. Recognition, strategy, and affect are learning networks in the brain (Rose & Meyer, 2002) that correlate to three core principles of UDL, which are stated in Table 3.1 (Hall, Strangeman, & Meyer, 2003, p. 7). Technology is another important aspect of UDL as it allows for continuous flexibility within the framework of the three principles.

Tomlinson (2000) defined differentiation as "simply attending to the learning needs of a particular student or small group of students rather than the more typical pattern of teaching the class as though all individuals in it were basically alike" (p. 4). This philosophy complements UDL by providing specific elements that can be differentiated. Tomlinson (2001a, 2001b) reviewed content, process, and products as some potential ways to differentiate instruction as UDL relies on its core principles to guide the instructional process (see Table 3.2).

One can see from Tables 3.1 and 3.2 that the relationship of UDL and DI to life skills instruction is a supportive and integrated one. This becomes increasingly relevant as inclusive educational opportunities across the program continuum focus on an "all children" agenda as opposed to "my children versus your children." The central themes and core beliefs of both UDL and DI are readily adaptable to life skills instruction and indeed lend themselves to the concepts and beliefs that are integrated into both.

Table 3.1
Core Principles of UDL as Related to Life Skills Instruction

Three core principles of UDL	Guiding principles of life skills instruction
To support recognition learning, provide multiple, flexible methods of presentation.	Everything we do with students should be considered in the context of where they will likely be in the near future.
To support strategic learning, provide multiple, flexible methods of expression and apprenticeship.	Treat each instructional day as if it were the last day in a student's scholastic life.
To support affective learning, provide multiple, flexible options for engagement.	Reevaluate what you do with students on a regular basis.

Note. The information in column 1 is adapted from *Differentiated Instruction and Implications for UDL Implementation* (p. 7), by T. Hall, N. Strangeman, and A. Meyer, 2003, Washington, DC: Office of Special Education Programs, Office of Special Education and Rehabilitative Services.

Table 3.2
Differentiation and Life Skills Instruction

Ideas for effective differentiation	Life skills instruction and effective differentiation
Effective curriculum	Focus is on improving outcomes for students and making links to post-secondary experiences.
Flexible teaching	Teachers can differentiate based on content, process, and products depending on the needs of the students.
Shared responsibility for learning	Students are active participants in the program.
Building community	Individual strengths are honored and needs reviewed and strengthened.
Emphasis on individual growth	The student's Individualized Education Program details the student's progress.

Note. The information in column 1 is adapted from *How To Differentiate Instruction in Mixed-Ability Classrooms* (2nd ed., p. 51), by C. A. Tomlinson, 2001, Alexandria, VA: ASCD. Copyright 2001 by Association for Supervision and Curriculum Development.

Life Skills Instructional Opportunities Across the Program Continuum

During the past decade the program continuum for students with special needs has focused increasingly on the best practices of providing a free and appropriate education in the least restrictive environment. A wide range of inclusive educational models that embrace heterogeneous groups and the principles of UDL and DI are successfully being practiced in schools throughout the country in addition to the more traditional self-contained classes. Across the board this range presents an exciting opportunity to provide life skills instruction for all students.

The identification of major life demands and the specific life skills that accompany them is a major component of the top-down model of curriculum development. Working with students to differentiate instruction based on their interests, strengths, and needs is also critical to a proactive grass roots or bottom-up model. When the two approaches are integrated, a successful and comprehensive approach to teaching life skills begins to emerge. The practice or application of this information is the next critical step after the generation of major life demands. Individuals involved in curriculum development or, more precisely, those responsible for what is actually taught to students, can begin to integrate life skills topics and instruction into the curriculum structure within which they operate.

The case has been made for the importance of covering life skills before a student's exit from formal schooling. Now the case must be made that it is possible to do this regardless of the educational environment in which the student is placed. This chapter provides suggestions for teaching life skills regardless of the student's educational environment.

Educational Placements

Past and current reauthorizations of the Individuals with Disabilities Education Act (IDEA) have focused on educating individuals in the least restrictive environment appropriate to their needs. The *Twenty-Sixth Annual Report to Congress on the Implementation of the Individuals with Disabilities Education Act* (U.S. Department of Education [USDOE], 2004) reflected the various educational placements of students with disabilities. Aggregate data on the placements are presented in Table 3.3. This table includes data from the 50 states, District of Columbia, and U.S. territories. Table 3.3 represents the percentages of students (ages 6–21) from a specific categorical group who are placed in the three most common settings: general education, resource room, or a separate (self-contained) class.

Table 3.3 shows variability across the categorical groups as well. Examining the extent of time that students spend in general education settings (the categories labeled "general education" and "resource room") some interesting differences begin to emerge. The majority of students with learning disabilities (86%) are receiving the

Table 3.3
Percentage of Students Age 6 to 21 Served in Different
Educational Environments During 2000–2001 School Year

Environment	All disabilities	Learning disabilities	Emotional disturbance	Mental retardation
General education class	48.2%	46.9%	28.8%	16.9%
Resource class	28.7%	58.6%	23.0%	30.5%
Separate class	19.0%	13.5%	30.7%	52.6%

Note. From *Twenty-Sixth Annual Report to Congress on the Implementation of the Individuals with Disabilities Education Act,* by U.S. Department of Education, 2004, Washington, DC: Office of Special Education Programs, Office of Special Education and Rehabilitative Services.

majority of their education in general education settings (combining the general education and resource room figures), whereas fewer students who have been identified as having mental retardation (47%) find themselves in similar arrangements. Not surprisingly, only half (52%) the students classified as having emotional disturbance spend the better part of their educational day in general education environments. This is the same trend that presented itself with data from the early 1990s. The main difference between the data now and the data then is that across the board, in all three categories (learning disabilities, emotional disturbance, and mental retardation) the percentage of students being educated in the general education environment (general education and resource room) has increased. Comparing the USDOE's (2004) *Twenty-Sixth Annual Report to Congress* to the *Sixteenth Annual Report to Congress* (USDOE, 1994), students who have learning disabilities went from 79% to 86% of their time in general education settings, students having emotional disturbance went from 44% to 52%, and those with mental retardation had the largest increase from 31% to 47% of their day spent in general education settings.

The logical implications of these data for teaching life skills to such students suggest that options for delivering instruction, particularly in the general education settings, are needed. For students who spend all of their instructional day in general education settings and receive consultant services from special education personnel, life skills topics have to be worked into the established curriculum. While this suggestion holds for students receiving resource services when they are in general education settings, special education teachers can infuse life skills topics into the designated content they must cover with these students when they are in the resource room. They can also augment prescribed instruction with additional life skills topics that may be related but are separate from what they must cover. This view aligns nicely with the philosophies of UDL and DI discussed in the beginning of this chapter by which all students will benefit from the instruction provided.

For students who are in special education settings for at least the greater part of their instructional day, other more comprehensive options such as life skills coursework may be viable. The other options described above (infusion and augmentation) are also possible. Overriding issues such as credit versus noncredit courses or the particular philosophy of a school (i.e., school-based decision making) or school district (i.e., focus on literacy) may dictate the nature of certain programs.

Options for Organizing Integration of Life Skills Content in Instruction

A realistic appraisal of the adult outcome needs of students, the current educational placements of students, and various school restructuring movements suggests that a continuum of options for delivering life skills instruction is warranted. A potential continuum is represented in Figure 3.1, which represents variations in the amount of time available for covering life skills topics. The option at the bottom of the continuum is life skills oriented. The option at the top of the continuum represents a scenario in which content other than life skills is emphasized. Between these two ends of the continuum are other viable options depending on the nature of the teaching situation and curriculum.

One should not speculate that the continuum reflects the distinction between inclusive educational programs and those that are self-contained. It is very possible

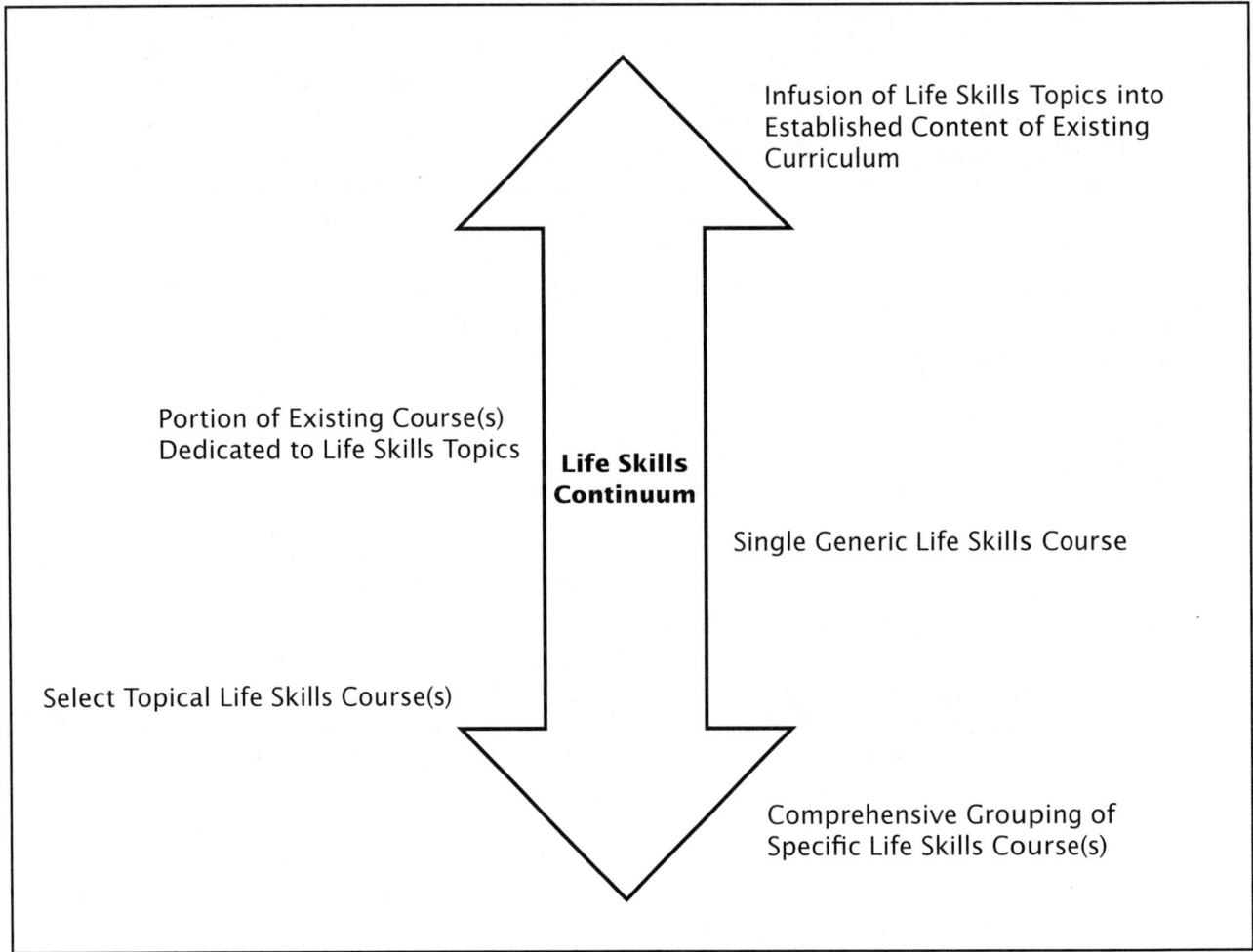

FIGURE 3.1. Options for integrating life skills content into the curriculum.

that a diploma-generating general education program might have a life skills orientation or that the infusion approach may have to be implemented in a vocational program that does not cover essential life skills.

The primary message is that teaching life skills to students with special needs is needed and that it can be accomplished regardless of the educational setting in which the students' needs are being met. From the continuum in Figure 3.1, one can also apply the principles of differentiated instruction and universal design of learning. Some students may be able to access what they need from an infusion approach, whereas others may need more of an augmentation approach or even a specific course on a particular topic. The natural flexibility of the continuum is conducive to meeting the needs of students with diverse learning needs.

The remainder of this section provides examples of how the various options highlighted in Figure 3.1 can be implemented. As shown in Table 3.4, the continuum has been arbitrarily categorized into three types of approaches for integrating life skills content into the curriculum: infusion approach, augmentation approach, and coursework approach. Table 3.4 summarizes the different options presented in the following discussion.

Table 3.4
Comparison of Various Options for Teaching Life Skills Content

Curricular options	Nature of curricular approach	Inclusive settings	Self-contained settings	Elementary level	Secondary level	Curricula examples
Infusion into existing content	infusion	yes	yes	yes	yes	working in a discussion of how to treat athlete's foot when the topic of fungus is covered in a general science textbook
Dedicated portion of course	augmentation	yes	yes	yes	yes	unit on "the financial implication of dating" in addition to the general content of a unit on fractions
Generic life skills course	distinct course	yes	yes	no	yes	elective course titled "Career Exploration 1"
Topical life skills course	distinct course	yes	yes	no	yes	course titled "Math in the Real World"
Comprehensive arrangement of life skills courses	distinct set or series of courses	yes/no (situation specific)	yes	no	no	set of courses such as: • personal finance • practical math • health and hygiene • greenhouse science • practical communication • community awareness and involvement • occupational development • interpersonal relations

Infusion Approach

Rationale. The infusion approach is used when students are in a curricular orientation that is highly structured and allows for neither elective life skills coursework nor the allocation of time to cover additional topics. Frequently, it will apply to situations where students are fully included in general education classes and, if they are on the secondary level, are likely to be in diploma-track programs.

Implementation. Two requirements are needed for teachers to infuse life skills instruction into existing course content. First, teachers need to be familiar with various major life demands and resulting specific life skills such as those presented in previous chapters. Second, teachers must be aware of the specific topics presented in the instructional material being used. It is critical to capitalize on the "teachable moments" created by existing content. Once a topic is identified as having life skills relevance, attention must be directed to it and then coverage can ensue. Interdisciplinary or thematic units also provide a fertile foundation for identifying life skills relevance and making connections to a variety of topical areas (Meyer-Meinbach, Fredericks, & Rothlein, 2000; Williams & Deal-Reynolds, 1993; Willis, 1995).

Ideally, teachers (especially special education teachers providing consultation services to general education teachers) would preview materials to identify all the topics that could be expanded into a discussion of functional values. Once these values are identified, some preparation may be needed. If done with enough lead time, teachers could obtain materials that may serve as resources for the discussion. Appendix A of this guide can be used for this purpose. Special education teachers will find that having knowledge about life skills and how to make existing content more relevant to students is a valuable asset in their work with general education teachers.

A limitation of the infusion approach is that the life skills addressed are dictated by the topics in the instructional materials. Hence, this approach leads to incomplete coverage of the many life demands for which students need to be prepared. There are, however, some positive benefits of the infusion approach for both students and teachers. Minimally, students will learn about some important life skills, and infusing life skills topics into the existing curriculum will enhance the relevancy of the instruction for students. A secondary outcome is that students are likely to be more excited about the topics being presented.

Examples. Given the current regulatory mandates previously discussed, the infusion option is both relevant and timely. Because of this relevancy, we are providing four examples of how teachers can use the infusion technique with their students. A similar format is used in representing each of the examples. First, the title of the course is given, with an indication of whether the course is credit or noncredit; second, the specific topic being covered in the course is highlighted; third, selected life skills activities that could be chosen to infuse into the topic, along with any appropriate major life demands, are offered.

1. **Course:** General Math Course (credit)
   Topic Being Covered: "Keeping Financial Records"
   Life Skills Activities To Be Infused [Major Life Demands]
   • Discuss record-keeping systems needed for managing family finances. [Maintaining a budget, paying bills, and paying taxes]
   • Examine occupations that require financial record-keeping skills. [Seeking and securing a job]
   • Examine various types of community involvement that involve financial record-keeping skills. [Creating change in the community (e.g., volunteer work on a community fundraiser)]

2. **Course:** United States History (credit)
   Topic Being Covered: "Women's Rights"

Life Skills Activities To Be Infused [Major Life Demands]
- Discuss the topics of discrimination. [Being sensitive to the needs of others]
- Identify the procedures to register to vote. [Using all levels of government agencies]
- Discuss the issues and candidates' positions of an upcoming election. [Knowing major events at the local, regional, national, and international levels]
- Write to the League of Women Voters and the National Organization for Women to share concerns. [Sharing personal feelings, experiences, concerns, and desires with other people]

3. **Course:** General Science (credit)
   Topics Being Covered: "Fungus" in a section titled "All Living Things Are Made of Cells"
   Life Skills Activities To Be Infused [Major Life Demand]
   - Discuss how one can contract, treat, and prevent athlete's foot. [Understanding illnesses and medical/dental needs across age levels]

4. **Course:** Greenhouse Science (noncredit)
   Topic Being Covered: "Ecosystems"
   Life Skills Activities To Be Infused [Major Life Demands]
   - Discuss the balance needed in a terrarium. [Engaging in individual hobbies and crafts]
   - Discuss environmental issues of local concern. [Understand all sides of public opinion on community issues]

These examples are presented to give a taste of what can be done to make content life skills relevant and meaningful for both teachers and students.

Augmentation Approach

Rationale. Augmentation can be used when there is some class time available to cover topics that are not prescribed by course description. This option allows the integration of life skills topics that usually relate to a similar topic being covered in the course. In some cases, one class period each week may be specifically dedicated to covering life skills; in other situations, life skills will be covered when there is relevance to course content. The distinguishing feature between this option and infusion is that a great portion of allocated course time is dedicated to covering life skills in augmentation.

Procedures. What teachers need to do is quite simple: Identify the life skills areas, develop or identify a unit on the topics, plan for teaching the unit, and deliver the instruction. Again, familiarity with the major demands of adulthood may be helpful. The same strengths and limiting features described for the infusion approach apply to this approach. One difference, however, is that more teacher preparation time may be needed in an augmentation approach because more class time is being devoted to this instruction.

Examples. All of the scenarios used to exemplify the infusion approach could be used with augmentation as well. Where cursory attention is given to the life skills topics in an infusion approach, more in-depth coverage is given to such topics in an augmentation approach. For instance, on the topic of "Women's Rights," the teacher could present a comprehensive unit on discrimination "then and now." Such a unit could provide extensive coverage of this topic and would be of great value to students with special needs, some of whom may have experienced the personal insult that accompanies discriminatory practices. The athlete's foot topics could be expanded into a unit on how to proactively prevent health problems.

Another example that shows how a topic could be augmented to cover real-world needs is to spend some time on the "economics of dating" when teaching a mathematics course. Few topics spark more interest and enthusiasm in adolescents than this one, as it has real meaning to most of them. The teacher would differentiate the approach to meet the learners' needs; thus, the topic could be done as an augmentative approach in a mathematics course that had more of a life skills approach, or as an infusion approach in an Algebra I or II class. An intriguing unit could be developed that would examine the cost of going on a date. Activities could be planned to have students decide with whom they want to go, where they want to go, what they want to do, what they think it will cost, and ultimately what is the actual cost to go on this date. This example serves two important purposes: (a) the outcomes of examining the monetary costs associated with dating would reinforce the math principles presented in the Algebra I or II class and (b) the unit teaches some meaningful life skills.

Life Skills Classes: Coursework

Rationale. Classes that are focused on life skills and are substantially integrated into existing coursework can be an integral aspect of a student's school experience. In some cases, one class period each week may be specifically dedicated to covering life skills; in other situations, life skills will be covered when there is relevance to course content. The distinguishing feature between this option and augmentation is that a greater portion of allocated course time is dedicated to covering life skills in this option.

Many schools offer an array of existing courses that incorporate life skills curricula. Their monikers can vary, such as specials, cocurriculars, exploratory times, and elective classes, but regardless of the name, they serve the similar purpose of allowing students to learn more about a topical area that interests them and is often linked to life skills (Wolk, 2001). These courses are available to all students (special education and general education) and typically include consumer and family science, health, computers, and business. Some schools have gone further and linked student needs to course requirements. For example, some middle schools require all students to pass basic keyboarding or computer classes before transitioning to high school. This was done in response to the need for students at the high school level to have basic proficiency in keyboarding. Other courses focus on overall life skills through coping strategies, social–emotional health, and school personalization (Wenz-Gross, Anderson, Parker, O'Meara, & Carreiro King, 2002). More typical courses target adaptive daily living skills and other life skills activities for students with special needs. These courses offer students who may need a more comprehensive life skills program the opportunity to fully explore this curriculum.

Another opportunity for embedding life skills activities into an existing school structure is through advisory time (also referred to as advisory/advisee time or mentoring time). Advisory time is when a teacher has consultation time (or chat time) with the same core group of students for anywhere from 20 minutes to a full class period. The amount of advisory time varies from school to school, but the focus is typically on social–emotional development (Coleman, 2001; Esposito & Curcio-Cole, 2002; Schoenlein, 2001), which can be easily aligned with a variety of life skills activities.

Procedures. Like the previously discussed options, the development of coursework should be based on the future needs of students. A recommended procedure for the development of the content to be covered in life skills courses, presented in Figure 3.2, is discussed below. We recognize that other administrative requirements may be necessary; they are addressed in Chapter 4.

1. *Decide the major goals for the course in terms of both content and instruction.* What outcomes are students to demonstrate? How is instruction going to be delivered and content covered (i.e., textbooks, community-based)?

2. *Develop a scope and sequence of the content to be covered.* Content should be based on students' current and future needs, as determined by a realistic appraisal of probable subsequent environments. Identification of potential topics for inclusion in coursework might involve selecting topics from existing resources, such as the list of major life demands contained in Table 1.6 of this guide, or a listing of competencies and subcompetencies, such as Brolin's (1991) *Life-Centered Career Education* program.

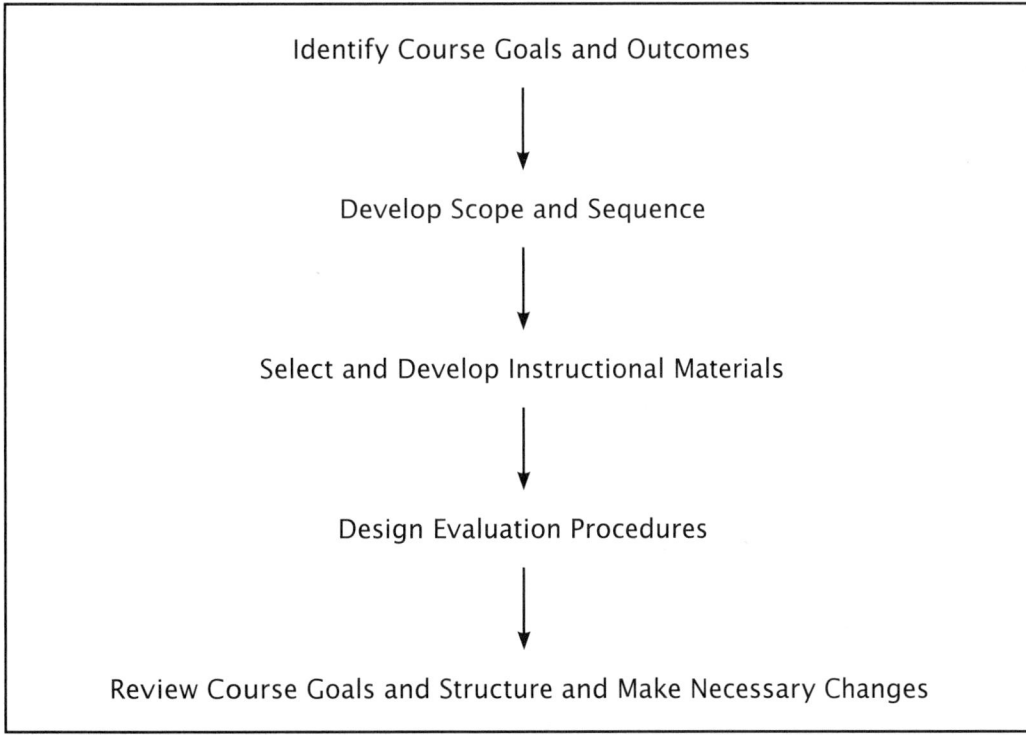

FIGURE 3.2. Course development process.

3. *Select instructional materials that will be helpful in accomplishing the goals of the course.* (Appendix A of this guide should be helpful with this task.) It is possible that teachers will want to use a textbook in a certain course. Many districts have detailed protocols for textbook review and purchase. We recommend working with the district's administrators (school-based and central-office) to assist in facilitating this process. It may be necessary to develop one's own materials or solicit materials from community sources if commercial ones are unavailable. Ways of dealing with this problem are discussed in Chapter 4.

4. *Design a procedure to evaluate the effectiveness of the life skills coursework.* It is extremely important to create mechanisms for assessing how well life skills are being taught and how well students are learning them. The social validity of any course rests in how well the content benefits the students either immediately or at some later point. As a result, it might be necessary to conduct follow-up studies of students to determine whether the life skills taught are indeed important in their lives and whether the students show competence in performing them. Assessment is extensively reviewed in Chapter 2.

5. *Review course goals and structure and make changes as necessary.* All programs should be considered temporary offerings. Curricular change and innovation should be a scheduled part of all programs. It will be essential to revise life skills courses to adapt to an ever-changing world.

Examples. As suggested in Figure 3.1, there are three options for the coursework approach: a single generic life skills course, selected topical life skills courses, and a comprehensive grouping of specific life skills courses. A single generic life skills course is one option that many high schools have made available for students. This course would present a comprehensive life skills curriculum for which students receive credits. This approach is used when the curriculum allows for the development of a separate course. There are a number of variations related to this option, from a year-long life skills class that covers a myriad of topical areas to a set of different topical life skills courses that could be offered as quarterly electives depending on students' needs. Often typical peers who may need support in learning about life skills or who have an interest in the field of education take life skills coursework in an inclusive setting. The advantage of the coursework option is that more time can be devoted to functional content, and it can be organized according to adult need rather then being dictated by other course content.

Some districts break their program into Life Skills I and Life Skills II. Students may take Life Skills I during the freshman or sophomore year of high school and Life Skills II during the junior or senior year. When this occurs, the first part of the coursework (i.e., Life Skills I) focuses on having students apply academic skills in the natural environment. Practicing money identification, giving change, using calculators, decision making, and studying appropriate vocabulary for each of these life skills are examples of tasks that can be introduced and practiced in the classroom. Teachers can also prepare students by inviting resource people from the community (e.g., bankers, medical personnel, store or business managers) into the classroom. A resource person can be any individual who has experience and knowledge relevant to the life skills being taught in the classroom. These people can introduce concepts, describe their jobs associated with their business, outline the training needed to obtain a position similar to theirs, or share information on specific topics (e.g., substance abuse, first aid). This is discussed in depth in Chapter 4. The second part of the curriculum (i.e., Life Skills II) connects the skills learned to application through job-related experiences both on and off the school site. This can be an integrated and integral aspect of developing life skills coursework and is also discussed in Chapter 4.

A topical life skills course could take one of two different formats. One format is a course designed entirely around an adult domain. For instance, an entire course could easily address the topic of home and family. In many schools, courses along these lines already exist and should be considered for inclusion in a student's program of studies. The second format focuses on a more traditional area. An example of a math course along these lines is "Math in the Real World"—a course designed to cover math that has real-world relevance. Some of the possible topics that could be part of this course are presented in Figure 3.3.

The third option for coursework relates to the situation in which a series of life skills courses is offered. This option is useful in schools that provide innovative alternative functional curricula that generate credit toward graduation or functional curricula for students who are not in diploma-track programs.

Living within one's means

Estimating   Profit and loss

Areas, surface, and volumes

Percentages   Hire and purchase

Signed numbers   Taxes

Interest   Tables and graphics

Ratios and proportions   Geometry

Travel and transportation

Games and chance

Math for home maintenance and repair

FIGURE 3.3. Possible topics for "Math in the Real World."

A suggested series of life skills courses is presented under this option in Table 3.4. The organizational scheme for the development of this series is an attempt to cover the areas of math, science, social studies, and communication. Each course includes coverage of the major life demands we all must face. Selected examples of some of the content from each of the courses are provided in Table 3.5.

Table 3.5
Suggested Life Skills Courses and Select Sample Topics

Life skills courses	Samples of topics covered
Personal finance	maintaining a budget filing tax forms submitting an application for a loan using credit cards
Practical math	performing home repairs and maintenance estimating travel time cooking measuring dosage of prescribed medicine
Health and hygiene	dealing with illness administering first aid maintaining one's personal appearance handling stress
Everyday science	gardening identifying how things work controlling pests using science in the kitchen
Practical communication	using resource materials requesting information writing personal cards and notes taking phone messages
Community awareness and involvement	registering to vote using community resources (e.g., library) attending neighborhood association meetings knowing one's legal rights
Occupational development	identifying personal interests and aptitudes preparing a career-planning packet practicing interview skills identifying available jobs in the community
Interpersonal relations	getting along with others accepting criticism complimenting others engaging in social conversation

Community-Based Instruction

One of the most important aspects of a life skills curriculum is the practice or application of the life skills in the natural environment. This type of experience is valuable for students. It builds confidence and self-esteem needed to function in the community environment. We suggest that teachers start with in-school experiences and move to community experiences when the students reach a certain level of success with the school-based experiences. These experiences also enable teachers to continuously review and assess their students' strengths and needs and to adjust the program accordingly. Further in-depth discussion and selected examples of community-based instruction are provided in Chapter 4.

Relationship of Scholastic and Social Skills to Life Skills

Understanding the relationship of scholastic and social skills to acquisition of life skills is important. One must comprehend the concerns and fears of significant individuals (parents, students, teachers, administrators) that may affect each student's mastery of basic competencies before leaving school.

Importance of the Relationship

One has to simply read the newspaper or watch the news to see the national and local concern about students' acquiring basic academic, social, and survival skills. In this age of accountability, everyone wants to ensure that students can successfully read, write, listen, speak, solve problems, and use math concepts. The concern also extends to the students' ability to survive in different situations and environments and get along with those they meet. The acquisition of these skills is paramount to a student's success on the job and as a community member. As teachers, we work hard to see that these skills are instilled in every student prior to their exit from formal schooling. A source of additional support comes from parent engagement in the life skills process. Parents and guardians are the first teachers of their children and can serve to strengthen what their children learn at school as well as to connect the concepts learned to their home and community environment.

The selected examples, activities, and recommendations throughout this chapter, and indeed the entire book, can be adapted for either the classroom or home and community environment. In recent years, after-school programs have been able to incorporate valuable life skills activities into their repertoire through theme-based programming (Bergstrom & O'Brien, 2001). Encouraging and educating parents and others in regard to life skills application and development in the classroom, as well as providing opportunities for home-based or after-school activities, is paramount to successful acquisition and, hopefully, generalization of the acquired life skills in a variety of settings. Technology is one valuable tool that can be used to assist both educators and parents in developing activities appropriate for either the school or home environment. Chapter 5 discusses information on instructional materials, including technology, that are adaptable for both teachers and parents.

As educators, parents, and community members, we want each student to leave the formal school experience with the skills to be successful as an adult in the community. Life skills instruction fulfills that wish. The merging of scholastic instruction and life skills instruction for adult outcome–based programs provides a likely solution to critical concerns for all. Figures 3.4 and 3.5 provide examples of how these concepts can be integrated into students' programs. These integrated activities can be modified for either school or home.

Selected Examples Across School Levels

Figures 3.4 and 3.5 present sample activities that incorporate scholastic skills with adult domains (under which major life demands and life skills are identified). These matrices exemplify the application of scholastic skills and social and survival skills to everyday adult tasks or life skills. The suggested activities illustrate these functional applications.

Activities emphasizing functional application of scholastic skills can be found at any grade level. Figure 3.4, the elementary matrix, outlines examples of activities that are appropriate at the elementary level. These examples are relatively simple types of tasks that are, in many cases, preliminary to other activities that students are expected to master later in their programs. In many cases, the activities are introductory to a concern that will be mastered within the next few years.

Figure 3.5. the secondary matrix, illustrates activities that would more commonly be associated with older students who are a few months to a few years from exiting their programs. These tasks represent a level of performance that is expected of any successful adult in the community. These matrices provide teachers, parents, and others a working idea of the range of ability, age, and type of tasks that can be found in a life skills program. In addition, they offer an illustration of the relationship between needed scholastic skills and the real-life application of those skills to everyday situations.

This chapter provided suggestions for organizing and delivering life skills in varying academic, school, or home situations. In addition, the relationship to teaching scholastic skills in solving real-life tasks at the elementary and secondary level was discussed.

	Employment/ Education	Home and Family	Leisure Pursuits	Community Involvement	Emotional/ Physical Health	Personal Responsibility and Relationships
Reading	Read library books on various occupations.	Read directions to prepare brownies from a mix.	Look for ads in the newspaper for toys.	Read road signs and understand what they mean.	Locate poison control numbers in the phone book.	Read a story to a younger child.
Writing	Write to the school board about a pothole in the school driveway.	Make a list of items needed from the grocery store.	Fill out a magazine order form completely.	Complete an application to play Little League.	Keep a daily diary of food you eat in each food group.	Write a thank-you note to a relative for a gift.
Listening	Listen to a lecture by a bank official on savings accounts.	Listen to a lecture on baby-sitting tips.	Listen to radio/TV to see if a ball game is rained out.	Listen to a lecture on how children can recycle.	Listen to the school nurse explain the annual eye exam for your class.	Listen to a family describe their family vacation.
Speaking	Discuss reasons we work.	Ask parents for permission to stay at a friend's house.	Invite friends over to play Monopoly.	Discuss park and playground improvements with the mayor.	Ask the school nurse how to care for mosquito bites.	Discuss honesty, trust, and promise. Define them.
Math Applications	Calculate how much you would make babysitting at $3.25 an hour for 3 hours.	Compute the cost of a box of cereal using a coupon.	Compute the cost of going to the movies.	Compute tax on a video game.	Calculate and compare the cost of different types of adhesive bandage. Include tax.	Ask a friend to share a candy bar. Calculate your part of the cost.
Problem Solving	Decide which environment you work best in: out or in; quiet or noisy; active or at a desk, etc.	Decide how to share TV time with a sibling.	Given $20 for the afternoon, which would you do: go to the movies, go bowling, or play DVDs?	Role-play types of scenarios in which you would use the 911 emergency number.	Decide how many hours of sleep you need per night.	Decide if you have enough money to purchase a vending-machine soda for you and your friend.
Survival Skills	Keep homework assignments in a special notebook.	Develop a checklist of what to do before and after school.	Use a map to find the best way to the mall.	Draw a map of the way you go to and from school.	Mark the calendar for your next dental appointment.	Identify important table manners.
Personal/ Social	Ask a classmate to assist you with a job.	Settle a dispute with a sibling.	Call a multimedia store to see if they have a specific movie.	Role-play asking a police officer for help if you're lost.	Ask a friend to go bicycling with you.	Role-play appropriate behavior for various places (movies, church, restaurant, ball park).

FIGURE 3.4. Elementary matrix: Relationship of scholastic and social skills to adult domains.

	Employment/ Education	Home and Family	Leisure Pursuits	Community Involvement	Emotional/ Physical Health	Personal Responsibility and Relationships
Reading	Read classified ads for jobs.	Interpret bills.	Locate and understand movie information in a newspaper.	Follow directions on tax forms.	Comprehend directions on medication.	Read letters from friends.
Writing	Write a letter of application for a job.	Write checks.	Write for information on a city to visit.	Fill in a voter registration form.	Fill in your medical history on forms.	Send thank-you notes.
Listening	Understand oral directions of a procedure change.	Comprehend oral directions for making dinner.	Listen to a weather forecast to plan outdoor activity.	Understand campaign ads.	Attend lectures on stress.	Take turns in a conversation.
Speaking	Ask your boss for a raise.	Discuss morning routines with your family.	Inquire about tickets for a concert.	State your opinion at a school board meeting.	Describe symptoms to a doctor.	Give feedback to a friend about the purchase of a CD or DVD.
Math Applications	Understand the difference between net and gross pay.	Compute the cost of doing laundry in a laundromat versus at home.	Calculate the cost of a dinner out versus eating at home.	Obtain information for a building permit.	Use a thermometer.	Plan the costs of a date.
Problem Solving	Settle a dispute with a coworker.	Decide how much to budget for rent.	Role-play appropriate behaviors for various places.	Know what to do if you are the victim of fraud.	Select a donor.	Decide how to ask someone for a date.
Survival Skills	Use a prepared career planning packet.	List emergency phone numbers.	Use a shopping center directory.	Mark a calendar for important dates (e.g., recycling, garbage collection).	Use a system to remember to take vitamins.	Develop a system to remember birthdays.
Personal/ Social	Apply appropriate interview skills.	Help a child with homework.	Know the rules of a neighborhood pool.	Locate self-improvement classes.	Get a yearly physical exam.	Discuss how to negotiate a price at a flea market.

FIGURE 3.5. Secondary matrix: Relationship of scholastic and social skills to adult domains.

COMMUNITY-BASED INSTRUCTION

Community-based programs have become a staple in the U.S. educational system. They have evolved over a period of time from work–study experiences to distributive education in the 1950s, 1960s, and 1970s to field experiences in the 1980s (Cronin, Wendling, Lord, & Palmisano, 1991) and service learning during the late 1980s (Kinsley & McPherson, 1995) and throughout the 1990s to the present (Kaye, 2004; Kinsley & McPherson, 1995; Lewis, 1995). In most locations, community-based options are now available in most public and nonpublic school systems.

Several terms and definitions can be found in the literature in reference to using the community in some way, shape, or form for instructional use. Over the last several decades, the community has become a significant resource for all students in school. This chapter outlines the various aspects of community-based instruction as it relates to applying life skills to everyday life. This includes defining community-based instruction, identifying who is involved in community-based instruction, making the connection and engagement of community-based instruction with the community, knowing the community and its resources, and discussing the components of community-based instruction.

What Is Community-Based Instruction?

Several terms appear in the literature to convey the concept of community-based instruction (CBI). A few of those terms include community instruction, community participation, community-based interactions, and community-based programs or programming. These terms and others describe a programming option in schools that helps students make the connection between academic content and real-life experiences. Current definitions include the following:

> CBI is a strategy used to promote functional skills in natural, nonschool environments that students frequent individually, with their families, or with peers. (Beakley, Yoder, & West, 2003, p. 1)

> Community experiences allow a student to have hands-on experiences in (1) employment, (2) recreation, (3) recreation/leisure, and (4) community functioning (e.g., accessing community resources, such as medical, travel, safety, banking). (Flexer, Simmons, Luft, & Baer, 2005, p. 222)

Community-based training ... involves educators implementing instruction and requiring students to perform behaviors in work sites, recreational areas, restaurants, grocery stores, shopping malls, and other places in the local community that they are likely to frequent as adults. (Sabornie & deBettencourt, 2004, p. 346)

Community-based instruction ... should be provided in the community in which the student lives and in the businesses frequented by the student and his or her family. (Wehman, 2001, p. 152)

As you can see, the above definitions have similarities and differences. Simply put, community-based instruction is the application of knowledge in its natural environment (e.g., instruction on the Dewey decimal system should be in the library, punching a time clock in an employment setting, baking cookies in a kitchen, vacuuming a carpet in an independent living situation, completing a personal information form in a doctor's office, registering to vote in a county or parish voter registration office, and signing up for a soccer team in a recreation gym). By learning real-life skills in their natural environments, students benefit for a lifetime from the experiences. Authentic learning in the natural or nonschool environment is very powerful and not easily forgotten. Several federal mandates (e.g., the No Child Left Behind [NCLB] Act, the Individuals with Disabilities Education Act [IDEA]), individual state standards (Bassett & Kochhar-Bryant, 2003), school reform movements (e.g., NCLB), and accreditation bodies (e.g., National Council of Accreditation of Teacher Education, Southern Association of Colleges and Schools) require or strongly suggest that schools use performance-based learning and assessment techniques with students. Every student, regardless of academic functioning level, is able to benefit from performance-based experiences. The experience of learning how to sail a boat is much different from reading about sailing or watching a film on sailing. Getting out in a boat on the water is the real learning experience. Many children and adolescents will beg their parents for the experience of learning to play baseball, dance a ballet, perform gymnastics, or play a musical instrument. Many times the inspiration to do these activities comes from their reading about or observing others doing the activity. Learning to play baseball or dancing a ballet takes place in the natural environment for each of these activities and not in contrived situations. Why not teach as many skills as we can in natural environments?

Who Should Be Involved in Community-Based Instruction?

Everyone interacting with students on a daily basis or who has the potential of impacting their lives should be involved with some aspect of assisting students in understanding the application of academic information to real-life experiences. These people would include but not be limited to their parents, siblings, extended families, neighbors, friends, peers, teachers, all other school personnel (principal, related service personnel, paraprofessionals, librarians, clerical staff, cafeteria workers, janitors, bus drivers, volunteers), and workers in community government, businesses, and agencies.

A growing body of literature supports community-based instruction for students with disabilities (Agran, Snow, & Swaner, 1999; Beck, Broers, Hogue, Shipstead, & Knowlton, 1994; Brolin & Loyd, 2004; Falvey, 1989; McDonnel, Wilcox, & Hardman, 1991; Wilcox, 1988) as well as for all students (Beakley et al., 2003; Cronin, 1996; Dymond, 2004; Sabornie & deBettencourt, 2004). Community-based instruction needs to be available to every student regardless of functioning level, disability, age, grade level, or other characteristics. Offering this option of instruction in the community to only a select group of students would be limiting the number of individuals who can benefit from a very worthwhile and, for many, a much needed applied learning experience. All students can benefit from problem-solving situations as they happen in the natural environment. These experiences will build self-esteem and confidence in future encounters. Authentic learning in the natural environment is a richer, more meaningful learning experience and one that is not easily forgotten.

Participating in community experiences provides opportunities that cannot be planned or created in another venue. As many teachers can attest, participation is a function of the opportunities presented by the environment, as well as of the individual's skills, as the following scenario demonstrates (Wilcox, 1988, pp. 120–122):

A teacher and four boys from an area high school were visiting three local discount stores with the objective to collect data on the prices of various toiletries to compare the prices of each product at the various stores. They traveled to the stores via public bus. Because it was a cold January day, everyone was wearing a coat. This was an activity they had done earlier in the week in their classroom using empty toiletry containers (e.g., shampoo bottles, toothpaste box and tube, deodorant container). The students were divided into teams of two. Each team had a clipboard, data collection sheets for each product, and pencils. The teacher urged them to use a shopping cart as they had to gather several different brands of toiletries. The boys answered by saying, "Real men don't use shopping carts" and declined the offer of the cart.

As one team of boys was gathering items to start entering data, they could not carry all the items and began putting items in their coat pockets. I am sure you can guess what happened next. Yes, they were caught on the security camera. Needless to say what happened next could never be captured in a classroom lesson. The security guard hauled them off to the manager's office and located the teacher and the other team. The teacher, realizing this was the ultimate teachable moment, asked the manager to proceed as if they were actually shoplifting. The manager gave them the serious "this is what happens when you shoplift" speech, stopping short of calling the sheriff's office. After he had their full attention to the point of tears, he asked them what kind of class assignment they were doing in his store. After they described the activity, the manager asked whether it was possible for them to share the data they collected with him. He then explained why he was interested in that kind of information. He also asked them to come back to his store anytime, but to let him know when they were coming and what the focus of their activity would be, and he said they must use shopping carts. The teacher took him up on his offer. Every time they visited after that experience, the manager greeted them at the door, facilitated their visit, and had refreshments for them. Eventually, two of the boys were placed there for job exploration experiences and several students have been hired as employees at that store.

The teacher realized at that point that everyone learned that day. The boys learned that the prices of various brands of toiletries are different at each store, that they should always use a shopping cart, and, more important, that shoplifting is a no-nonsense, serious matter. They also requested that their class go on a field experience to the sheriff's office to see what happens when people are arrested. The manager learned that his store was an extension of the high school and took a vested interest in the students and teachers at that school. After all, the students were current and future customers, as well as potential employees.

The teacher learned that she needed to do more up-front work with all the businesses and agencies that she used in the community. In addition, she realized that the students needed to be part of the planning process. Their individual and group choices became vital to her facilitating their community learning and participation.

Making the Connection and Engagement of Community-Based Instruction with the Community

Students need to make a connection between learning in the classroom and learning in the natural environment. Community-based instruction allows students to understand the application of academic content to the following real-life skills and experiences in the natural environment: (a) learn or master a skill; (b) solve problems in a variety of situations; (c) make adjustments to their behaviors in social situations; (d) draw relationships between cause and effect in various situations; (e) model or imitate behaviors of peers; (f) provide venues for job sampling; and (g) provide age-appropriate experiences.

Schools, teachers, and parents need to work together to identify students' community needs and the options and opportunities in their communities for engagement. This can happen only when collaboration occurs with the involvement of all parties.

Knowing Your Community and Its Resources

As you are planning the CBI program at your school, it is imperative to become acquainted with significant people and resources in the community. This includes, but is not limited to, people and their jobs, community resources, community agencies, and government resources and programs that you can call upon to assist in the implementation of your CBI program. One way to introduce your program to the community is to create an introductory packet of information. This packet might include information about your school, such as the instructional programs, the students who attend the school, the purpose of nontraditional programs, demographic information about the school, the curriculum, transportation options and issues, the type of performance-based activities you expect of each student, and the expectations that you and your principal have for the employees and volunteers of businesses, community agencies, and programs. Also very important is the necessity to have insurance coverage for both the students and school personnel who will work with the community contacts or visit the community-based sites. You also need to interview the potential contacts and identify and visit community resources, agencies, and programs to inquire about their concerns, questions, and guidelines that you and your students will need to follow as potential visitors to their establishments.

To use your community effectively to implement a community-based program and coordinate community activities with your classroom instructional program, you must get to know your community on several levels. This involves identifying potential locations or sites that will provide hands-on experiences for your students and contacting the manager or director to set up an appointment to visit the site. The information packet described above will be a very important document to share with the managers, supervisors, and employees when you visit the potential community-based sites. While you are at the site, if possible, you might also want to observe the various job tasks and interview the managers, supervisors, and employees.

It is also important to familiarize yourself with your district guidelines regarding collaborative activities with businesses, community agencies, and local, state, and federal government offices. Many school systems have outlined the steps for working with entities outside the system including the do's and don'ts of what they can and cannot do. In many cases, an interagency, community partnership, or cooperative agreement must be drafted, reviewed by school system legal personnel, and signed by both parties.

As you are identifying the potential community-based sites in your school district, you might want to align the community-based sites with the domains of adulthood (see Figure 1.3 in Chapter 1) and major life demands (see Table 1.6 in Chapter 1) to ensure balanced coverage of a variety of experiences. In addition, you might want to consider the following targeted options:

• Identify the connections that are possible with the employers of the parents in your school. This connection is an important one and, many times, the most valuable option for all involved.

• Identify businesses and government offices and agencies that will work with you to provide assistance in learning about careers and seeking employment in doing any of the following:

1. Provide placements for students to do observation or job shadowing of various positions in their company and interview current employees about the expectations of their jobs.
2. Provide positions for job sampling experiences.
3. Provide placement opportunities for community vocational training (CVT) sites.

• Identify businesses and government offices and agencies, such as the following, that will assist with instructional situations:

1. grocery stores, drug stores, discount stores, department stores, clothing stores, electronics stores, DVD/video stores, hardware stores, car dealerships, and post offices to assist with such activities as comparison shopping and purchasing items

2. fast food establishments, restaurants, cafeterias, and bakery shops to practice language skills, money skills, choice making, eating skills, and social skills
3. laundromats to learn and practice washing and drying clothes
4. card and gift shops to choose greeting cards or gifts appropriate for specific people for various occasions
5. gas stations, new or used car dealers, and mechanics to learn about the purchasing and maintenance of cars and trucks

• Introduce the students to community services, resources, or government agencies such as these:

1. services at the public libraries such as free use of computers and access to the Internet; checking out books, videos, DVDs, and CDs; and obtaining IRS forms and other government forms or documents
2. recreation programs and facilities such as public parks, playgrounds, swimming pools, Little League baseball, soccer, basketball, swimming, hockey, football, and noncredit classes at community centers
3. community colleges and university campuses for classes in financial management, painting, photography, or dance
4. a public transportation facility to purchase a transit pass
5. utility and other services, including water, garbage, recycling, electricity, gas, cable TV, cellular phone providers, emergency, fire, and police
6. government offices to learn about getting a driver's permit or license, car registration, automobile safety inspections, voter registration, food stamps, or a building permit
7. community agencies and services to learn about their function and purpose: rehabilitation services, Red Cross, League of Women Voters, Salvation Army, Veterans of Foreign Wars, Urban League, or YMCA/YWCA

• Identify possible business, agency, or community organization partnerships in the local community that will assist educational programs in the long haul. These would include but are not limited to doctors, dentists, lawyers, hospitals, local corporations, local merchants, community recreation centers, Social Security office, sororities, fraternities, nonprofit entities, Rotary Clubs, Kiwanis, Elks, Jaycees, Lions Clubs, chambers of commerce, Telephone Pioneers, Knights of Columbus, Boys and Girls Clubs, church or synagogue groups, or any other local civic group.

Several of the contacts, community service organizations, and civic organizations mentioned above will provide speakers to visit your class to discuss their functions and purposes. Others offer financial assistance to schools, educational programs, and other needy groups. Many of these groups also offer financial support to a specific program, such as assisting with the expenses of transportation for a field experience, entrance fees, or meals in the community. In addition, some civic groups will provide assistance in acquiring materials by either purchasing them or helping to gather them in the community. Contact the various organizations for support in your community. Figure 4.1 outlines examples of community resources as they relate to the adult domains.

	Employment/ Education	Home and Family	Leisure Pursuits	Community Involvement	Physical/ Emotional Health	Personal Responsibility and Relationships
Businesses	continuing education workshops	grocery stores	company picnic; sports store; bowling alley	partnership with a K–12 school	drug store; pharmacy	stress workshops at a community center; counseling services
Agencies	employment agency; Department of Labor	local family network organizations	Humane Society	Red Cross; Salvation Army	food stamp programs; food pantry	family support services (e.g., Families Helping Families)
Public Facilities	Social Security office	picnic at a park	outdoor concerts	recycling center	public health flu shot program	
Recreation Facilities	office softball team	zoo	public tennis courts; swimming pools	county fair; Mardi Gras parade		

FIGURE 4.1. Relationship of community resources to adult domains.

Components of Community-Based Instruction

There are several ways community-based instruction can be infused or incorporated into the academic programs of all students. Four techniques that incorporate community-based instruction are currently being used throughout this country. Those include in-school learning opportunities (Beakley et al., 2003; Wehman & Kregel, 2004), community-based opportunities (Beakley et al., 2003; Cronin, 2000; Wehman & Kregel, 2004), volunteerism (Beakley et al., 2003; Kaye, 2004), and service learning (Lewis, 1995; Wehman, 2003; Wehman & Kregel, 2004). Each of these options can be infused or incorporated into the general education curriculum, thereby providing access for all students to community instruction and the opportunity to make the connection of what they learn in school to real-life situations.

In-School Opportunities

Simple experiences that are naturally occurring events around your school can be good introductory community preparation experiences for students before they actually go into the community. Brainstorming a list of all of the potential job experiences available on a particular campus provides a starting point for the teacher to make contacts among the school faculty and staff for possible participation in the program. Figure 4.2 shows a worksheet to assist with this activity.

On-campus field experiences or applied learning experiences provide the best "first" experience to prepare students for off-campus encounters and opportunities. When planning and setting up on-campus field experiences, teachers should adhere to the same procedures they would use for off-campus field experiences. Figures 4.3 and 4.4 provide guidelines for a community resource person's visit and an applied learning experience, respectively.

(text continues on p. 72)

In-School Job Opportunities Brainstorm Activity

Adult Domain:

Subdomain:

Major Life Domain:

School Contacts	Potential Job Experiences

FIGURE 4.2. Organizer for brainstorming for in-school job opportunities.

Preparing for a Community Resource Person's Visit

Teachers must prepare both the class and the community resource person for the visit to their class. The following lists provide basic guidelines for the teacher, the students, and the resource person, both before the visit to the classroom and after the visit is completed.

BEFORE THE VISIT

Prepare Yourself

☐ Determine the instructional goals of your class and how the resource person can help you achieve them.

☐ Study the resource person's field so you will be informed about what he or she does. You might ask for some materials about the person's job, business, agency, or hobby.

☐ Think of some questions or topics of discussion that may be of interest to your students.

☐ Be prepared to support the resource person in the classroom.

Prepare Your Students

☐ Share with your students the resource person's experience and expertise in the area they are studying.

☐ Brainstorm with your students to develop a list of questions for your resource person.

☐ Have the students discuss appropriate behavior.

☐ Have materials, displays, or projects available to share with the resource person.

Prepare Your Resource Person

☐ Inform the resource person of what the instructional goals are for the class and what you want the students to do.

☐ Share with the resource person information such as the size of your class, the age of your students, and the amount of preparation you will do for the visit.

☐ Send a reminder to the resource person concerning time, date, location of the school, and the phone number where you can be reached. Inquire about any needs he or she may have.

☐ Encourage the resource person(s) to do something other than simply lecture. Suggest they wear their work clothes, bring some tools of their trade, publications, handouts, videos/DVDs, or other items that would be of interest to your students.

Other Things to Prepare

☐ Media needs

☐ Someone to greet the resource person

☐ Break time

☐ Unknown factors: a boring speaker, a no-show, or an inappropriate presentation

(continues)

FIGURE 4.3. Checklists for community resource person's visit. *Note.* Adapted from "The Resource Person," a handout by Roxy Smarzik, Instructional Services Department, Region X Education Service Center, Richardson, TX.

☐ Notifying the principal and other teachers
☐ If appropriate, invite other interested students and teachers

AFTER THE VISIT

For the Students

☐ Discuss the presentation and relate it to the concepts being studied.
☐ Ask the students to evaluate the presentation, both in writing and in discussion.
☐ Plan a follow-up activity that will enable the students to study the concept more or put it into action.
☐ Ask students to write thank-you notes to the resource person(s).

For the Resource Person

☐ Personally thank the resource person orally and follow up with a written note.
☐ Inform the resource person of positive feedback from the student evaluations.

For Yourself

☐ Establish a file of resource persons, student evaluations, and follow-up activities.
☐ Note anything you would do differently next time.

FIGURE 4.3. *Continued.*

Placing students with other teachers, staff in the main office, cafeteria workers, media specialists, librarians, counselors, social workers, building engineers, custodians, groundskeepers, coaches, or the athletic director for a specified amount of time each week is a beginning (e.g., one hour, once a day, three times a week). The number and types of positions will vary from campus to campus. The experiences gained will give both the teachers and the students a feel for the students' strengths and potential challenges that might occur when placed in a community setting. In addition, collaborative ventures with other classes or departments can produce beneficial results for all. Table 4.1 provides a sampling of opportunities that are available in most school settings. Examples such as assisting in the school supply store or a snack store can provide additional opportunities for students to work with typical peers in work-related ventures.

Community Opportunities

Community opportunities encompass applied learning experiences that can be sustained with career and job exploration experiences or short-term job shadowing experiences. Students can be matched to job experiences in the community, such as volunteering at a local hospital or nursing home, working at local retail stores or offices, or assisting in preschool centers, just to name a few. Job shadowing can last for a specified number of weeks and give the student a reality-based opportunity to engage in job exploration activities. For example, at one high school in New England, students have the opportunity to participate in job shadowing experiences in

Preparing for an Applied Learning Experience

One of the most important things a teacher can do when taking his or her class into the community is to plan every detail of the experience. Following are checklists of suggested planning tasks for yourself, students, the community site, and final preparation before you go plus follow-up activities after you return.

BEFORE YOU GO

Prepare Yourself

☐ Determine why you want to go. How does the applied field experience fit into your instructional goals?

☐ Visit the site before the field experience. Talk with the people there to tailor the trip for your students, class content, and instructional goals.

Prepare Your Students

☐ Explain the purpose of the applied learning experience and how it relates to their class work.

☐ Ask for their input concerning what they think they will see.

☐ Identify on-site points of interest to anticipate.

☐ Explain and identify proper field experience behavior. Let students know what you expect from them.

Prepare the Site

☐ Consult with the site managers or directors about your intended applied field experience. Plan to have them meet the group. Ask if personnel will be available for a tour.

☐ Inform them of your instructional goals and the focus of your curriculum.

☐ Follow up with a confirmation note.

Complete Your Preparations

☐ Take care of such details as administrative approval, parental notification and approval, transportation, bus passes, chaperones, notification of other teachers, lunch plans, restroom stops, and scheduling. Depending on your instructional goals, any resource lends itself to multiple explorations. For example, a field experience at a supermarket or department store could involve the following topics:

- product comparison
- price comparison
- weights and measures
- transportation of materials
- budgeting
- product display
- store design

(continues)

FIGURE 4.4. Checklists for an applied learning experience. *Note.* Adapted from "The Field Trip," a handout by Roxy Smarzik, Instructional Services Department, Region X Education Service Center, Richardson, TX.

- store location
- selection and varieties of products
- job availability and application procedures
- departments

WHILE YOU'RE THERE

☐ Supplement your guide's information at the site by relating what the students see to their class activities.

☐ Offer the students different ways of viewing and experiencing the visit. Design an on-site activity (e.g., price comparison); assign them to interview a person while they are there, or ask one student to be the on-site reporter.

☐ Encourage direct experiences. Students enjoy wearing hard hats or lab coats. Demonstrations or hands-on activities are a refreshing change from the lecture approach.

☐ Keep on schedule and watch your time!

☐ Make sure the group acts as a team with the same goals.

☐ Assign a student to photograph the trip. Pictures could be useful for a review of the trip.

AFTER YOU RETURN

☐ Have students write a thank-you note to appropriate individuals at the site.

☐ Have students evaluate the field experience. Compare student expectations before and after the trip.

☐ Plan a follow-up activity that will enable students to apply what they have learned both in school and on site.

☐ Keep a file of field experiences with information about location, contact people, evaluation, and follow-up activities. Note anything you would do differently.

FIGURE 4.4. *Continued.*

a given area that correlates to Career and Technical Center strands. This allows the students to make an informed decision before committing to a particular Career and Technical Center program. Some examples of these job shadowing or work sampling experiences can be found in Table 4.2.

There are times when teachers, administrators, and parents are hesitant to extend teaching into the community environment. Much of this hesitation is the result of past experiences they have had with field trips, the various negative connotations of these types of excursions (e.g., fun, play, unstructured, no application to academics), transportation problems (e.g., no funds for public transportation or school buses), and the lack of understanding of the relationship of the field trip or learning experience to the curriculum. We have found that a simple change of language better communicates the objectives or goals of the field trip or field experience. Instead of referring to a field trip, referring to an applied learning experience clearly gives the indication of an academic exercise with a performance-based aspect in which students must be able to demonstrate competency if they are to meet the applied

Table 4.1
In-School Job Opportunities

Classroom	Office	Cafeteria	Library	Athletic Department	Other
serve as class office runner	deliver mail	collect meal tickets	shelve books	clean equipment	serve as safety patrol
clean black-boards	collect attendance from classroom teachers	roll silverware in napkin	check books in and out	put equipment away	work on school newspaper
pass out papers	stuff envelopes	serve as lunch monitor	read to younger students	sell tickets to athletic events	work on yearbook
collect papers	assist with candy drive	prepare for lunch (fill silverware containers, arrange tables and chairs)		serve as team manager	participate in student council
sharpen pencils				keep score	work in school store

Table 4.2
Community Learning Opportunities by Adult Domains

Employment/ Education	Home and Family	Leisure Pursuits	Community Involvement	Physical/ Emotional Health	Personal Responsibility and Relationships
day care center	grocery store	sports store	recycling center	drug store	stress workshops at community center
school (read to younger children)	lawn and garden center	bowling alley	food pantry	fitness center	counseling services
library (read to younger children)	any retail store	movie theater	library	hospital	
office		museum		doctor's office	
		humane society		hair salon/ barber shop	
		outdoor concerts		nursing home	
		swimming pool			
		zoo			

learning standards or state standards for the life skills knowledge and applied skills. For those students who participate in their state's alternate assessment, this can be an additional opportunity to showcase the students' interactions with the community and, perhaps, with typical peers in natural environments.

An important component of ongoing involvement with the community is continued communication with the family. Appendix C contains three sample permission letters adapted from the St. Bernard Parish Public Schools in Louisiana. As you can see from these examples, attention to details in a permission letter is reassuring to the parents and reinforces the importance of relating academic concepts to real life. The letters also are a subtle suggestion of the types of community activities that parents can model or emulate on a daily basis with their son or daughter.

Teachers generally do not have difficulty finding applied learning sites. Any place, large or small, in the community is a potential site. Figure 4.5 is a brainstorming organizer for identifying contacts who can bring the community to your class if you are not able to go to them. The availability of possible field experiences will vary in each community. Coordinating applied learning experiences to the community with life skills topics being studied by one or more of the students in their classes is also easily done. The curriculum sets the pace and creates the need to visit the natural environment in which the life skills occur in order to practice the skills learned or introduced in the classroom. A matrix of potential community field experiences as they relate to each of the adult domains is provided in Table 4.3.

The logistics of planning and coordinating applied learning experiences in the community involves many details. Preparation of the students for their community experience is extremely important, as is the preparation of your contact people in the field. Figure 4.6 will assist you in preparing your students before they go and provide for instructional activities at the site and follow-up activities when you return. You can give copies of the completed form to your school administration, parents of the students, and the contact at the community site. This will ensure that all involved parties are informed of the plan. Figure 4.4 outlines suggestions for preparing yourself, the students, and the individuals at the applied learning site, as well as suggestions for follow-up after the applied learning experience has been completed. Many of these suggestions can also be applied when implementing school-based experiences.

Teachers who have ventured into the community realize the need for students to be evaluated on these nontraditional experiences. A simple evaluation instrument can be developed to assess students on any number of variables (e.g., social skills, decision making, appropriate dress, use of academic skills or target life skills). Three samples of field experience checklists can be found in Figures 4.7, 4.8, and 4.9. Additional classroom assessment techniques can be found in Chapter 2.

Volunteerism

Another option students can experience in terms of applying knowledge taught in schools to real-life activities is volunteerism. Volunteers come in all sizes, ages, and skill ability levels. Volunteer experiences can occur at any time during one's life and can take place in different formats and venues. For many older children and adolescents, volunteer activities are a prelude to paid employment. Many schools and church-related youth groups are the stimulus for volunteer activities. These can be in the form of group volunteer options or individual activities. Many times volunteer activities surface around holidays (e.g., making food baskets at Thanksgiving, organizing a "Santa" holiday party for children at Christmas, making valentines for residents of a nursing home or assistive living facility, or placing American flags on the graves of veterans on Memorial Day). The range of experiences can include serving Thanksgiving dinner at a homeless shelter or delivering meals to shut-ins to volunteering on a regular basis at a hospital or clinic. Volunteer experiences can also be done as a group such as gathering food donations for a food bank or assisting a group with building a home for Habitat for Humanity. See Table 4.4 for a listing of potential volunteer sites. As with the on-campus experiences, the number and types of volunteer positions will vary from community to community.

Community Experiences Brainstorm Activity

Adult Domain:

Subdomain:

Major Life Domain:

Contacts (people who can bring the community to your class)	Community Sites (places your students can visit)

FIGURE 4.5. Organizer for brainstorming for community experiences.

Table 4.3
Community Field Experiences by Adult Domains

Employment/ Education	Home and Family	Leisure Pursuits	Community Involvement	Physical/ Emotional Health	Personal Responsibility and Relationships
day care center	laundromat	humane society	recycling center	fitness center	stress workshops
school or library (read to younger children)	furniture store	zoo	food pantry	hospital	at community center
	bank	community theater	library	nursing home	counseling services
school office	restaurant	sport teams	fire department	Red Cross (first aid training)	
community college or vocational training facility	retail outlet (comparison shopping)	Mardi Gras parade	public gardens	dentist's office	
	hardware store	hotel or motel	post office	fire department	
personnel department of a business	baby sitting training	toy store	newspaper		

Service Learning

Service learning has become a staple in many school systems as not only an opportunity to apply concepts learned in the classroom to real-life experiences but also an opportunity to give back to the community. Using the service learning concept as part of an academic program can enhance students' learning in several ways. Bessier (1998) and Kaye (2004) have identified several convincing variables that support the incorporation of service learning into the curriculum for all students of every age. Those variables include addressing the local issues and needs; integrating academic content with community and school needs; collaborating with peers, school, and community; using problem-solving skills; promoting a sense of caring for others; and applying academic skills and content to real-life situations and dilemmas.

According to the National and Community Service Act of 1990, service learning is an instructional method

> under which students learn and develop through active participation in thoughtfully organized service experiences that meet actual community needs and that are coordinated in collaboration with the school and the community;

> that is integrated into the students' academic curriculum or provides structured time to think, talk, or write about what the student did and saw during the actual service activity;

> that provides students with opportunities to use newly acquired skills and knowledge in real-life situations in their own communities; and

Field Experience Preparation Worksheet

Academic subject: _____

Adult domain: _____

Subdomain: _____

Major life domain: · _____

Life skill: _____

Date of visit: _____

Site/contact: _____

Address: _____ Phone number: _____

_____ E-mail _____

Transportation: _____

Parent volunteers: _____

Administration/staff involvement: _____

Goals and objectives of visit:

1. _____
2. _____
3. _____

Discussion points:

1. _____
2. _____
3. _____

Preparation activities:

1. _____
2. _____
3. _____

Field activities (site):

1. _____
2. _____
3. _____

Evaluation options:

1. _____
2. _____
3. _____

Follow-up activities:

1. _____
2. _____
3. _____

FIGURE 4.6. Field experience preparation worksheet.

Field Experience Checklist
Register to Vote at the Police Jury Building

Name: _____ Date: _____

	A	NA
1. Dresses appropriately	_____	_____
2. Brings appropriate personal information	_____	_____
3. Walks on sidewalks	_____	_____
4. Has correct change for the bus	_____	_____
5. Presents bus card to driver and places money in change receptacle	_____	_____
6. Politely asks for voter registration form to fill out	_____	_____
7. Completes form with little or no assistance	_____	_____
8. Selects and orders items from Ed and Mike's Mexican Cantina	_____	_____
9. Uses appropriate table manners	_____	_____
10. Leaves appropriate tip for the server	_____	_____
11. Rings bell at the appropriate stop	_____	_____
12. Waits for bus to move before crossing the street	_____	_____

Grade: _____

Comments:

_____

_____

_____

_____

FIGURE 4.7. Sample field experience checklist: Register to vote. *Note.* A = Acceptable; NA = Not acceptable. This field experience checklist was adapted from the St. Bernard Parish (Louisiana) School System Alternative Program. We wish to give special acknowledgment to Deborah Lord and Kathy Wendling for sharing this information.

that enhances what is taught in school by extending student learning beyond the classroom into the community and helps to foster the development of a sense of caring for others.

Why Is Service Learning Important? The importance of service learning cannot be underestimated. Several groups including the U.S. Congress have

Field Experience Checklist
Using Public Transportation

Name: _____ Date: _____

	A	NA
1. Dresses appropriately	_____	_____
2. Gives coupons to the bus driver	_____	_____
3. Gives correct change for city bus	_____	_____
4. Places change in receptacle	_____	_____
5. Asks driver for transfer	_____	_____
6. Walks on sidewalks when available	_____	_____
7. Rings bell at appropriate stop	_____	_____
8. Gets off bus and waits until bus passes before crossing street	_____	_____

Grade: _____

Comments:

_____

_____

_____

_____

FIGURE 4.8. Sample field experience checklist: Using public transportation. *Note.* A = Acceptable; NA = Not acceptable. This field experience checklist was adapted from the St. Bernard Parish (Louisiana) School System Alternative Program. We wish to give special acknowledgment to Deborah Lord and Kathy Wendling for sharing this information.

recognized the need to formalize and offer options for young people to participate in service learning activities through formal school-related activities and other venues (e.g., church groups, Boy Scout and Girl Scout troops). Kaye (2004) presented these reasons supporting the importance of service learning:

- provides meaningful ways for everyone in a school (all students, teachers, and administrators) and community agencies and contacts to come together for a common purpose that is mutually beneficial
- provides many benefits for students such as academic, social, and emotional learning experiences; development of skills in several areas; exploration of career options; and appreciation of civic responsibility and community participation

Field Experience Checklist
Don's Wholesale Club Comparison Shopping

Name: _____ Date: _____

	A	NA
1. Appropriate dress: collared shirt; jeans in good condition	_____	_____
2. Clean shaven	_____	_____
3. Well-groomed hair, nails, and ears	_____	_____
4. Smells nice	_____	_____
5. Makes polite conversation	_____	_____
6. Refrains from name-calling	_____	_____
7. Talks in a soft voice	_____	_____
8. Does comparison shopping in an orderly manner	_____	_____
9. Handles equipment (TV, stereos, VCRs) with care	_____	_____
10. Orders in a clear voice at Bill's Famous Hamburgers	_____	_____
11. Says "thank you" after ordering	_____	_____
12. Uses appropriate table manners	_____	_____
13. Waits for everyone to finish eating before getting up to leave	_____	_____
14. Cleans up table after eating	_____	_____
15. Returns to the bus at the right time	_____	_____

Grade: _____

Comments:

_____

_____

_____

_____

FIGURE 4.9. Sample field experience checklist: Comparison shopping. *Note.* A = Acceptable; NA = Not acceptable. This field experience checklist was adapted from the St. Bernard Parish (Louisiana) School System Alternative Program. We wish to give special acknowledgment to Deborah Lord and Kathy Wendling for sharing this information.

Table 4.4
Potential Volunteer Opportunities by Adult Domains

Employment/ Education	Home and Family	Leisure Pursuits	Community Involvement	Physical/ Emotional Health	Personal Responsibility and Relationships
day care center	homeless shelter	humane society	recycling center	fitness center	stress workshops at community center
school (read to younger children)	adopt a grandparent	zoo	food pantry	hospital	counseling services
library (read to younger children)	yard sale for distressed family	community theater	library	nursing home	
school office	Meals on Wheels	community sport teams	fire department	Red Cross	
new student mentor	holiday gift baskets	museum	community vegetable gardens	disaster relief	
		beach clean-up	voter registration		

- provides a venue to demonstrate the relevance of the content they are learning in school and develop collaboration skills within a diverse situation
- provides help for community members

Definitions of Service Learning. There are many misconceptions about service learning. Service learning is not additional content to teach in the classroom, an isolated activity, a one-time volunteer activity, nor a one-time good deed or random act of kindness (Bessier, 1998; Lewis, 1995). Service learning should not be perceived as just another activity done in school, but as an important integrated component of the overall curriculum that is an inclusive, collaborative effort among members of the school, families, businesses, agencies, and community members. Definitions of service learning reflect these sentiments.

Sawyer (1991), as cited in Kinsley and McPherson (1995), describes service learning as a powerful educational experience where interest collides with information, values are formed, and action emerges. The learning part has two dimensions: an inner dimension—learning about yourself, your motivation, your values—and an outer dimension—learning about the world and its ways.

Kaye (2004, p. 7) suggests that we need to define service learning by what it does for students. She advocates using service learning in a way that connects classroom content and skills to community needs. In doing so, students will use their skills gained through academic, social, and personal experiences to improve their community; base decisions on real situations and results; be a better person, have respect for their peers, and develop civic responsibility; be successful regardless of their functioning ability; develop a better understanding of self and others; and become leaders who collaborate, strive to creatively solve problems, and assist others.

Categories of Service Learning. Kaye (2004) identifies several different approaches to setting up service learning projects. The first is *direct service* to others, such as tutoring younger students or reading the newspaper to an older person.

This approach helps the student learn about caring for those who are different from them. They might be older or younger or come from a different part of the country or the world, to name a couple of differences. Another option is *indirect service*. Involvement in indirect service is providing a service to a group or community rather than an individual and learning how to work cooperatively on a team, organizing and prioritizing. Types of indirect service include developing a recycling program, making sandwiches for a disaster relief team, or collecting food, clothing, and toys for a homeless shelter. The third option is *advocacy,* which involves bringing awareness of an issue or situation to a group or the community. Examples of advocacy projects include collecting signatures to put in a traffic light at a dangerous intersection or writing letters to the editor of the community newspaper to bring attention to the need for new computers in the public libraries. The last option is *research.* A research service learning project would involve collecting information or data on a topic or need in the community. An example would be counting the number of potholes in a specific neighborhood to document the extreme need for the streets department to repair the streets. In doing so, students learn how to organize, gather information, and assess a situation.

Process of Service Learning.
Kaye (2004) suggests a four-step process to set up a service learning project after contemplating the meaning of service learning and the type of service project to pursue. She identifies four essential and interdependent stages to guide a project: preparation, action, reflection, and demonstration. Kaye identifies the following aspects to consider during the preparation stage: identify a need, draw upon experiences, seek out new information, analyze the problem, collaborate with community representatives, develop a plan, be aware of the integration of service and learning, and define the guidelines for implementation.

For the action phase, Kaye outlines the need to recognize value, purpose, and meaning; use prior learning plus new academic skills and knowledge; recognize unusual or new learning experiences; experience real-life consequences; and provide a safe environment for learning, making mistakes, and success. The third stage, reflection, offers the opportunity for students to outline what happened, identify people and situations different from their own experiences, ponder their thoughts and feelings from the experience, look at the experience from a broad perspective, identify aspects of the project that could be changed or improved, brainstorm questions pertinent to the experience, and seek feedback. The final phase of service learning, demonstration, involves sharing the results or outcomes of the project with others. This might include reporting or making a presentation to groups (their class, community groups, parents, etc.), writing an article or a letter to the community newspaper, or posting the information on an appropriate Web site (e.g., a local governmental body such as the city or town Web page or a community forum).

Challenges of Service Learning.
Kinsley and McPherson (1995) observe that service learning is both a mindset and pedagogy. They suggest that service learning as a mindset not only influences the way we develop courses but also provides a venue for students to give to their community and others. Service learning is also a way to teach community citizenship and problem solving of local issues. This pedagogical opportunity provides students with a lifetime of understanding their responsibilities as citizens in their community. This connection of applying academic content to everyday problem solving is a lesson that will play itself out over the course of one's life.

Keeping in mind that service learning is both a mindset and pedagogy, Kinsley and McPherson (1995) suggest pondering the following when implementing any program or curriculum:

- Students might have experiences with others who are different from themselves. This presents an opportunity for discussions on building an understanding and sensitivity to expanding their relationships to others they would otherwise not meet.
- Open service learning opportunities to real-life problem solving as opposed to Band-Aid approaches to problems. This would include identifying and acting on preventive measures in addition to solutions.
- Work toward institutionalizing service learning with an emphasis on new and creative possibilities and solutions.
- Assist students in clarifying their motivations and interest in service learning.
- Facilitate a venue in which the community openly shares, participates, and collaborates with schools in the responsibility for all students' education.

Family Involvement in the CBI

The involvement of a student's family in the community-based instruction cannot be emphasized enough. They are major partners with school-based personnel in the CBI process and have responsibilities in the collaborative agreement with the school that include but are not limited to the following:

- Understand and act on the goals set for their son or daughter. Follow through on goals at home.
- Indicate the level of involvement and commitment they can make in the planning, implementation, and home follow-up of their son's or daughter's community-based instructional program.
- Demonstrate support of other school programs such as volunteering as a chaperone for a social event at school, participating in a school fundraiser, or offering to be a parent volunteer during an applied field experience activity.
- Brainstorm and identify CBI activities and community sites that need to be addressed in the student's IEP and transition plan.
- Participate in brainstorming during problem-solving sessions on variables that impact the student's community-based instructional program.
- Assist in problem-solving transportation issues to and from CBI sites when they arise.
- Supervise follow-up activities that complement CBI activities done in the community—both in the home environment and in additional community environments when necessary for the maintenance and generalization of community skills.
- Report on the observation and data collected of tasks their child performed in the natural environment.
- Identify future concerns about their son's or daughter's functioning in the community.

- Continue ongoing two-way communication with their son's or daughter's teachers and other school-based personnel through notes, e-mails, phone calls, planning meetings, newsletters, and questionnaires.

Additional discussion regarding family involvement with various aspects of community involvement can be found in Chapter 6.

Obstacles and Challenges to Community-Based Instruction

We would be remiss if we did not address the issues surrounding the obstacles and challenges of community-based instruction. Staffing, scheduling, safety, budget, insurance, and transportation are a few of the concerns that are important to address (Beakley et al., 2003; Cronin, 1996; Dymond, 2004; Wehman, 1992; Wilcox, 1988).

Staffing. One of the most challenging aspects of community instruction is staffing. The functioning level of the students and the activities that are involved will dictate the number of adults needed in the field with the students. Many school systems use a 1:4 ratio (teacher or other adult to students). Other suggestions include utilizing team teachers, support personnel (e.g., speech–language pathologist, occupational or physical therapist, school nurse, social worker, counselors, or physical education teachers), administrators, disciplinarians, peers, volunteers, paraprofessionals, nondisabled peer tutors, university students, service organizations, or senior citizens.

Scheduling. The challenge of scheduling varies from campus to campus. In many ways, scheduling depends on the staffing situation at the school. Many schools are struggling with the dilemma of noncertified personnel. In this scenario, many principals and chairs of the special education departments call upon a number of the individuals listed above to assist in community skills instruction.

Budget. The cost of community-based instruction is always a problem. School systems usually budget as much as they can for community activities. Sometimes money can be redirected or reclassified so monies traditionally used for petty cash, instructional materials, supplies, or equipment can be used instead for community-based instruction. Many times supplemental funds are warranted. In addition, creative strategies to acquire funding might include soliciting contributions from parent–teacher organizations or civic or community groups (e.g., Rotary Club, Lions Club, Kiwanis, chamber of commerce), fundraisers sponsored by the school, or donations from philanthropic groups.

Liability. Many factors need to be considered when addressing issues of liability and neglect. These include but are not limited to developing district policies on community skills instruction (to include interagency agreements with all community contacts and sites), insurance coverage for both the students and the school personnel under all community conditions they might experience during school hours, training programs for all who will be involved in the off-campus programs (e.g., CPR, first aid, local policies regarding jaywalking, street crossing procedures, protocol in the community when an accident happens).

Safety. Training in safety is a must for both students and any staff or volunteers who participate in the community-based instructional program. Safety procedures should include but not be limited to students carrying their identification and emergency information on themselves, crossing streets, getting on and off various forms of public transportation appropriate to the community (e.g., bus, train, streetcar, trolly, taxi, subway, ferry, boat), having procedures to follow if they get lost, and knowing how to protect themselves during rain or storms. A detailed outline of the field experience, the itinerary, the students and adults involved, mode of transportation, and departure and return time should be filed in the office at least a day (or more) before the day of the outing.

Transportation. The needs for transportation are unique to the community in which you live. Students should have experiences on all forms of transportation available in their community. Factors such as their ability level, distance, destination, cost, and number of individuals involved will dictate the form of transportation they use. In rural communities the general lack of public transportation for everyone is challenging. Creative problem solving is needed in these situations. Options might include share-a-ride programs, carpooling, bicycles, or shared shuttle van services for commuters.

MATERIALS IDENTIFICATION, SELECTION, AND DEVELOPMENT

The teacher's role in any life skills class will shift as the teacher becomes integral in bringing real-life tasks, materials, and experiences to students and in taking the students into the community. Life skills content and information may not always come out of the traditional textbook but instead from items found in everyday life. One of teachers' most important and time-consuming jobs is reviewing, researching, ordering, preparing, making, and soliciting materials for instruction. Obtaining materials for a life skills program is no different. Organizing life skills materials involves resourcefulness, creativity, and a substantial amount of planning, start-up, and effort.

Sources of Instructional Materials

Resources for life skills materials are as varied as the features of the community in which instruction occurs. Materials used for life skills instruction should reflect the subsequent environments in which the students will eventually function and use that skill. The type of materials should also vary to provide motivation, stimulation, and variety to the students. When selecting materials for instructional purposes, the teacher should consider each source equally. The following discussion outlines considerations for acquiring a variety of life skills materials for the classroom. Considerations include the correlation of each material with a real-life task, the use and availability of commercially made materials, teacher- or student-generated materials, the resources available in the community, and technology used in the community.

Real-Life Task Correlation

As teachers consider materials for use in a life skills lesson, they need to reflect on the use of that material in real life. Is the material used in a real-life setting? Is it up-to-date, and does it reflect the best use for the student? Is this material a substitute for the real item? Is the real thing accessible to these students on site or do they have to go into the community to use it? Ultimately, teachers will want to use the real item in the natural environment or the next best substitute for it.

Commercially Available Materials

In recent years, a deluge of commercially prepared materials focusing on life skills information and activities has flooded the market. Due to the recent focus on improved student outcomes via standards-based instruction, many have addressed the problems that have for years plagued materials used in high schools for students with special needs and those who are at risk. Problems such as low reading levels, lack of relevancy to student needs and interests and "juvenile-looking" illustrations and concepts have been addressed by authors and publishers in currently available materials. Although the quality and appropriateness of materials available for students have expanded, building a life skills library in a classroom still can be time consuming and expensive.

A great deal of time can be spent sorting through the myriad of available materials to determine reading level, content, cost, and other criteria. Although each teacher should have the opportunity to review materials before purchasing them, this is rarely possible. In addition, teachers often are not aware of what is available, as they have not been able to review catalogs (or even received any), meet with publishing representatives, or attend conferences that have material exhibits. In addition, many teachers have very little, if any, money designated for them to spend on materials. Limited budgets require that money be spent wisely. Having as much information about materials as possible beforehand makes material selection easier.

Appendix A provides a listing of many commercially available materials, although it is not designed to be a comprehensive list. This listing provides a general source for teachers on the availability of materials relating to the major life demands and subdomains identified in Table 1.6 (see Chapter 1). Columns 1 and 2 in Appendix A contain the title of the material and the publisher's three-letter code, respectively. If they are stated in the publisher's catalog, the recommended age and reading level are listed in columns 3 and 4, respectively. The type of material (e.g., workbook, video, DVD, flash cards) can be found in column 5. Figure 5.1 is an excerpt from Appendix A. This information should be useful in purchasing commercially produced materials.

Teacher- or Student-Generated Materials

In some instances the materials needed for a particular lesson or task may not be commercially available. Teachers must then consider other alternatives. Creating the material is one option. A popular method of making teacher-generated materials is using file folder lessons or topical instructional packets. The teachers can obtain cartons, labels from cans, applications, ads from newspapers and magazines, or any other items that have life skills relevancy from home or a business in the community. Information from the cartons, labels, or ads can be written on note cards and stored in the folder or packet. Students can write the answers to questions about the cards on paper or do the activity orally with the instructor, paraprofessional, or peers in the class. The file folders or instructional packets can provide individualization for students who have specific needs or require additional work on specific life skills. In addition, these teacher-made materials are the perfect way to customize the materials and the curriculum to local needs.

Teachers often have a difficult time finding the extra hours to develop folders or instructional packets. Calling on students or assigning students to be assistants

Home Management

Material	Publisher	Age Level	Reading Level	Type
Everyday Household Items	SAD	MS–AD	4.0	WB
Grocery Store Foods Words	PCI	EL	—	SW
Home Cooking	ATT	—	—	K
Janus Life Skills: Staying Healthy	GLF	JH–HS	3.0	B, TR
A Special Picture Cookbook	PRO	EL	—	B

Publishers

Code	Name
ATT	Attainment Company
GLF	Globe Fearon/Pearson Learning Group
PCI	Programming Concepts
PRO	PRO-ED
SAD	Saddleback Educational

Types of Materials

Code	Type
B	Book
K	Kit
SW	Software
TR	Teacher resource
WB	Workbook

Age Levels

Code	Level
EL	Elementary School
MS	Middle School
JH	Junior High School
HS	High School
AD	Adult

FIGURE 5.1. Excerpt from Appendix A, Materials List.

in putting together folders or packets not only involves them in the process but can also give them the opportunity to suggest topics for materials and allow them to show their creativity and ingenuity. Students could also work individually or in groups to create materials. As they observe other students using materials they have made, students feel a sense of satisfaction and a boost in self-esteem.

Community-Derived Resources

One rich and extensive source of materials is the community, which can offer many types of free or inexpensive materials. Any business or government office or agency (local, state, or federal) is a potential source of classroom materials. Forms, booklists, pamphlets, applications (job, housing, utility service, medical and dental histories, services, Social Security, food stamps, voter registration), checks and deposit and withdrawal forms from a bank, restaurant menus, apartment and housing guides, postal forms, phone books, maps from realtor offices, menus from restaurants (fast food, sit-down, cafeterias, snack bars), driver's manuals from the department of motor vehicles, mall maps and directories, and newspapers are gold mines of educational materials that are available at little or no cost.

Materials can also be solicited from students, parents, family members, teachers, and the school's parent organization. Materials such as magazines, empty boxes and containers, "junk mail," catalogs, or coupons can be used to make file folders or teaching packets. Anything that has the potential for teaching or demonstrating a skill used in everyday living is valuable to a person teaching life skills. The list of items that can be collected from community sources or individuals can be lengthy, but it ensures that the materials used are community specific.

Technology

Technology has become a significant part of our daily lives, jobs, home, community, and education. Teachers who address life skills topics need to incorporate into their lessons whenever possible the technology found in everyday environments. Examples of technology encountered on a daily basis are automatic teller machines (ATMs), voice mail, microwaves, automated gas pumps with debit/credit options, cell phones, video and DVD players, compact disc players, personal computers and laptops, computerized dictionaries and thesauruses, fax machines, and remote controls for the garage, TV, and home entertainment centers.

Classroom technology has changed dramatically in recent years. Computers, e-mail, and the Internet/World Wide Web are obligatory assets in most schools. Technology is a viable part of students' school and home environments. Additionally, technology could involve low-tech assistive devices (Ciampa Stoller, 1998) that are relatively easy to make and use or intricate assistive technology (Galvin & Scherer, 1996) designed for very specific needs. Teachers routinely use e-mail to communicate with parents and students. School Web sites are often interactive, with teachers being able to post weekly or monthly assignments and semester syllabi.

Educationally related software options currently on the market are numerous and growing. They run the gamut from tutorials, simulations, drill and practice games, problem solving, tests, reference and information, and utilities (Lindsey, 2000). All are designed to provide the user with information, activities, or both. To make these software programs meaningful, teachers need to align them with the needs of the students. This alignment will assist in making the link between knowledge and skills used both in classroom and in community-based settings. There are also computerized programs that have a real-life or career awareness focus. These range from student-selected life choices in a computer-simulated city to programs assessing a student's life skills strengths and needs (i.e., SimCity, Choices, System of Interactive Guidance, and InfoPlus). Many high schools have all incoming ninth graders complete an interest inventory with a guidance counselor. This is a great opportunity for the guidance counselors to begin to know the students they serve and for the ninth graders to begin to think about their own goals.

The wealth of software options and Web-based applications can be overwhelming to teachers, students, and parents. Lindsey (2000) explored several elements that are necessary to consider when reviewing and selecting software, as well as using it in the classroom:

1. The technology chosen is compatible and aligned with the curriculum.
2. Principles of quality instruction are evident in the scope and sequence of the software program and application.
3. Students can readily understand how to use the program(s).
4. Student collaborative efforts are structured to maximize teaching and learning in group activities that use software.
5. Adequate time and preparation are allowed for any project-based learning (which often involves technology) activities.
6. The deluge of information that can be garnered from software and the World Wide Web does not equate to knowledge. Students need to be able to use the technology appropriately and effectively in order to gain meaning from it.

These considerations are especially relevant in today's rapidly changing world of technology. Teachers and parents alike have to be vigilant in their scrutiny of materials, software programs, and Web-based applications that students and children access.

Guidelines for Selecting Life Skills Materials

According to Hammill and Bartel (2004), much time has been devoted to determining the content of curriculum used in schools and deciding the evaluative techniques used to determine students' strengths and needs. They estimate that, by comparison, little time is spent selecting instructional materials. In addition, Hammill and Bartel suggest that between 75% and 99% of a student's instructional time is arranged around some type of material. Care needs to be exercised when selecting materials to ensure compatibility with the curriculum, the student, and the teacher.

Selecting and Evaluating Materials

Materials selection involves a variety of elements. Hammill and Bartel (2004) suggest several aspects to consider when selecting appropriate materials. Their suggestions parallel the differentiated instruction discussion in Chapter 3. They recommend ensuring that the materials are both flexible enough to target more than one student and adaptable to accommodate an array of learning styles (visual, kinesthetic, auditory, tactile). Durability and ease of use are also factors to consider. It becomes even more important to develop criteria for selection of materials when using a life skills curriculum to ensure the materials will address the adult outcomes, interest level, reading levels, and so forth, reflected in each student's Individualized Education Program (IEP) or Individualized Transition Plan (ITP).

Many professionals have suggested ways of selecting and evaluating educational materials (Neugebauer, 2000; J. O. Wagner, 1999). Some material evaluations consist of checklists or forms with five or six questions. Other material evaluations are two to three pages long with numerous questions to consider. Several evaluation forms suggest specific variables such as cost, readability, target age, durability, task levels, interest levels, format, sequence and organization of the materials, and clarity of directions (Minner, 2002; Thier, 2001). Others include an overall evaluative approach that considers the adaptability of the materials for students (Handal, Leiner, Gonzalez, & Rogel, 1999), laterality of instruction, and compatibility of the materials with the learning theory of the teachers and learning styles of the students (Schneider & Krajcik, 1999). Some are specific to evaluating and using materials on the World Wide Web (Lee & Small, 1999; Mohler, 2001; Potter, 2003; Schmitz, Staab, Studer, Stumme, & Tane, 2002). We suggest using a combination of the above to evaluate materials used to teach life skills.

Hammill and Bartel (2004) suggest examining a variety of factors in reviewing and evaluating material (see Figure 5.2). Several of the factors they suggest should be addressed when any material, whether purchased, teacher made, or community based, is being considered for use with specific students. Knowing such information as the level of the material, format, and time requirements will impact the success of using that material with students.

In addition to the items suggested by Hammill and Bartel (2004), we suggest one more. Teachers should review the material for bias, stereotyping, and discrimination. Having the material reflect diversity as to gender, race, and disability is important. Students need to see the material as relevant to them, to their environment, and to their envisioning themselves performing life skills in their community. Materials also need to be culturally sensitive and reflect society's diversity.

Figure 5.3 lists the variables relating to the curriculum–student–teacher triad (Hammill & Bartel, 2004). These variables are important to consider when trying to match the material to the content being taught as well as to students' academic and cultural needs. Teachers also need to consider the methods used and the time involved in using the material. In addition, some materials involve training and education on the part of the teacher that are not always feasible. Utilizing both the materials analysis and evaluation of the curriculum–student–teacher triad would be a good start in customizing an appropriate review for selecting life skills materials.

Identifying Materials

One of the most arduous tasks for teachers is locating materials. We have tried to assist teachers in identifying different types of materials with the resources indicated in Appendix A in this book. There are other ways in addition to this type of listing

Materials Analysis

1. *Bibliographic and price information.* This information is necessary for future reference or purchase, as well as to make determination that may assist in analysis. The teacher may consider such items as the following:

    Title—The name of the product may help identify the content area and whether the product is part of a set or series.

    Author—Is it someone known for his or her work in a specific area or someone associated with a particular approach?

    Copyright date—Is it current? Does the work reflect new trends and facts?

    Price—Is it within the budget limitations? Is it in keeping with other materials prices, and does it appear reasonable for the work's teaching value?

    Publisher—Does the company have a reputation for producing a certain kind or quality of material?

2. *Instructional area and skills, scope and sequence.* Does the material cover the content area or specific components of the area? Does it address the specific skills needed? Does the material present initial instruction, remediation, and practice or reinforcement activities for the skills? Are the skills presented in the appropriate sequence?

3. *Component parts of the material.* Does the material have multiple pieces? Can the pieces be used independently? Can the pieces be used for other purposes? Are the pieces consumable? Can the piece be purchased independently? Will keeping track of all components be a problem?

4. *Level of the material.* Does the publisher state the readability level of the material? Is it consistent throughout the material? Is the interest level appropriate to the content, pictures, and publisher's statements?

5. *Quality.* Is the material (e.g., paper, tape, acetate, film) of good and durable quality? Is the print clear and of appropriate size and contrast with the background color? Are the illustrations clear and relevant to the content? Do they add to rather than detract from the instruction?

6. *Format.* Is the form (e.g., workbook, slide, tape) appropriate? Does it use the appropriate receptive and expressive modes for the content? Is the material clear and easy to follow? Is special equipment (e.g., projector, recorder) required?

7. *Support materials.* Does the material include additional components (e.g., placement test, check tests, resource files, objective cluster)? Are there teacher's guides or teacher's editions? Are there teacher-training materials?

8. *Time requirements.* Is the task of an appropriate length? Does the material allow flexibility for scheduling? Does it allow flexibility in instructional procedures?

9. *Field-test and research data.* Does the publisher offer any research to support the validity or reliability of the material? In essence, do the data support the contention that the material will do what the publisher says it will do for the type of student indicated?

10. *Methods, approach, or theoretical bases.* Does the material employ a specific approach or method, or is it based on a specific theoretical concept? Is it one that meets the end of the curriculum–teacher–student triad? Is it compatible with other ongoing instruction? Is the method, approach, or basic theory substantiated by any published research?

FIGURE 5.2. Factors to consider when analyzing materials. *Note.* From *Teaching Students with Learning and Behavioral Problems* (pp. 412–413), by D. D. Hammill and N. R. Bartel, 2004, Austin, TX: PRO-ED. Copyright 2004 by PRO-ED. Reprinted with permission.

Student Variables

1. *Needs of the student.* What skills and concepts are required of the student for immediate success?
2. *Current levels of functioning.* What is the student's level of performance within the sequence of skills? What is the student's current reading level for instructional purposes?
3. *Grouping.* How well does the student work in groups of varying sizes (e.g., in small groups, in large groups, individually)?
4. *Programming.* What is the best way to approach the student? Can the student work independently? Is the student self-directed and motivated? Does the student require direct teaching or frequent reinforcement?
5. *Methods.* Have any particular methods been used successfully? Does the student react positively or negatively to particular modes of instruction (e.g., multimedia vs. print only)?
6. *Physical, social and psychological characteristics.* Do factors such as orthopedic restrictions, family problems, or ethnic or cultural diversity imply unique needs?

Teacher Variables

1. *Method.* What method does the teacher want to employ? What is the teacher's philosophy toward the teaching of a particular content?
2. *Approach.* What approach is required by the teacher (e.g., group instruction or individual instruction; phonetic approach)?
3. *Time.* Does the teacher have time constraints for delivery of instruction? Does the teacher have someone else who can deliver the instruction?
4. *Training.* Has the teacher been trained to use certain materials?
5. *Education.* Has the teacher been trained in the content area?

FIGURE 5.3. Variables related to the curriculum–student–teacher triad. *Note.* From *Teaching Students with Learning and Behavioral Problems* (pp. 409–410), by D. D. Hammill and N. R. Bartel, 2004, Austin, TX: PRO-ED. Copyright 2004 by PRO-ED. Reprinted with permission.

that teachers use to locate instructional materials. Hammill and Bartel (2004) offer the following suggestions as a guide for teachers in this pursuit:

1. Ask other colleagues. Networking with other life skills teachers will help you identify what they use with students who are working on skills similar to those your students are working on.

2. Seek help from special resource personnel. These individuals devote most of their time to reviewing materials and media for classroom use and have access to individuals who are using similar materials. They may also know representatives of publishing companies. They may be librarians, media or materials specialists, or curriculum coordinators.

3. Locate information from publishers. Access catalogs, mailed brochures, and representatives of publishing companies. Many companies have toll-free numbers that you can call to have a catalog sent to you. Most

companies publish new catalogs at the beginning of the school year or in January. Note that the price and availability are always subject to change.

4. Visit the nearest media/materials centers in your school system. Identify the local or regional media center serving your schools. These centers house various collections of materials that teachers may borrow to use in their classes so they can evaluate that material before purchasing it. This is a cost-effective and efficient way to evaluate materials.

5. Avail yourself of the resources of your local colleges and universities. Many have resource centers or courses in methods and materials. Some faculty members may be involved in testing of materials.

6. Locate prepared materials lists. Lists can be found in teacher resource books or textbooks, disseminated during workshops or conference sessions, or requested from school districts or state departments of education. Most of these lists include basic information only. They normally do not evaluate materials.

7. Attend conferences. Sessions and exhibits at conferences can provide an opportunity to look at materials. They also provide the chance for teachers to confer with each other regarding materials used in their classes.

8. Use an electronic retrieval system. Internet (World Wide Web) searches are commonplace and one way to search for subject-specific information. In addition, there are retrieval systems developed by commercial companies that provide information on the physical characteristics of the materials, as well as their cost and availability.

In summary, this chapter has outlined some considerations that teachers need to address when identifying, selecting, and developing materials for use in their life skills programs. Attention to this process of acquiring materials will, hopefully, ensure the best possible tools for teaching students life skills concepts. There a number of important instructional considerations that also need to be reviewed when one is in the process of selecting and purchasing materials. These considerations are applicable to teachers, parents, and administrators. Everyone wants to get the most out of their educational budgets, and that means thinking strategically to best meet the needs of students.

FAMILY ENGAGEMENT

A partnership between home, school, and community can be a viable and meaningful way to encourage and support family engagement in the educational process (Decker, 2001; L. Taylor & Adelman, 2000) and to utilize community resources (Grubbs, 2003; Ziegler, 2000). Family engagement in a child's education can take on many different appearances along a continuum of involvement opportunities. All of the points on this continuum focus on strengthening home, school, and community partnerships with the overall goal of improving outcomes for children. This continuum is similar to viewing the ocean along the horizon. There is no point on the horizon that is better than another point. There are just different places depending on where one is located at the time. The continuum is individualized and fluid because family engagement is subject to change as opportunities for participation change. Figure 6.1 illustrates the different continuum points and provides examples of options for involvement.

Family engagement in the application of life skills targets several points on the continuum. It facilitates dialogue between parent and, if appropriate, family members regarding life skills information by allowing the family to both receive and provide information on their child. They are actively participating in the ongoing education of their child through the teaching of life skills as well as making decisions regarding their child and the life skills process. All of these continuum points could lead to family input regarding overall life skills programs and policy-related decisions. This would, of course, depend on the interest and involvement choices of the parents and other family members. In any case, a myriad of points along this continuum are addressed through family engagement in the life skills process.

Family Engagement in the Life Skills Process

Family engagement is an important and positive component of a student's school life (Baker & Soden, 1998; Kucher, Smith-Rockhold, Bemis, & Wiese, 1998; Scott-Stein & Thorkildsen, 1999). There have been scores of books, brochures, articles, and newsletters on strategies and techniques to strengthen and sustain a strong home and school collaboration (Elias, Bryan, Patrikakou, & Weissberg, 2003; Kucher et al., 1998; G. Taylor, 2000; Wittreich, Jacobi, & Hogue, 2000). Our focus in particular is on family unit engagement in the life skills process.

Previous chapters discussed the abundance of opportunities for the development and teaching of life skills both in classroom and in community-based settings. Both teachers and families are united in their desire for students to learn about

**Home/School/Community Partnership:
Continuum of Opportunities for Family Engagement**

*Families as
passive
participants*

*Families as
active
participants*

Receiving information about their child or school	*Receiving information and support for parenting*	*Participating in decisions about their child*	*Participating in the education of their child*	*Providing information, supporting others*	*Engaging in decision making about programs and policies*
(e.g., progress report; phone call, daily notebook; parent–teacher conference; bulletin board)	(e.g., workshop; fact sheet; special events for families; networking with other parents at pot-luck event; family day; attending parent support group)	(e.g., serving as an active team member in creating their child's IEP; developing life skills activities; collaborating or problem solving with teacher about learning and behavioral strategies for their child)	(e.g., expecting well of the child; participating in life skills activities with their child; reading to the child; developing language and life skills through dinner conversation; sharing learning experiences with the child through play; carrying out learning activities in the IEP; supporting their child with materials or help for homework)	(e.g., serving as contact for other families; sharing experiences at a family event; shared problem solving with professionals; providing information to teacher through daily notebook, phone call, visit to class, parent–teacher conference, etc.)	(e.g., member of advisory board or school improvement team; input in creating a family involvement continuum; input in program evaluation; creating events relating to life skills opportunities)

FIGURE 6.1. Continuum of opportunities for family engagement. *Note.* From Burgess & Wood, 2004. Unpublished figure.

life skills and to be able to apply those skills on a consistent basis at home and in real-life settings. Teachers are with their students during the school day. Parents or other caregivers are with their children the remainder of the time. Thus, families are integral partners in maximizing opportunities for learning life skills. A simple way to get started is for a family member to have a conversation with the child's teacher as to what current life skills are being addressed. This information can then be translated into everyday discussions and opportunities for application in the home or family life. The following section provides some examples of home activities and adaptations that families can use. It is by no means all-inclusive, as the options are as endless as one's creativity.

Home-Based Activities and Adaptations

Every home or community activity can be easily adapted into a minilesson on life skills. Families can choose one of the life skills domains based on discussions with the child's teacher or begin with a domain area with which they feel comfortable. The six domains (employment/education, home and family, leisure pursuits, community involvement, physical/emotional health, and personal responsibility and relationships) offer a wide range of family choices. The subdomains assist in narrowing down specific life demands that serve as springboards for specific life skills activities in which families and children can engage. We encourage readers to refer back to the major life demands listed in Table 1.5 in Chapter 1. Perusing this table, particularly in the life demands column, one can immediately see the opportunities for applying specific life skills in which parents or caregivers and children can engage on a daily or weekly basis. For example, in the home and family domain, there is the subdomain family life. One of the life demands of family life is planning and preparing meals. Each family procures groceries regularly. Typically, multiple steps are involved in this process. Think of the times people go to the grocery store, complete their shopping, and return home only to realize they have forgotten one essential item. These steps may include preparing a list of items to purchase at the grocery store. The child can be involved in looking in the refrigerator to see what items the family needs to replenish. This can be followed up by going to the grocery store and locating each type of item on the shopping list, comparing the sizes and prices, and then purchasing all the items. Depending on the individual needs of the child and the family, the focus may be on a variety of different steps (reviewing the store circular or the grocery store ads published in the newspaper, cutting the coupons, comparing products and prices, selecting items, understanding the checkout process, using the coupons, paying for the items, bringing them home, and putting them away in their appropriate places in the home). It is easy to take for granted many of the steps in this activity, which actually involves multiple steps and thoughtful consideration for successful completion. The practice of these life demands can be valuable and enjoyable life skills application opportunities for parents or caregivers and their children.

Another example could involve the domain area of leisure pursuits. Any of the subdomains (indoor activities, outdoor activities, community/neighborhood activities, travel, and entertainment) offers a host of opportunities for continued life skills application. One of the major life demands listed for indoor activities in Table 1.5 is playing table or electronic games. Many families routinely engage in group activities such as board games, puzzles, or electronic games such as Xbox, PlayStation, Game Boy, and others. Here again, there are multiple steps involved in preparing to play indoor games. Some of these involve setting up, reviewing game rules, discussing who will go first, employing appropriate social skills interactions while playing the game, cleaning up after the game concludes, and so forth. Discussing the steps involved in an activity with one's child or children also can be applied to the leisure pursuits subdomain of outdoor activities for softball, basketball, football, or tennis, whether the game is played informally in a backyard or as part of an organized team sport in school or in a community Little League situation. One can make this case over and over again for all life skills activities. Table 6.1 presents a selection of life skills opportunities that typically present themselves at some point in the course of daily life in most homes.

Getting Started

Table 1.6 and Figure 1.2 in Chapter 1 offer examples of and guidelines for identifying specific life skills. From Table 1.6 one can also garner ideas for specific life skills. One of the strengths of life skills identification and home or community applications is the individualization to the child and family. There is no limitation on what one can identify as a specific life skill. When faced with so many choices, however, it can become daunting for a parent or caregiver to pick a starting point. Here are some guiding questions they can use in selecting specific life skills to address. They are designed to encourage discussion and reflection of the child's strengths and needs and hence the selection of specific life skills to address.

1. **Adult Domain.** *In which life skills adult domains is my child already actively participating?* This question focuses on examining the child's strengths and needs. It sets the stage for examining the child's present level of performance in terms of life skills. A student in middle school would in all likelihood have different life skill needs than a graduating senior. Still, both individuals can benefit from continued opportunities to apply their life skills knowledge to real-life situations.

2. **Specific Subdomain and Major Life Demands.** *What do I hope my child will accomplish this year in terms of life skills?* What are the family's wishes for the child for both the present and the future? In thinking about a child's long-term goals, it is relevant to consider what the child should be able to do now or in the near future so that he or she can, at some point, meet the long-term goal. For example, the long-term goal may be to become involved in community issues that support good citizenship, such as voting in elections. The next question takes that long-term goal and breaks it down into specific life skills.

3. **Specific Life Skills.** *What life skills will my child need for this year to make progress toward his or her goals?* Following the community involvement example from question 2, the specific life skill focus could be to understand the voting process, obtain information on the candidates and issues, register to vote if age appropriate, go with a parent to a polling place, and so forth. The parents or caregivers will have thought about the child's long-term goals; now what specific life skill activities can they and the child engage in this year for the child to make progress and be successful?

Parents all have busy lives and may not be able to recall on demand all the wonderful and meaningful life skills activities in which they have engaged over a number

Table 6.1
Home-Based Life Skills Opportunities as Related to Adult Domains

Employment/ Education	Home and Family	Leisure Pursuits	Community Involvement	Physical/ Emotional Health	Personal Responsibility and Relationships
Call the homework hotline when needed.	Change a light bulb.	Locate and read the movie section of the newspaper to select a movie and time.	Gather recycle materials for pick-up.	Prepare a healthy lunch.	Settle a dispute with a sibling.
Check the want ads for a summer job.	Clip coupons from the Sunday paper.	Use a map to locate the nearest park with a swimming pool.	Decide on which Little League sport to play each season.	Identify the appropriate clothing for the weather.	Write a thank-you note to a relative for a gift.
Complete an application for employment.	Make a list of items needed from the grocery store.	Search the Internet for information on a city to visit.	Role play the possible situations in which you would call 911.	Decide how many hours of sleep you need per night.	Take turns in a conversation.
Practice interview skills.	Make a list of emergency phone numbers.	Use a shopping center directory.	Read road signs and discuss what they mean.	Negotiate an appropriate bedtime.	Send a get-well card to a friend who is ill.
Understand the difference between net and gross pay.	Discuss morning routines with family members.	Check the weather forecast on the Internet or TV to plan an outdoor activity.	Obtain information for a building permit.	Comprehend directions on medications.	Develop a system to remember birthdays.
				Describe symptoms to a doctor.	Read e-mail from a friend or relative.
					Plan the cost of a date.

of months. Figure 6.2 is a sample of a monthly worksheet that families and other caregivers can use to quickly and easily keep a record of the adult domains and major life demands that have been targeted for their child. This can be reviewed monthly and tweaked accordingly. Children should also be involved, not only in identifying the life skills activities to incorporate into home activities, but also to be actively involved with the record-keeping process. This worksheet can also provide written documentation and data to facilitate life skills discussions at parent–teacher conferences or when meeting to review a child's IEP.

Whenever possible, one should take advantage of everyday activities and events to engage in meaningful and ongoing discussions of the steps involved in learning, practicing, and applying life skills to everyday experiences. Integral to successfully completing these goals are (a) giving children a well-rounded life skills education and (b) thoughtful planning for and practicing of specific life skills in real-world situations and experiences.

Home/School/Community Partnership: Life Skills Worksheet

Month _____

Put a check (✓) each time you address a life demand in one of the domains. After the end of each week and month you will be able to do a quick visual scan to see which domains you have focused on and which domains you may need to address. If you need to review the life demands, please refer back to Table 1.5.

Domains (subdomains)	Life Demands Addressed (✓)
Employment/Education (general job skills, general education/training considerations, employment setting, career refinement and reevaluation)	Week 1 Week 2 Week 3 Week 4
Home and Family (home management, financial management, family life, and child rearing)	Week 1 Week 2 Week 3 Week 4
Leisure Pursuits (indoor activities, outdoor activities, community/neighborhood activities, travel, and entertainment)	Week 1 Week 2 Week 3 Week 4

(continues)

FIGURE 6.2. Home/school/community partnership: Life skills worksheet.

Domains (subdomains)	Life Demands Addressed (✓)
Community Involvement (citizenship, community awareness, and services/resources)	Week 1 Week 2 Week 3 Week 4
Physical/Emotional Health (physical health and emotional health)	Week 1 Week 2 Week 3 Week 4
Personal Responsibility and Relationships (personal confidence/understanding, goal setting, self-improvement, relationships, and personal expression)	Week 1 Week 2 Week 3 Week 4

Comments: _____

_____

_____

_____

_____

FIGURE 6.2. *Continued.*

FINAL THOUGHTS

The main theme of this guide is the importance of preparing youth with special needs for the challenges of adulthood. Our experiences suggest that many of the skills needed to enhance one's quality of life must be systematically addressed within the existing curricular structure of the school and within the context of standards-based education. To do this effectively, a number of actions must be carried out. First, an examination of the subsequent environments to which students likely will go after they exit school should be conducted (Kortering & Elrod, 1991). Second, the curricular needs of students should be based on this analysis (i.e., a top-down approach to life skills identification).

The primary purpose of the guide is to give teachers and other curriculum specialists a methodology for integrating life skills topics into the educational programs of students with special needs or those who are placed at risk for encountering school-related problems. By providing a framework, relevant examples, and resources, we feel that locally referenced and culturally responsive life skills can be identified and, ultimately, taught.

The Benefit of Life Skills Preparation for All Students

All students—not only those with special needs—need to acquire requisite life skills. The major demands of life, as discussed in Chapter 1, confront all of us. The difference is that many of us learn how to deal with them in a variety of ways—most notably through natural support systems (e.g., family, friends). For many students with special needs, these support systems do not exist, so they may never learn some very important life skills.

It is unrealistic, even in the best life skills–oriented program imaginable, to prepare students for every possible adult situation. However, it is possible to attend to many of the more probable ones. Because we cannot precisely foresee students' future experiences, it is very important to build a strong problem-solving component into programs. Teaching students strategies that they can use to handle new, difficult situations provides them with tools they can use throughout their lives. Remaining cognizant that students need not only factual and procedural knowledge (skills) but also the ability to apply what they know is a cornerstone of life skills instruction.

As emphasized many times throughout this guide, life skills preparation should begin at the elementary school level. Waiting until the last years of high school to get students ready for what lies ahead is ineffective and unconscionable. The Division on Career Development of the Council for Exceptional Children (Clark, Carlson, Fisher, Cook, & D'Alonzo, 1991) argues that

> a commitment to life-centered career development and transition preparation for students exclusively at the secondary level is not only inadequate, it is counterproductive. Such an exclusive approach ignores the possibility that school programs have not succeeded in the past because of providing *too little, too late* [emphasis added]. (p. 118)

The Continued Need for Curricular Review and Innovation in a Standards-Based World

A number of professionals who are concerned about the plight of youth with special needs as they move into adulthood argue that curricular changes are needed to ensure better adult outcomes for these individuals. The following three observations underscore the need for curricular review and innovation:

> The truth is that the secondary curriculum for special education students appears to have very little, if any, impact on their eventual adjustment to community life. (Edgar, 1987, p. 560)

> The problem is that too many young people in public schools, particularly youths with disabilities and youths who are not college-bound, are not well served by the traditional academic model. (Roessler, 1991, p. 59)

> Much of the curriculum that was being offered in the high schools could be characterized as an attempt to remediate basic academic skills and/or to provide intensive tutoring in the various content area subjects such as literature, social studies and science. Typically missing from the offerings were study skills or "learning strategies," and functional curricula aimed at independent living skills such as money management and meal preparation.... The impact of these curricular shortcomings was to deny a meaningful educational program for those who were not capable of succeeding in the regular academic curriculum. (Halpern, Benz, & Lindstrom, 1992, p. 111)

These comments describe the scenario for many students who are at risk for experiencing school failure and point out the need for reevaluating the relationship between what students need to be taught and what is being taught.

Programs must be sensitive to students' current and future needs (Polloway, Patton, Epstein, & Smith, 1989). They need to be meaningful to students in the short term to keep students in school, and they need to be relevant to students over the long term to help them function more successfully in their adult lives. As M. Wagner (1991) reports, the National Longitudinal Transition Study of Special Education (NLTS) findings imply "that if schools can give students powerful reasons to come to school and can help students achieve in their courses, they can help many students persist in school" (p. 108).

Throughout this guide, in our attempt to provide information to service providers to enable them to develop programs that include some degree of life skills instruction, we may have failed to emphasize the importance of involving students in their own life skills and transition planning. As Karge, Patton, and de la Garza (1992) conclude, "it is an inherent right to be involved in one's own life planning" (p. 65). Of course, such involvement is not always possible; however, for the vast majority of students with special needs, making decisions about their future is their right.

Because dealing with the demands of adulthood is a lifelong venture, it is essential that we teach individuals with special needs to make use of ongoing, natural support systems throughout their lives. This relates to the suggestion discussed earlier about teaching individuals to be functional problem solvers. The suggestion here is that some adults may need assistance in locating supports to help them to be successful—part of the linkage activity of the transition planning process. Edgar (1990) goes so far as to recommend that "we can replace teaching of skills with support of an individual" and that "by including ongoing support services as a possible intervention we do NOT give up instruction, rather we ADD an option to our intervention repertoire" (p. 13).

Because we live in a world that is changing very rapidly, those of us involved with life skills programming must address the realities of a complex world. Kolstoe's comments are as appropriate today as they were in 1976:

> Probably no final statement can ever be forthcoming concerning the skills and characteristics required to live successfully in this culture, primarily because society is characterized by constant change.... There seems, however, no alternative other than to use the best current information available for curricular guidelines and to modify those guidelines as new and better information becomes available. If society is constantly changing, it seems only reasonable that curricula should also change. (p. 33)

Personal Commitment to Students

Most of us who teach or who have taught students with special needs or who are at risk for school failure strive to provide skills and information to make their lives more enjoyable and fulfilling. Perhaps most important, we must strive to let these students know that we sincerely care about them and that they are important to us, which involves more than being an excellent teacher methodologically or a font of knowledge. It means that students should experience what Edgar (1990) calls "an atmosphere of caring, human dignity, and optimism" (p. 13).

Professionals concerned about what happens to students when formal schooling ends have to be alarmed by the outcome and dropout data that define the fate of many individuals. We must keep advocating for students, always guided by their best interests. Edgar's (1991) notion that educators have a sacred covenant with students is most compelling:

> We must provide them with the best services, every day, that we can offer. We must think about how our efforts affect the student not only today but also in the future. We must step back, now and then, to look at the overall role of

education, how we fit into the larger picture, and what changes we must make, in ourselves and in our system, so that our students will benefit from education. We must find ways to renew our own personal energy to keep doing this, day after day, year after year. It is our mission in life. (p. 39)

This guide for developing life skills instruction has evolved through that motivation.

MATERIALS LIST

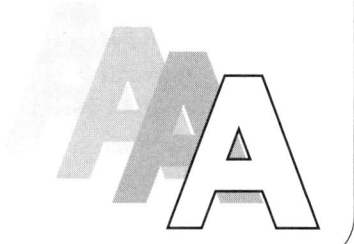

One of the most time-consuming tasks for teachers is identifying and gathering materials for instruction. To help alleviate that cumbersome job for teachers of life skills, we have put together the following life skills materials list. *This list comprises materials from selected publishers and is not considered to be comprehensive.* We offer it as a general source and a starting point for teachers. We encourage teachers who use this listing to write or call the publishers to obtain a recent catalog, as new materials are added constantly and older or outdated ones are removed. Publishers' addresses and phone numbers can be found in Appendix B. We have not listed prices, which are subject to change. We also encourage teachers to build on this list as they find publications in their search for materials to meet life skills instructional needs.

The list is organized by 22 of the 23 subdomains identified in Table 1.5. Column 1 contains the name of the material. The publisher's three-letter code is in column 2. The recommended age (if stated), the reading level (if stated), and the type of material (e.g., workbook, video, DVD, filmstrip, flash cards) can be found in columns 3, 4, and 5, respectively. The codes for the publishers, age levels, and types of material follow this discussion. The age codes listed are recommendations found in the publishers' catalogs.

Appendix A Contents

Abbreviations Used in This Appendix

Publishers

Code	Name
ACA	Academic Communication Associates
AGS	AGS Publishing
AKC	American Kennel Club
AQU	Aquarius Health Care Videos
ATT	Attainment Company
CEC	Council for Exceptional Children
CHB	Channing Bete
CPR	Continental Press
CSB	Communication Skill Builders
CUR	Curriculum Associates
ERE	Educational Resources
GAM	Gamco Industries
GLE	Glencoe/McGraw-Hill
GLF	Globe Fearon/Pearson Learning Group
HIN	High Noon Books
JMS	James Stanfield Publishing
KSA	KidSafety of America
LLS	Laureate Learning Systems
LSI	LinguiSystems
MHC	McGraw-Hill/Contemporary
NPR	National Professional Resources
NSP	National School Products
PBS	PBS Video
PCI	Programming Concepts
PDA	Program Development Associates
PRO	PRO-ED
REM	Remedia Publications
REP	Research Press

RPM	RPM Press
SAD	Saddleback Educational
SOW	Sopris West
STV	Steck-Vaughn
SUN	Sunburst Visual Media
TSP	Tom Snyder Productions
WAL	Walch Publishing

Types of Materials

Code	Type
A	Audiotape
B	Book
CP	Comprehensive program
DM	Duplication master
DVD	DVD
F	Film
FC	Flash cards
FS	Filmstrip
G	Game
K	Kit
MN	Manipulative
P	Poster
PH	Pamphlet
RB	Resource book
SW	Software
T	Test
TR	Teacher resource
V	Video
WB	Workbook

Age Levels

Code	Level
EL	Elementary School
MS	Middle School
JH	Junior High School
HS	High School
AD	Adult

General Job Skills

Material	Publisher	Age Level	Reading Level	Type
10 Golden Rules for the Workplace	PDA	HS–AD	—	V
61 Cooperative Learning Activities for Computer Classrooms	SAD	EL–AD	—	TR, DM
Ads & Coupons: Practical Practice Reading	REM	MS–HS	—	WB
Basic Life Skills at Work	NSP	MS–AD	—	SW
Better Writing for Better Jobs	SAD	HS–AD	—	WB, TR
Big Digit Desktop Calculators	PCI	EL–JH	—	MN
Breaking Out	LLS	HS	—	V
Build Your Own Website	SAD	MS–AD	—	TR, B
Building Success in the Workplace	STV	AD	3.0–4.0	WB
Career Awareness Plus	SAD	HS–AD	2.0–3.5	B
Career Exploration	SAD	MS–AD	3.0–4.0	B
Career Ideas Series	SAD	MS–AD	6.0	B
Career Planner's Portfolio	CUR	MS–HS	—	RB
Career Planning for the 21st Century	GLE	HS–AD	—	WB, TR
Career Skills	SAD	MS–AD	4.0–5.0	B, WB
Careers Without College	SAD	MS–AD	3.0–4.0	B
Careers Without College	SAD	JH–AD	7.0	B
Catalogs: Practical Practice Reading	REM	MS–HS	3.0–4.0	WB
Competitive Job Finding Guide for Persons with Handicaps	PRO	HS–AD	—	B, WB
Computer Dictionary	SAD	EL–AD	—	TR
Computer Graphics & Animation	SAD	MS–AD	—	TR, B
Computers at Work	NSP	EL–HS	—	SW
Computers at Work	PDA	HS–AD	—	SW
Coolcareers.com	SAD	EL–HS	5.0	B
Counseling Activities for Life Skills and Career Development	PRO	MS–HS	—	B
Daily Experiences and Activities for Living	PRO	MS–AD	3.0–5.0	K
Day-to-Day Life Skills: Speaking	ACA	MS–AD	—	B
Day-to-Day Life Skills: Writing	ACA	MS–AD	—	B
Developing Workplace Skills	CHB	MS–HS	—	PH
Developing Your Job Search Skills	SAD	JH–HS	—	WB

General Job Skills (*Continued*)

Material	Publisher	Age Level	Reading Level	Type
Directories & Guides: Practical Practice Reading	REM	MS–HS	3.0–4.0	WB
Disabilities in the Workplace	PDA	MS–AD	—	V
Dressing for Success	PDA	HS–AD	—	V
Effective Training at Work	PDA	HS–AD	—	SW
Employability Skills Books	STV	HS–AD	4.0–5.0	B
Employability Skills Program	SAD	JH–AD	2.5–4.0	B
Essential Life Skills Series	CSB	JH–AD	—	WB
Essential Vocabulary: Computer Words	REM	MS–HS	3.0–4.0	WB
Essential Vocabulary: Survival Words	REM	MS–HS	3.0–4.0	WB
Exploring Careers	GLE	HS–AD	—	CP
Filling Out Forms: Practical Practice Reading	REM	MS–HS	3.0–4.0	WB
From School to Work	SAD	MS–HS	6.0	B
Going to Work Center	CHB	MS–HS	—	P, PH
Grooming for Success	PDA	HS–AD	—	V
A Guide to Vocational Assessment	PRO	—	—	B
Handbook of Career Planning for Special Needs Students	AGS	—	—	TR
How to Get a Job and Keep It	STV	AD	5.0–6.0	WB
How to Hold Your Job	PRO	HS–AD	3.0	B, WB
Interview Skills for the Future	PDA	HS–AD	—	SW, V
The Interviewing Edge for Job Seekers with Disabilities	PDA	HS–AD	—	V
Interviewing Skills for Job Candidates with Learning or Other Hidden Disabilities	PDA	HS–AD	—	V
Interviewing Skills for Job Candidates with Physical Disabilities	PDA	HS–AD	—	V
Introduction to Skills for School Success	CUR	MS–AD	—	V
It's All Part of the Job	PDA	HS–AD	—	V
Janus Life Skills: Understanding Advertisements	GLF	JH–HS	3.0	B, TR
Janus Life Skills: Understanding Schedules	GLF	JH–HS	3.0	B, TR
Janus Life Skills: Using the Telephone	GLF	JH–HS	3.0	B, TR
Job Ads and Career Paths	PDA	MS–AD	—	SW, B
Job Box Key	SAD	JH–AD	2.5–3.0	B, DM

General Job Skills (*Continued*)

Material	Publisher	Age Level	Reading Level	Type
Job Club Counselor's Manual	PRO	AD	—	B
Job Coaching Strategies	PDA	HS–AD	—	B, V, SW
Job Interview Skills	CHB	HS–AD	—	B
Job Interviewing for People with Disabilities	PDA	HS–AD	—	V
Job Power	SAD	HS–AD	7.0	B
The Job Readiness/Job Success Series	NSP	HS–AD	—	SW
Job Readiness/Job Success Stories	PRO	HS–AD	4.0	SW
Job Readiness Skills CD-ROM Series	GLE	MS–HS	—	SW
Job Ready	CUR	HS–AD	—	B
Job Search	SAD	MS–AD	4.0	WB
Job Search Tactics for People with Disabilities	PDA	HS–AD	—	V
Job Skills & Career Exploration	GLF	HS–AD	2.0–6.0	WB, TR
Know-How Is the Key	PDA	HS–AD	—	B, RB
Labels & Packages: Practical Practice Reading	REM	MS–HS	3.0–4.0	WB
Learning for Earning	SAD	MS–AD	7.6	B, TR
Letters for Your Resume	ERE	—	—	SW
Life Skills Picture Math	PCI	EL	—	WB
Looking at Work	SAD	MS–AD	2.0–3.0	B
Mathematics Workshop Series: Math on the Job	GLF	MS–HS	5.0–6.0	B, TR
Mavis Beacon Teaches Typing	NSP	EL–HS	—	SW
Mavis Beacon Teaches Typing for Kids	NSP	EL	—	SW
The Newspaper: Practical Practice Reading	REM	MS–HS	3.0–4.0	WB
Occupational Aptitude Survey & Interest Schedule	PRO	JH–HS	—	K
On My Own with Language	LSI	MS–HS	4.5–5.5	DM
On Your Career	CHB	HS–AD	—	WB
Plan Your Day	NSP	EL–MS	—	SW
Planning Your Career—Find the Work That's Right for You	CHB	MS–HS	—	B
Practical Reading 1	SAD	MS–AD	4.0	B
Preparing for Career Success	GLE	MS–HS	—	B, WB, TR
Preparing Teens for the World of Work	PRO	MS–HS	—	B, DM

General Job Skills (*Continued*)

Material	Publisher	Age Level	Reading Level	Type
Reading-Free Vocational Interest Inventory	PRO	JH–HS	—	K
Real Life Math	PRO	JH–HS	4.5–6.0	K
Resumes and Applications for People with Disabilities	PDA	HS–AD	—	V
Roller Typing	NSP	EL–MS	—	SW
Six Steps to Employment	PDA	HS–AD	—	B
Slam Dunk Typing	NSP	EL–MS	—	SW
Social Skills at Work	NSP	MS–HS	—	SW
Social Skills at Work	PDA	MS–AD	—	SW
Social Skills at Work	PDA	MS–AD	—	V
Succeeding in the World of Work	GLE	HS–AD	—	B, WB, TR
"Success at Work" Job Search & Education Kit	CHB	MS–HS	—	K
Success at Work: Transitioning to the Workplace	PDA	HS–AD	—	V, PH
Success on the Job: Communicating Clearly	SAD	HS–AD	—	WB, TR
Success on the Job: Understanding What You Read	SAD	HS–AD	—	WB, TR
Success on the Job: Writing at Work	SAD	HS–AD	—	WB, TR
Supported Employment Six Pack	PDA	MS–HS	—	B, V
Talking Calculator	PCI	—	—	MN
Technology Tools for Terrified Teachers	SAD	EL–AD	—	TR
Thank You for Calling	PRO	EL–AD	—	A, WB
Transitions to Postsecondary Learning	PDA	HS	—	V, PH
Typing Tutor 10	NSP	EL–AD	—	SW
Understanding Occupational Vocabulary	PRO	MS–AD	—	TR
Using a Telephone	PRO	MS–AD	—	K
Vocabulary Builders for Daily Living	ACA	MS–AD	—	B
Vocabulary in Context—Workplace & Career	SAD	HS–AD	4.0	WB, TR
Vocational Curriculum for Developmentally Disabled Persons	PRO	—	—	B
Vocational Training Curriculums for Special Needs Students	REP	—	—	B
W.A.G.E.S. (Working at Gaining Employment Skills)	SOW	HS	—	B
A Way to Work	ATT	HS	—	K
What's Up with Your Future	CHB	MS–HS	—	WB

General Job Skills (*Continued*)

Material	Publisher	Age Level	Reading Level	Type
Workforce 2000 Video Library	GLE	HS–AD	—	V, TR
Working 1	JMS	—	—	V
Workplace Role-Play Series	SAD	MS–HS	5.0	B
Workplace Skills—Keys to Success	CHB	MS–HS	—	PH
Writing for a Reason	SAD	MS–HS	2.5	WB, B
Yes I Can … Get That Job	REP	—	—	K
Your First Resume & Interview	GLE	HS–AD	—	V
Your New Job—Tips for Success	CHB	MS–HS	—	PH

General Education/Training Considerations

Material	Publisher	Age Level	Reading Level	Type
61 Cooperative Learning Activities for Computer Classrooms	SAD	EL–AD	—	TR, DM
125 Ways to Be a Better Student	LSI	MS–HS	—	DM
125 Ways to Be a Better Test Taker—Elementary	LSI	EL–MS	—	DM
125 Ways to Be a Better Test Taker—Jr./Sr. High	LSI	MS–HS	—	DM
A+ Guide to Transitions from High School to College for Special Education	PDA	HS	—	V
Academic Survival Tips for Student Athletes	LLS	—	—	A
Advanced Skills for School Success	CUR	MS–HS	—	CP
Analogies	SAD	MS–HS	—	WB
Attending a Two-Year College	CHB	HS	—	B
Basic Skills/Study Techniques Program	LLS	—	—	K
Brain Cogs	NSP	EL–MS	—	SW
Build Your Own Website	SAD	MS–AD	—	TR, B
Cause & Effect Games	CSB	HS–AD	—	CP
Classification & Organization Skills—Developmental	CUR	HS–AD	6.0	WB
Communicate! Skills for Schools, Business, and Everyday Life	NSP	JH–AD	—	SW

General Education/Training Considerations (*Continued*)

Material	Publisher	Age Level	Reading Level	Type
Computer Dictionary	SAD	EL–AD	—	TR
Computer Graphics & Animation	SAD	MS–AD	—	TR, B
Computer Test Preparation	LLS	HS–AD	—	SW
Computers for Beginners	SAD	EL–AD	—	TR, B
Crash Course for Study Skills	LSI	MS–HS	—	DM
The Daily Detective	ACA	MS–HS	—	B
Day-to-Day Life Skills: Speaking	ACA	MS–AD	—	B
Day-to-Day Life Skills: Writing	ACA	MS–AD	—	B
Dictionary Skills Practice	CUR	MS–AD	4.0	WB
Did You Follow Directions?	REM	EL	—	B
The Dropout Prevention Program	LLS	—	—	K, TR
Effective Reading	LLS	—	—	A, WB
Employment Signs	ATT	—	—	SW
English at School & on the Job	GLF	MS–HS	7.0–9.0	B, TR, SW
English for Everyday Living	SAD	MS–HS	4.5–5.5	B
Essential Life Skill Series	SAD	JH–AD	5.0	WB, B
Essential Vocabulary: Computer Words	REM	MS–HS	—	WB
Essential Vocabulary: Survival Words	REM	MS–HS	—	WB
Everything You Need to Know About Financial Aid	LLS	—	—	V
Financing a College Education	CHB	HS	—	B
Following Directions	REM	EL	—	B
Following Directions—Advanced	CUR	HS–AD	6.0	WB
Foundation of Library Skills Series	ERE	—	—	SW
General Mathematics Project	SAD	HS–AD	—	WB
Guide to Standardized Test Preparation	GLF	MS–HS	3.0–4.0	B, WB, TR
Guide to Study Skills & Strategies	GLF	MS–HS	3.0–4.0	WB, TR
A Guide to Vocational Assessment	PRO	—	—	B
HELP for Memory	LSI	EL–HS	—	DM
How to Make the Right College Choice	LLS	—	—	V
How to Modify Voc Ed for Handicapped Students	LLS	—	—	TR

General Education/Training Considerations (Continued)

Material	Publisher	Age Level	Reading Level	Type
How to Study	AGS	JH–SH	—	WB
How to Succeed in College	LLS	—	—	V
How to Write the Best Reports	NSP	EL–JH	—	SW
Information Signs	ATT	—	—	SW
Introduction to Skills for School Success	CUR	MS–AD	—	V
Lazy Student's Guide to School Success	NSP	MS–HS	—	V
Learning for Earning	SAD	MS–AD	7.6	B, TR
Learning Strategies for School, Home & Work	WAL	HS–AD	—	DM
Making the Grade	LLS	—	—	SW
Making the Grade	SAD	JH–HS	—	WB
Map Skills	ERE	—	—	SW
Math Skill Pack	SAD	HS–AD	2.0–5.0	A
Mind Games: Puzzles in Logic	SAD	MS–HS	—	WB
Mind Your Manners—Social Success	JMS	—	—	V
Moving to Middle School	PRO	EL–MS	—	WB
My School: Language Activities for Daily Living	LLS	EL–MS	—	SW
Next S.T.E.P.–Second Edition	PRO	HS–AD	—	CP
Occupational Aptitude Survey & Interest Schedule	PRO	JH–HS	—	K
On Academic Integrity	CHB	HS	—	WB
On Building Study Skills	CHB	HS	—	WB
On Your Senior Year	CHB	HS	—	WB
Personalized Math	REM	EL–MS	—	WB
Problem Solving: In School	GLF	MS–HS	5.0	B, TR
Problem Solving: On the Job	GLF	MS–HS	5.0	B, TR
Programmed Study Technique and Study Habits Survey	AGS	JH–HS	—	WB, T
Reading Between the Lines	SAD	HS	—	WB
Reading-Free Vocational Interest Inventory	PRO	JH–HS	—	K
The Reference Reference	NSP	EL–HS	—	SW
Research & Reference Skills: Review Masters Across the Curriculum	GLF	MS–HS	4.0–5.0	TR, DM

General Education/Training Considerations (*Continued*)

Material	Publisher	Age Level	Reading Level	Type
Safety Signs	ATT	—	—	SW
Scholarships Today	LLS	—	—	SW
School & Basic Concept Words Software	PCI	EL	—	SW
School Rules Unit Book	PCI	EL	—	TR
Skills for Better Living (Volumes I, II, or III)	NSP	MS–AD	—	SW
Skills Pack	SAD	HS	2.0–4.0	A
Starting College—A Guide for First-Year Students	CHB	HS	—	B
Steps to Self-Determination	PRO	MS–AD	—	CP
Story Starters: Science	ERE	—	—	SW
Story Starters: Social Studies	ERE	—	—	SW
Strategies for Study	SAD	JH–HS	—	WB
Study Skills Book	AGS	—	gr 4–6	WB
Study Skills for Successful Learning	NSP	MS–AD	—	SW
Study Skills Series	SAD	MS–AD	4.5–7.5	WB
Study Skills: Strategies & Practice	CUR	HS–AD	1.0–7.0	DM
Study Strategies for Early School Success	LSI	EL–MS	—	DM
Study Strategies Made Easy	LSI	MS–HS	—	DM
Success in the Classroom	LLS	—	—	V
Success on the Job: Understanding What You Read	SAD	HS–AD	—	WB, TR
Success on the Job: Writing at Work	SAD	HS–AD	—	WB, TR
Survival Guide for Computer Literacy	GLF	JH–AD	5.0–7.0	B, TR
Survival Guide for Students	GLF	MS–HS	6.0–7.0	B, TR
Survival Words	ATT	—	—	SW
Tackling Teen Topics	CSB	HS	—	CP
Technology Tools for Terrified Teachers	SAD	EL–AD	—	TR
Ten Steps to College	PBS	MS–AD	—	V
Test Ready Mathematics	CUR	HS–AD	gr 1.0–8.0	WB
Test Ready Practice with Cloze	CUR	HS–AD	gr 3.0–6.0	WB
Test Ready Reading & Vocabulary	CUR	HS–AD	1.0–8.0	WB
The Test Taker's Edge	SUN	MS–AD	—	SW

General Education/Training Considerations (*Continued*)

Material	Publisher	Age Level	Reading Level	Type
Things to Know About Personal Paperwork	WAL	MS–AD	4.0	B
Tips & Tricks for Handhelds in the Classroom	SAD	EL–HS	—	DM
Tips & Tricks for Using the Internet	SAD	EL–HS	—	DM
Tools for Transition Program	AGS	JH–SH	—	K
Transitions to High School	PDA	EL–MS	—	V, PH
Transitions to Postsecondary Learning	PDA	HS	—	V, PH
Unlocking Test Taking	GLF	MS–HS	5.0–6.0	B, TR
The Video Test Preparation Review Series	LLS	HS–AD	—	V
A Way to Work	ATT	HS	—	K
What Is It? Things in a Classroom	PCI	EL	—	G
What Shall I Do Now, Teacher?	REM	EL	—	B
What's Up with Academic Integrity	CHB	MS–HS	—	WB
What's Up with Academic Success	CHB	MS–HS	—	WB
What's Up with Beating Test Anxiety	CHB	MS–HS	—	WB
What's Up with Study Skills	CHB	MS–HS	—	WB
What's Your Point of View on School Issues?	GLF	MS–HS	3.0	B, TR
Who Knew? The Study Smart Issue	CHB	EL–MS	—	WB
Workplace Skills—Keys to Success	CHB	MS–HS	—	PH
Write Your Research Report	GLF	MS–HS	5.0	B, TR
Writing Across the Curriculum	GLF	MS–HS	5.0–6.0	B, TR
Writing in the Real World	GLF	MS–HS	3.0–4.0	WB, TR, SW
You Can Survive Your Freshman Year	CHB	HS	—	B
Your Child's First Year of College—A Guide for Parents	CHB	HS	—	B
Your First Year in College	CHB	HS	—	B

Employment Setting

Material	Publisher	Age Level	Reading Level	Type
Basic Life Skills at Work	NSP	MS–AD	—	SW
Building Success in the Workplace	STV	AD	3.0–4.0	WB

Employment Setting (*Continued*)

Material	Publisher	Age Level	Reading Level	Type
Calculators at Work in Daily Living	WAL	MS–HS	—	DM
Career Awareness Plus	SAD	HS–AD	2.0–3.5	B
Career Exploration	SAD	MS–AD	3.0–4.0	B
Career Ideas Series	SAD	MS–AD	6.0	B
Career Skills	SAD	MS–AD	4.0–5.0	WB, B
Career–Life Skills Packs	SAD	HS	2.5–4.0	K
Careers Without College	SAD	MS–AD	3.0–4.0	B
Careers Without College	SAD	JH–AD	7.0	B
Communicate! Skills for Schools, Business, and Everyday Life	NSP	JH–AD	—	SW
Communication Skills Series	SAD	AD	2.6–2.8	B, WB
Computer Literacy	GLF	JH–AD	3.0–4.0	CP
Consumer Skills	SAD	—	3.0	WB
Coolcareers.com	SAD	EL–HS	5.0	B
Developing Workplace Skills	CHB	MS–HS	—	PH
Developing Your Job Search Skills	SAD	JH–HS	—	WB
Employability Skills Program	SAD	JH–AD	2.5–4.0	B
Employment Signs	ATT	—	—	SW
English Survival Series	SAD	MS–AD	2.0–5.0	WB
Essential Life Skill Series	SAD	JH–AD	5.0	WB, B
Everyday English	SAD	JH–AD	—	WB
From School to Work	SAD	MS–HS	6.0	B
General Mathematics Project	SAD	HS–AD	—	WB
Getting Ahead at Work	SAD	MS–AD	4.0	WB
Going to Work Center	CHB	MS–HS	—	P, PH
The Guide to Basic Skills Jobs, Volume I	REP	—	—	RB
A Guide to Vocational Assessment	PRO	—	—	B
How to Get a Job and Keep It	STV	AD	5.0–6.0	WB
Information Signs	ATT	—	—	SW
Introduction to Skills for School Success	CUR	MS–AD	—	V
Job Accommodation Handbook	REP	—	—	TR

Employment Setting (*Continued*)

Material	Publisher	Age Level	Reading Level	Type
Job Coaching Kit	RPM	—	—	K
Job Power	SAD	HS–AD	7.0	B
The Job Readiness/Job Success Series	NSP	HS–AD	—	SW
Job Ready	CUR	HS–AD	—	B
Learning for Earning	SAD	MS–AD	7.6	B, TR
Looking at Work	SAD	MS–AD	2.0–3.0	B
Math for the World of Work	AGS	MS–AD	3.9	CP
Math Skill Pack	SAD	HS–AD	2.0–5.0	A
Math Skills for the Workforce	STV	HS–AD	4.0–6.0	B
Medical Words	ATT	—	—	SW
Necessary Skills for the Workforce	STV	HS–AD	3.0–4.0	B
Picture This (Creates Flash Cards)	PDA	EL–AD	—	SW
Practical Arithmetic Series: Working with Sense	GLF	MS–HS	3.0–4.0	B
Practicing Occupational Reading Skills: Automotive	STV	AD	5.0–6.0	WB
Practicing Occupational Reading Skills: Business	STV	AD	5.0–6.0	WB
Practicing Occupational Reading Skills: Carpentry	STV	AD	5.0–6.0	WB
Practicing Occupational Reading Skills: Electronics	STV	AD	5.0–6.0	WB
Practicing Occupational Reading Skills: Health Care	STV	AD	5.0–6.0	WB
Practicing Occupational Reading Skills: Machine Trades	STV	AD	5.0–6.0	WB
Problem Solving: In School	GLF	MS–HS	5.0	B, TR
Problem Solving: On the Job	GLF	MS–HS	5.0	B, TR
Safety Signs	AQU	—	—	SW
Safety Training Kit	REP	—	—	K
Skill Packs	SAD	HS	2.0–4.0	A
Succeeding in the World of Work	GLE	HS–AD	—	B, WB, TR
"Success at Work" Job Search & Education Kit	CHB	MS–HS	—	K
Survival Vocabulary	SAD	JH–AD	2.0–4.0	B, WB
Survival Words	ATT	—	—	SW
Take Time	PRO	—	—	TR
The Time Is Now	PRO	EL–AD	1.0	WB
Transportation Signs	ATT	—	—	SW

Employment Setting (*Continued*)

Material	Publisher	Age Level	Reading Level	Type
Using a Telephone	PRO	MS–AD	—	K
Vocabulary Building	SAD	MS–HS	—	DM
W.A.G.E.S. (Working at Gaining Employment Skills)	SOW	HS	—	B
A Way to Work	ATT	HS	—	K
Workforce: Building Success	STV	MS–AD	4.0–6.0	B, TR
Working I	JMS	—	—	V
Working II	JMS	—	—	V, T
Workplace Role-Play Series	SAD	MS–HS	5.0	B
Workplace Skills	PCI	—	—	G
Workplace Skills—Keys to Success	CHB	MS–HS	—	PH
Worktales	GLF	HS	2.0–3.0	B
Yes I Can … Do the Job Right	REP	—	—	K
Yes I Can … Work with People	REP	—	—	K
Your New Job—Tips for Success	CHB	MS–HS	—	PH

Career Refinement and Reevaluation

Material	Publisher	Age Level	Reading Level	Type
9–5 Series	HIN	MS–HS	3.0	B
Able to Work	PDA	MS–AD	—	B
Breaking Out	LLS	HS	—	V
Bridges: Making the Transition from School to Work	SAD	MS–AD	—	WB, TR
Career Awareness Plus	SAD	HS–AD	2.0–3.5	B
The Career Box	GLF	MS–HS	4.0–6.0	PH, WB, TR
Career Clusters	GLE	HS–AD	—	WB
Career Discover	NSP	EL–MS	—	SW
Career Exploration	SAD	MS–AD	3.0–4.0	B
Career Exploration on the Internet	NSP	EL–HS	—	SW, B
Career Explorer	NSP	EL–HS	—	SW
Career Ideas Series	SAD	MS–AD	6.0	B

Career Refinement and Reevaluation (*Continued*)

Material	Publisher	Age Level	Reading Level	Type
Career Kids	NSP	EL	—	SW
Career Ladders: Transition from High School to Adult Life	PRO	MS–HS	—	K
Career Options for Women	LLS	—	—	B
Career Pathways	GLE	MS–AD	—	V, SW, WB, TR
Career Planet Launch Pad	NSP	EL–MS	—	SW
Career Planet Launching Connections	NSP	EL–MS	—	WB, TR
Career Planner's Portfolio	CUR	MS–HS	—	RB
Career Readers	SAD	JH–AD	2.0	B
The Career Search Programs	LLS	—	—	K
Career Skills	SAD	MS–AD	4.0–5.0	WB, B
Career–Life Skills Packs	SAD	HS	2.5–4.0	K
Careers	GLF	MS–HS	3.0–4.0	CP
Careers in Dogs Resource Guide	AKC	MS–HS	—	B
Careers Without College	REM	MS–HS	3.0–4.0	B
Careers Without College	SAD	MS–AD	3.0–4.0	B
Careers Without College	SAD	JH–AD	7.0	B
Children's Dictionary of Occupations	NSP	EL–MS	—	B
Choosing Employment Goals	SOW	MS–HS	—	K
Community Helpers	PCI	EL	—	B
Competitive Job Finding Guide for Persons with Handicaps	PRO	HS–AD	—	B, WB
Cool Jobs	REM	EL–HS	1.0–3.0	B
Coolcareers.com	SAD	EL–HS	5.0	B
Crash Course: Basic Accounting	NSP	HS	—	SW
Daily Experiences and Activities for Living	PRO	MS–AD	3.0–5.0	K
Developing Workplace Skills	CHB	MS–HS	—	PH
Disabilities in the Workplace	PDA	MS–AD	—	V
Dressing for Success	PDA	HS–AD	—	V
Essential Life Skills Series	CSB	JH–AD	—	WB
Exploring Careers	GLE	HS–AD	—	CP
Exploring the World of Work CD-ROM	GLE	HS	—	SW

Career Refinement and Reevaluation (*Continued*)

Material	Publisher	Age Level	Reading Level	Type
From School to Work	SAD	MS–HS	6.0	B
Going to Work Center	CHB	MS–HS	—	P, PH
Grooming for Success	PDA	HS–AD	—	V
The Guide for Occupational Exploration	AGS	—	—	RB
Handbook of Career Planning for Special Needs Students	AGS	—	—	TR
The Harrington O'Shea Career Decision-Making System	AGS	HS–AD	—	T
INFO Job	SAD	JH–HS	—	B
Insights	PRO	EL–MS	—	B
Interview Skills for the Future	NSP	HS–AD	—	SW
Interview Skills for the Future	PDA	HS–AD	—	SW, V
Interviewing Skills for Job Candidates with Physical Disabilities	PDA	HS–AD	—	V
It's All Part of the Job	PDA	HS–AD	—	V
Job Ads and Career Paths	PDA	MS–AD	—	SW, B
The Job Box	GLF	MS–HS	2.0–3.0	WB, PH, TR
Job Box Key	SAD	JH–AD	2.5–3.0	B, DM
Job Power	SAD	HS–AD	7.0	B
Job Readiness Skills CD-ROM Series	GLE	MS–HS	—	SW
Job Ready	CUR	HS–AD	—	B
Job Search Skills for the 21st Century	NSP	HS–AD	—	SW
Job Search Tactics for People with Disabilities	PDA	HS–AD	—	V
Job Interviewing for People with Disabilities	PDA	HS–AD	—	V
Job Skills & Career Exploration	GLF	HS–AD	2.0–6.0	WB, TR
Job Tips	LLS	—	—	P
Job Tips	SAD	JH–AD	2.7	B
Learning for Earning	SAD	MS—AD	7.6	B, TR
Lifetimes	GLF	HS	—	B
Looking at Work	SAD	MS–AD	2.0–3.0	B
Math Word Problems: Careers	NSP	EL–JH	—	SW
Multimedia Career Center	NSP	MS–HS	—	SW
Know-How Is the Key	PDA	HS–AD	—	B, TR

Career Refinement and Reevaluation (*Continued*)

Material	Publisher	Age Level	Reading Level	Type
Occupation Cards	PCI	EL	—	FC
Occupation Words: Life-Skill Lessons	REP	EL–HS	4.0–5.0	B
Occupational Outlook Handbook: 2002–2003	NSP	EL–HS	—	SW
Occupational Outlook Handbook: 2004–2005	PRO	MS–AD	—	SW
Occupations	PRO	EL–AD	—	FC
On Your Career	CHB	HS–AD	—	WB
Planning Your Career—Find the Work That's Right for You	CHB	MS–HS	—	B
Practical Reading 1	SAD	MS–AD	4.0	B
Practicing Occupational Reading Skills: Automotive	STV	AD	5.0–6.0	WB
Practicing Occupational Reading Skills: Business	STV	AD	5.0–6.0	WB
Practicing Occupational Reading Skills: Carpentry	STV	AD	5.0–6.0	WB
Practicing Occupational Reading Skills: Electronics	STV	AD	5.0–6.0	WB
Practicing Occupational Reading Skills: Health Care	STV	AD	5.0–6.0	WB
Practicing Occupational Reading Skills: Machine Trades	STV	AD	5.0–6.0	WB
Preparing for Career Success	GLE	MS–HS	—	B, WB, TR
Preparing Teens for the World of Work	PRO	MS–HS	—	B, DM
Punch the Time Clock, Not Your Coworkers	NSP	MS	—	SW
Reading About Careers	REM	EL–MS	2.0–5.0	B
Ready to Work: Agriculture	GLF	MS–HS	4.0–9.0	B, TR
Ready to Work: Business	GLF	MS–HS	4.0–9.0	B, TR
Ready to Work: Health Occupations	GLF	MS–HS	4.0–9.0	B, TR
Ready to Work: Service & Retail	GLF	MS–HS	4.0–9.0	B, TR
Ready to Work: Technology	GLF	MS–HS	4.0–9.0	B, TR
Ready to Work: Trade & Industry	GLF	MS–HS	4.0–9.0	B, TR
Real Life Math	PRO	JH–HS	4.5–6.0	K
Resume Pro 3.0	NSP	HS–AD	—	SW
Resumes and Applications for People with Disabilities	PDA	HS–AD	—	V
The Right Job	SUN	MS–AD	—	SW
School-to-Work Career Center	NSP	HS–AD	—	SW
The School-to-Work Library	GLF	MS–HS	4.0–6.0	B

Career Refinement and Reevaluation (*Continued*)

Material	Publisher	Age Level	Reading Level	Type
Self-Directed Employment	PDA	HS–AD	—	B
Six Steps to Employment	PDA	HS–AD	—	B
Social Skills at Work	PDA	MS–AD	—	SW
Social Skills at Work	PDA	MS–AD	—	V
"Success at Work" Job Search & Education Kit	CHB	MS–HS	—	K
Success at Work: Transitioning to the Workplace	PDA	HS–AD	—	V, PH
Success in the World of Work (Volume 1)	NSP	HS–AD	—	SW
Take This Job and Love It	NSP	HS–AD	—	SW
Transition Planning Inventory	PRO	HS–AD	—	K
Vocabulary Builders for Daily Living	ACA	MS–AD	—	B
Vocabulary in Context—Workplace & Career	SAD	HS–AD	4.0	WB, TR
Vocational Curriculum for Developmentally Disabled Persons	PRO	—	—	B
Vocational Readers	SAD	JH–AD	2.0	B
Vocational Training Curriculums for Special Needs Students	REP	—	—	B
What's My Job	NSP	MS–JH	—	SW
What's Up with Your Future	CHB	MS–HS	—	WB
What's Your Point of View on Careers?	GLF	MS–HS	3.0	B, TR
Who Am I? Community Helpers	PCI	EL	—	G
The Woman Entrepreneur: Do You Have What It Takes?	LLS	—	—	V
Women in Non-Traditional Occupations	LLS	—	—	FS, V
Work Adjustment Inventory	PRO	HS–AD	—	K
Work Place Words: Life-Skill Lessons	REP	EL–HS	4.0–5.0	B
Worker Trait Group Guide	AGS	—	—	RB
Workforce 2000 Video Library	GLE	HS–AD	—	V, TR
Workplace Role-Play Series	SAD	MS–HS	5.0	B
Workplace Skills—Keys to Success	CHB	MS–HS	—	PH
Workplace Success Series: Applied Communication Skills	GLF	HS	6.0–9.0	B, TR
Workplace Success Series: Applied Math Skills	GLF	HS	6.0–9.0	B, TR
The World of Work: Animal Care	GLF	MS–HS	4.0–6.0	B
The World of Work: Banking & Finance	GLF	MS–HS	4.0–6.0	B

Career Refinement and Reevaluation (*Continued*)

Material	Publisher	Age Level	Reading Level	Type
The World of Work: Computers	GLF	MS–HS	4.0–6.0	B
The World of Work: Cosmetology	GLF	MS–HS	4.0–6.0	B
The World of Work: Film, Television & Video	GLF	MS–HS	4.0–6.0	B
The World of Work: Helping Professions	GLF	MS–HS	4.0–6.0	B
The World of Work: Hotels, Motels & Resorts	GLF	MS–HS	4.0–6.0	B
The World of Work: Law Enforcement	GLF	MS–HS	4.0–6.0	B
The World of Work: Music	GLF	MS–HS	4.0–6.0	B
The World of Work: Nutrition	GLF	MS–HS	4.0–6.0	B
The World of Work: Restaurant Industry	GLF	MS–HS	4.0–6.0	B
The World of Work: Transportation	GLF	MS–HS	4.0–6.0	B
You Are ... Series	HIN	MS–HS	4.0–5.0	B, WB
Your Career Adventure	GLE	HS–AD	—	B, TR
Your New Job—Tips for Success	CHB	MS–HS	—	PH

Home Management

Material	Publisher	Age Level	Reading Level	Type
25 Life Skill, Math & Language Programs	PDA	EL–HS	—	SW
Ads & Coupons: Practical Practice Reading	REM	MS–HS	—	WB
Baby Sitting	LLS	MS–HS	—	V
Be Your Own Plumber	LLS	—	—	V
Beginning Market Math	REM	EL–HS	1.0–2.0	B
Beginning Menu Math	REM	EL–HS	1.0–2.0	B
Being with Housemates, Part 1 & 2	JMS	—	—	V
Body & Fender Parts	LLS	—	—	V
Calculators at Work in Daily Living	WAL	MS–HS	—	DM
Car and Driver	SAD	MS–AD	4.0	WB
Career–Life Skills Packs	SAD	HS	2.5–4.0	K
Choosing & Preparing Foods	WAL	MS–HS	3.0	DM

Home Management (*Continued*)

Material	Publisher	Age Level	Reading Level	Type
Clock Faces	NSP	EL	—	SW
Clock Shop	NSP	EL–MS	—	SW
Clothing Photo Cue Cards	PRO	EL–AD	—	FC
Clothing Kit	PRO	EL–MS	—	K
Colorcards Everyday Objects	PRO	EL–AD	—	FC
Colorcards Color Library Food	PRO	EL–AD	—	FC
Colorcards Verbs	PRO	EL–AD	—	FC
Communicate! Skills for Schools, Business, and Everyday Life	NSP	JH–AD	—	SW
Community Skills	PCI	—	—	G
Consumer Skills	SAD	—	3.0	WB
Consumer Skills: Math and Economics	SAD	JH–AD	2.5–3.0	WB
Cooking Class	PCI	—	—	G
Cooking to Learn (I or II)	PCI	El–MS	—	TR, WB
Crime Prevention in the Home	LLS	—	—	V
Daily Experiences and Activities for Living	PRO	MS–AD	3.0–5.0	K
Department Store Math	REM	EL–HS	1.0–2.0	B
Discover Time	GAM	EL–MS	—	SW
Discover Time	NSP	EL	—	SW
Don't Get Hurt in the Kitchen	WAL	MS–HS	—	P
Electrical Appliances Kit	PRO	EL–MS	—	K
Employability Skills Program	SAD	JH–AD	2.5–4.0	B
Equipped for Life	REM	JH–HS	—	G
Everyday Activities Photo Cue Cards	PRO	EL–AD	—	FC
Everyday Household Items	SAD	MS–AD	4.0	WB
Fire Safety	PDA	MS–AD	—	V
Focus on Problem Solving	CPR	EL–MS	—	B, TR
Focus on Transition	PRO	HS–AD	—	WB
Following Directions: Around the House	REM	EL–MS	—	B
Food & Drink Photo Cue Cards	PRO	EL–AD	—	FC
Food for Today	GLE	HS–AD	—	CP

Home Management (*Continued*)

Material	Publisher	Age Level	Reading Level	Type
Food for Thought	SUN	MS–AD	—	SW
Fruits, Nuts, & Vegetables Kit	PRO	EL–MS	—	K
Furniture Kit	PRO	EL–MS	—	K
The Good & Easy Cookbook	WAL	MS–HS	3.0	B
Granny Applebee's Cookie Factory	NSP	EL–MS	—	SW
Graph Master	NSP	EL–HS	—	SW
Grocery Store Foods Words	PCI	EL	—	SW
Haircutting at Home	LLS	—	—	V
Health & Safety	SAD	MS–AD	4.0	WB
Home & Family Life Education	WAL	MS–AD	—	DM
Home Cooking	ATT	—	—	K
Home Video System Maintenance	LLS	—	—	V
Household Objects Photo Cue Cards	PRO	EL–AD	—	FC
How to Buy a Home with Nothing Down	LLS	—	—	V
How to Care for Your Home	WAL	MS–AD	3.0	B
How to Care for Your Lawn	LLS	—	—	V
How to Design & Build a Vegetable Garden	LLS	—	—	V
How to Design a Flower Garden	LLS	—	—	V
How to Grow & Cook Herbs	LLS	—	—	V
How to Grow & Nurture Seedlings	LLS	—	—	V
How to Grow Cool-Weather Vegetables	LLS	—	—	V
How to Grow Flowers	LLS	—	—	V
How to Grow Healthy Houseplants	LLS	—	—	V
How to Grow Plants in a Greenhouse	LLS	—	—	V
How to Grow Plants in Sunspaces	LLS	—	—	V
How to Grow Roses	LLS	—	—	V
How to Grow Warm-Weather Vegetables	LLS	—	—	V
How to Set Up a Home	WAL	MS–AD	3.0	B
In the Kitchen: Understanding Instructions	REM	EL–MS	3.0–4.0	WB
Information Signs	ATT	—	—	SW

Home Management (*Continued*)

Material	Publisher	Age Level	Reading Level	Type
James Discovers Math	NSP	EL	—	SW
Janus Life Skills: Budgeting & Buying	GLF	JH–HS	3.0	B, TR
Janus Life Skills: Getting From Here To There	GLF	JH–HS	3.0	B, TR
Janus Life Skills: Shopping & Caring for Cars	GLF	JH–HS	3.0	B, TR
Janus Life Skills: Staying Healthy	GLF	JH–HS	3.0	B, TR
Keeping House	AQU	—	—	K
Kitchen Math	WAL	MS–HS	4.0	DM, TR
Kitchen Utensils Kit	PRO	EL–MS	—	K
Labels & Packages: Practical Practice Reading	REM	MS–HS	—	WB
Language for Living Series	PRO	EL–MS	—	B
Learning to Budget	AGS	MS–AD	—	B
Let's Go Shopping!	REM	EL–HS	—	G
Life Coping Skills Series: Facts & Sources	STV	MS–JH	2.0–4.0	WB
Life Coping Skills Series: Forms & Messages	STV	MS–JH	2.0–4.0	WB
Life Coping Skills Series: Signs & Labels	STV	MS–JH	2.0–4.0	WB
Life Skills Math Game: Department Store Math	REM	EL–MS	—	G
Life Skills Math Game: Grocery Cart	REM	EL–MS	—	G
Life Skills Math Game: Shopping Bag	REM	EL–MS	—	G
Light & Tasty Cooking Labs	WAL	HS–AD	—	B
Living in the U.S.A.	SAD	JH–AD	—	B, WB
Look 'n Cook	AQU	—	—	K
Looking Good Key	PCI	—	—	G
Make Math More Real	PBS	EL–MS	—	V, SW
Math for Everyday Living	SAD	JH–HS	4.5–5.0	B
Math for the Real World	NSP	EL–JH	—	SW
Math Life Skills Series	CUR	MS–HS	—	WB
Math VIP	NSP	MS–JH	—	SW
Money Challenge	GAM	EL–MS	—	SW
Money Matters Guides	SAD	MS–AD	2.5	WB
Money Smarts	WAL	HS–AD	7.0	DM

Home Management (*Continued*)

Material	Publisher	Age Level	Reading Level	Type
Moving Out on Your Own	SAD	MS–AD	4.0	WB
My House: Language Activities of Daily Living	LLS	—	—	SW
Oil Change, Filters, & Lube	LLS	—	—	V
On My Own at Home	LSI	MS–HS	5.5–6.5	DM
On My Own with Language	LSI	MS–HS	4.5–5.5	DM
Out in the World–Second Edition	PRO	EL–MS	—	B
Parts of the House Kit	PRO	EL–MS	—	K
PCI Photo Bingo—Foods	PCI	EL	—	G
PCI Photo Bingo—Household Items	PCI	EL	—	G
PCI Photo Library	PCI	EL	—	FC
Picture This	PRO	EL–AD	—	SW
Picture This (Creates Flash Cards)	PDA	EL–AD	—	SW
Plan Your Day	AQU	—	—	K
Practical Food Safety	WAL	MS–HS	—	B
Practical Reading 2	SAD	MS–AD	4.0	B
Prepared Foods Kit	PRO	EL–MS	—	K
Problem-Solving Picture Cards	PRO	MS–AD	—	FC
Professional Tips for Easy Wallpapering	LLS	—	—	V
Reading Problems in Mathematics	CPR	EL–HS	—	B, TR
Real World Learning	NSP	EL–MS	—	SW
Real World Reading	PCI	MS–HS	—	CP
Replacing Exhaust Systems	LLS	—	—	V
Replacing Shocks and Struts	LLS	—	—	V
Safety Around Dogs: Your Safety Begins with You!	AKC	EL–HS	—	V
Safety in and Around the Home, Set One	PRO	EL–AD	—	FC
Safety in and Around the Home, Set Two	PRO	EL–AD	—	FC
Safety in the Home: How to Prevent Falls	PDA	MS–AD	—	V
Safety Signs	ATT	—	—	SW
Safety Skills	PCI	EL	—	G
A Safety Training Kit	REP	—	—	K

Home Management (*Continued*)

Material	Publisher	Age Level	Reading Level	Type
Seasons	TSP	EL–MS	—	SW, TR, WB
Select-A-Meal	ATT	—	—	K
Special Needs Curriculum—Math Resources	CPR	EL	—	CP
Special Picture Cookbook	PRO	EL	—	B
Survival Math	SAD	JH–AD	2.0–4.0	DM, A
Survival Words	ATT	—	—	SW
Take Time	PRO	—	—	TR
Things to Know About Cars & Driving	WAL	MS–AD	4.0	B
Things to Know About Housing	WAL	MS–AD	4.0	B
Things to Know About Personal Paperwork	WAL	MS–AD	4.0	B
Time Concepts Series	PRO	MS–AD	—	WB
The Time Is Now	PRO	EL–AD	1.0	WB
Tool Factory Applications	NSP	EL–HS	—	SW
Tools Kit	PRO	EL–MS	—	K
Toward Independence	PDA	MS–AD	—	SW
Tune Up & Maintenance, Parts I & II	LLS	—	—	V
Using a Telephone	PRO	MS–AD	—	K
Using a Telephone–Second Edition	PRO	EL–AD	—	K
Vocabulary in Context—Everyday Living Words	SAD	HS–AD	4.0	WB, TR
Vocabulary in Context—Media & Marketplace	SAD	HS–AD	4.0	WB, TR
What Is It? Things in a House	PCI	EL	—	G

Financial Management

Material	Publisher	Age Level	Reading Level	Type
41 Activities in Basic Money Management	SAD	JH–AD	4.0	DM
41 Activities in Basic Money Management	WAL	MS–AD	4.0	DM
Basic Coins	PCI	EL	—	SW
Basic Menu Math	PCI	EL	—	G, WB

Financial Management (*Continued*)

Material	Publisher	Age Level	Reading Level	Type
Basic Menu Math Game	PCI	EL	—	G
Basic Menu Math Software	PCI	EL	—	SW
Before You Buy a Dog Brochure	AKC	EL–HS	—	PH
Beginning Market Math	REM	EL–HS	1.0–2.0	B
Beginning Menu Math	REM	EL–HS	1.0–2.0	B
Being with Housemates, Part 1 & 2	JMS	—	—	V
Best Buys	REM	EL–HS	3.0–4.0	WB
Better Money Management—A Guide for Reaching Your Goals	CHB	HS–AD	—	B
Bonds	LLS	—	—	V
Budgets Aren't for Push-Overs: Budgeting, Goal Setting, & Record-Keeping	GLE	HS–AD	—	V
Building Your Money Pyramid: Financial Planning	GLE	HS–AD	—	V
Career Math	REM	EL–HS	3.0–4.0	WB
Check Writing	PCI	EL	—	K
Checkbook Math	REM	MS–HS	—	WB
Coin Abacus	PCI	EL	—	MN
Coin Abacus Worksheets	PCI	EL	—	WB
Coin Counting Bingo	PCI	EL	—	G, MN, WB
Coin-u-lator	PCI	EL–MS	—	MN, G
Coin-u-lator Activity Cards	PCI	EL–MS	—	FC
Coin-u-lator Worksheets	PCI	EL–MS	—	WB
The Confident Consumer	SAD	MS–AD	6.0	B
Consumer Education & Economics	GLE	HS	—	CP
Consumer Math	AGS	MS–AD	3.5	B
Consumer Math Success Kit	WAL	HS–AD	7.0	DM
Consumer Spending	SAD	MS–AD	4.0	WB
Counting Money	PRO	EL–AD	1.0	WB
Counting Money & Making Change	WAL	MS–HS	7.0	DM
Crash Course: Personal Finance	NSP	MS–AD	—	SW
Credit Card Cautions	GLE	HS–AD	—	V

Financial Management (*Continued*)

Material	Publisher	Age Level	Reading Level	Type
Daily Experiences and Activities for Living	PRO	MS–AD	3.0–5.0	K
Deluxe Banking Software	NSP	MS–AD	—	SW
Department Store Math	REM	EL–HS	1.0–2.0	B
Department Store Math	REM	EL–HS	3.0–4.0	B
Directory for Federal Aid	LLS	—	—	B
Discount & Drug Store Software	PCI	EL	—	SW
Dollars & Cents	NSP	EL–MS	—	SW
Dollars & Cents	PDA	EL	—	SW
Dollars & Cents Bundle	ATT	MS–HS	—	SW
Dollars & Cents Software	ACA	EL–HS	—	SW
Don't Shop 'Til You Drop: Credit & Consumerism	GLE	HS–AD	—	V
Everyday Math	REM	EL–HS	3.0–4.0	WB
Everything You Need to Know About Financial Aid	LLS	—	—	V
First Money	PCI	EL	—	SW
Focus on Problem Solving	CPR	EL–MS	—	B, TR
Get What You Pay For	GLE	HS–AD	—	V
Grocery, Discount & Drug Store Software	PCI	EL	—	SW
Grocery Store Game	PCI	EL	—	G
Grocery Store Software	PCI	EL	—	SW
Hamburger Hut	REM	EL–HS	3.0–4.0	B
How to Buy a Home with Nothing Down	LLS	—	—	V
How to Finance a College Education	LLS	—	—	V
How to Make the Right College Choice	LLS	—	—	V
How to Use Money Wisely	WAL	MS–AD	3.0	B
Income Tax Made Easy	WAL	HS–AD	6.0	WB
Instant Internet Activities Folder—Stock Market	SAD	EL–HS	—	TR
Kick the Tires … Finding & Financing a Used Car	GLE	HS–AD	—	V
Know Your Government	LLS	—	—	B
Learning for Earning	SAD	MS–AD	7.6	B, TR
Learning to Budget	AGS	MS–AD	—	B

Financial Management (*Continued*)

Material	Publisher	Age Level	Reading Level	Type
Life Skills Personalized Math	REM	EL–MS	—	WB
Life Skills Math Game: Bank Account	REM	EL–MS	—	G
Life Skills Math Game: Menu Math	REM	EL–MS	—	G
Life Skills Math Game: Purchase	REM	EL–MS	—	G
Making Change	PCI	EL	—	G, MN, WB
Managing Money	SAD	MS–AD	4.0	WB
Market Math	REM	EL–HS	3.0–4.0	B
The Marketplace	LLS	—	—	V
Math at Home	REM	EL–HS	3.0–4.0	WB
Math for the Real World	NSP	EL–JH	—	SW
Math for the World of Work	AGS	MS–AD	3.9	CP
Math in Everyday Life	WAL	MS–AD	—	TR, B
Math in the Mall	REM	EL–HS	3.0–4.0	WB
Math Life Skills Series	CUR	MS–HS	—	WB
Math Skills for the Workforce	STV	HS–AD	4.0–6.0	B
Math Word Problems: Money	NSP	EL–JH	—	SW
Math VIP	NSP	MS–JH	—	SW
Money Calc	PCI	EL	—	MN
Money Calc Worksheets	PCI	EL	—	WB
Money Challenge	NSP	EL	—	SW
The Money Management Series	NSP	MS–AD	—	SW
Money Math	PCI	EL	—	WB, MN
Money Math Kit	REM	EL–MS	—	K
Money Matters Guides: Be Ad-Wise	GLF	MS–HS	2.0	B, TR
Money Matters Guides: Be Credit-Wise	GLF	MS–HS	2.0	B, TR
Money Matters Guides: Insure Yourself	GLF	MS–HS	2.0	B, TR
Money Matters Guides: Know Your Rights	GLF	MS–HS	2.0	B, TR
Money Matters Guides: Make Your Money Grow	GLF	MS–HS	2.0	B, TR
Money Matters Guides: Master Your Money	GLF	MS–HS	2.0	B, TR
Money Matters Guides: More for Your Money	GLF	MS–HS	2.0	B, TR

Financial Management (*Continued*)

Material	Publisher	Age Level	Reading Level	Type
Money Matters Guides: Pay by Check	GLF	MS–HS	2.0	B, TR
Money Sense	REM	EL–HS	3.0–4.0	WB
Money Smarts	WAL	HS–AD	7.0	DM
Money Station	PDA	EL	—	MN, SW
Money Tray & Assorted Coin Pack	PCI	EL–HS	—	MN
Money Unit Book	PCI	EL	—	TR
Moneytown	NSP	EL	—	SW
Moving Out on Your Own	SAD	MS–AD	4.0	WB
Mutual Funds	LLS	—	—	V
Name Your Price	REM	EL–HS	—	K, MN
Next Dollar Shopping	PCI	EL–MS	—	G, MN, WB
Old-Fashioned Ice Cream Parlor	REM	EL–HS	3.0–4.0	B
Personalized Math	REM	EL–MS	—	WB
Practical Arithmetic Series: Buying with Sense	GLF	MS–HS	3.0–4.0	B
Practical Arithmetic Series: Money Makes Sense	GLF	MS–HS	3.0–4.0	B
Practical Arithmetic Series: Using Dollars & Sense	GLF	MS–HS	3.0–4.0	B
Practical Arithmetic Series: Working with Sense	GLF	MS–HS	3.0–4.0	B
Practical Math	AGS	MS–AD	3.5	WB
Practical Mathematics for Consumers	GLF	MS–HS	3.0–4.0	B, WB
Practical Reading 1	SAD	MS–AD	4.0	B
Reading Problems in Mathematics	CPR	EL–HS	—	B, TR
Real-Life Math	PRO	JH–HS	4.5–6.0	K
Real Numbers	MHC	HS–AD	—	WB
Real World Learning	NSP	EL–MS	—	SW
Scholarships Today	LLS	—	—	SW
Shopping Around the Town	REM	EL–MS	—	WB
Shopping at the Mall	PCI	EL	—	G
Shopping Basket	PCI	EL	—	MN
Shopping Basket Worksheets	PCI	EL	—	WB
Shopping Mall Math	REM	EL–MS	—	WB

Financial Management (*Continued*)

Material	Publisher	Age Level	Reading Level	Type
Shopping Smart	ATT	—	—	K
Simply English	HIN	EL–AD	—	B, WB
Skills for Better Living (Volumes I, II, or III)	NSP	MS–AD	—	SW
Special Needs Curriculum—Math Resources	CPR	EL	—	CP
Stashing Your Cash: Financial Service	GLE	HS–AD	—	V
Stepping Out	ATT	—	—	K
Success in Math: Consumer Math	GLF	MS–HS	6.0–7.0	B, TR
Survival Math Skills	WAL	MS–HS	5.0	DM
Teaching Consumer Concepts	SAD	HS	—	DM
Things to Know About Cars & Driving	WAL	MS–AD	4.0	B
Things to Know About Housing	WAL	MS–AD	4.0	B
Things to Know About Personal Paperwork	WAL	MS–AD	4.0	B
Things to Know About Spending & Saving Money	WAL	MS–AD	4.0	B
Touch Money	PCI	EL–MS	—	MN, WB
Touch Money Big Coin Activities	PCI	EL–MS	—	MN
Trading Up	PCI	EL–MS	—	G, MN, WB
Understanding the Business World and Stocks	LLS	—	—	V
Using Money	AGS	MS–AD	—	WB
Vocabulary in Context—Media & Marketplace	SAD	HS–AD	4.0	WB, TR
Where Does My Money Go?	PCI	EL–MS	—	G
Where Does My Money Go?	PCI	EL–MS	—	SW
Your Checking Account: Lessons in Personal Banking	SAD	HS	4.0	WB, TR
Your Checking Account: Lessons in Personal Banking	WAL	HS–AD	—	DM

Family Life

Material	Publisher	Age Level	Reading Level	Type
All Kinds of Families	KSA	EL	—	B
Be Cool: Play It Safe	KSA	EL–MS	—	V

Family Life (*Continued*)

Material	Publisher	Age Level	Reading Level	Type
Before You Buy a Dog Brochure	AKC	EL–HS	—	PH
Child Safety at Home	KSA	HS–AD	—	V
Child Safety Outdoors	KSA	HS–AD	—	V
Clock & Calendar Skills	SAD	MS–AD	—	DM
Clock & Calendar Skills	WAL	MS–HS	—	DM
Clocks & Calendars	REM	EL–MS	—	B
The Complete Dog Book for Kids	AKC	EL–MS	—	B
Consumer Words: Life-Skill Lessons	REM	EL–HS	4.0–5.0	B
Cooking Class	PCI	—	—	G
Day-to-Day Life Skills: Reading	ACA	MS–AD	—	B
Day-to-Day Life Skills: Speaking	ACA	MS–AD	—	B
Day-to-Day Life Skills: Writing	ACA	MS–AD	—	B
Emergency Family Preparedness	KSA	HS–AD	—	V
Environmental Action Series	GLF	MS–HS	—	B, TR
Essential Vocabulary: Department Store Words	REM	MS–HS	—	WB
Essential Vocabulary: Restaurant Words	REM	MS–HS	—	WB
Essential Vocabulary: Supermarket Words	REM	MS–HS	—	WB
Everyday Health: Exercise	GLF	MS–HS	3.0–4.0	B, TR
Everyday Health: Family Living	GLF	MS–HS	3.0–4.0	B, TR
Everyday Health: Insurance Basics	GLF	MS–HS	3.0–4.0	B, TR
Everyday Health: Nutrition	GLF	MS–HS	3.0–4.0	B, TR
Everyday Health: Safety	GLF	MS–HS	3.0–4.0	B, TR
Everyday Health: Wellness	GLF	MS–HS	3.0–4.0	B, TR
Everyday Household Items	SAD	MS–AD	4.0	WB
Families Today	GLE	HS–AD	—	CP
Family Life & How It Works	WAL	HS–AD	—	DM
Family Ties ... Strengthening the Family Unit	GLE	HS–AD	—	V
Fire Safety for Kids	KSA	EL–MS	—	V
Globe Health Program: AIDS & Other STDs	GLF	MS–HS	6.0	B, TR
Globe Health Program: Alcohol & Other Drugs	GLF	MS–HS	6.0	B, TR

Family Life (*Continued*)

Material	Publisher	Age Level	Reading Level	Type
Globe Health Program: Family Living & Sex Ed	GLF	MS–HS	6.0	B, TR
Globe Health Program: Nutrition & Dieting	GLF	MS–HS	6.0	B, TR
Globe Health Program: Self-Esteem	GLF	MS–HS	6.0	B, TR
Health	GLF	MS–HS	3.0–4.0	CP
Heath & Safety	SAD	MS–AD	4.0	WB
Home & Family Life Education	WAL	MS–AD	—	DM
The Home Alone Video for Kids	KSA	EL–MS	—	V
How to Set Up a Home	WAL	MS–AD	3.0	B
Independent Living Words: Life-Skill Lessons	REP	EL–HS	4.0–5.0	B
Interfact: Plants	SAD	EL–MS	2.0–3.0	B, SW
Interfact: Storms	SAD	EL–MS	2.0–3.0	B, SW
Interfact: Weather	SAD	EL–MS	2.0–3.0	B, SW
Jumbo Primary Time Teacher Kit	PCI	EL	—	K
Life Horizons II	JMS	—	—	SW
Life Skills for Teens	PRO	MS–HS	—	K
Lifetimes	GLF	HS	—	B
Looking for Words	ACA	EL–HS	—	SW
The Marriage Partnership	GLE	HS–AD	—	V
Money	REM	EL	—	B
Money Management Words: Life-Skill Lessons	REP	EL–HS	4.0–5.0	B
Money Smarts	WAL	HS–AD	7.0	G
Moving Out on Your Own	SAD	MS–AD	4.0	W
My Life	NSP	MS–HS	—	SW
Nutrition: Personal Care	REM	JH–HS	3.0–4.0	B
On Fire: A Family Guide to Fire Safety	KSA	HS–AD	—	V
The Parent Coach	SOW	EL–MS	—	B, FC
Parenting: Rewards & Responsibilities	GLE	HS–AD	—	CP
Picture Cue Dictionary: Shopping	ACA	EL–HS	—	SW
PREP for Effective Family Living	AGS	HS	—	K
Real World Reading	PCI	MS–HS	—	CP

Family Life (*Continued*)

Material	Publisher	Age Level	Reading Level	Type
Recognizing Coins	REM	EL	—	WB
Responsible Driving	GLE	HS–AD	—	CP
Seasons	TSP	EL–MS	—	SW, TR, WB
Skills for Better Living (Volumes I, II, and III)	NSP	MS–AD	—	SW
Special Needs Curriculum—Math Resources	CPR	EL	—	CP
Steps to Independent Living	REM	EL–AD	3.0–4.0	B, TR
Strong Kids, Safe Kids	KSA	EL–MS	—	V
Talk It Up! Bingo	PCI	EL	—	G
Talking Clever Clock	PCI	EL	—	MN, WB
Teaching Telephone	PCI	EL	—	MN, WB
Teenage Parents	LLS	HS	—	V
Things People Do	PCI	EL	—	G
Time Concepts	REM	EL	—	WB
Time Families Games	PCI	EL	—	G
Tough Decisions	SAD	MS–AD	7.0	RB
Vocabulary Builders for Daily Living	ACA	MS–AD	—	B
Vocabulary of Community & Living	ACA	MS–HS	—	WB
Water Safety for Kids	KSA	EL–MS	—	V
Weather and Seasons	PCI	EL	—	B
When Mom & Dad Break Up	KSA	HS–AD	—	V
Writing: A Reason to Write	REM	EL–HS	3.0–4.0	WB
Writing: Business Communication	REM	EL–HS	3.0–4.0	WB

Child Rearing

Material	Publisher	Age Level	Reading Level	Type
The Art of Creating Crafts for Children	LLS	—	—	V
The Art of Making Pictures for Children	LLS	—	—	V
Child Development	WAL	HS–AD	8.0	B

Child Rearing (*Continued*)

Material	Publisher	Age Level	Reading Level	Type
Child Development: Birth to One Year	GLE	HS–AD	—	V
Child Development: One to Three	GLE	HS–AD	—	V
Child Development: Three to Five	GLE	HS–AD	—	V
Child Development: Five to Eight	GLE	HS–AD	—	V
Child Development: Adolescence	GLE	HS–AD	—	V
Child Development: The First Two Years	KSA	HS–AD	—	V
Child Development Series	KSA	HS–AD	—	V
Common Childhood Illnesses	KSA	HS–AD	—	V
Common Childhood Injuries	KSA	HS–AD	—	V
Creating a Clean & Healthy Home	KSA	HS–AD	—	V
The Developing Child	GLE	HS–AD	—	CP
Everyday Health: Exercise	GLF	MS–HS	3.0–4.0	B, TR
Everyday Health: Family Living	GLF	MS–HS	3.0–4.0	B, TR
Everyday Health: Insurance Basics	GLF	MS–HS	3.0–4.0	B, TR
Everyday Health: Nutrition	GLF	MS–HS	3.0–4.0	B, TR
Everyday Health: Safety	GLF	MS–HS	3.0–4.0	B, TR
Everyday Health: Wellness	GLF	MS–HS	3.0–4.0	B, TR
Families Today	GLE	HS–AD	—	CP
Family Ties … Strengthening the Family Unit	GLE	HS–AD	—	V
Globe Health Program: AIDS & Other STDs	GLF	MS–HS	6.0	B, TR
Globe Health Program: Alcohol & Other Drugs	GLF	MS–HS	6.0	B, TR
Globe Health Program: Family Living & Sex Education	GLF	MS–HS	6.0	B, TR
Globe Health Program: Nutrition & Dieting	GLF	MS–HS	6.0	B, TR
Globe Health Program: Self-Esteem	GLF	MS–HS	6.0	B, TR
Good Enough to Eat	KSA	HS–AD	—	B
Healthy Habits	KSA	EL	—	V, B
Introduction to Computers for Children	LLS	—	—	V
Learn to Use Money Wisely for Children	LLS	—	—	V
My Body, My Buddy	KSA	EL	—	V
My Health	KSA	EL–MS	—	B

Child Rearing (*Continued*)

Material	Publisher	Age Level	Reading Level	Type
The Parent Coach	SOW	EL–MS	—	B, FC
Parenting	GLE	HS–AD	—	CP
Parenting: Rewards & Responsibilities	GLE	HS–AD	—	CP
Planning Activities for Children	GLE	MS–AD	—	V
Reading Realities	ERE	EL–HS	2.0–6.0	SW
Science Discovery for Children	LLS	—	—	V
Skills for Childcare Workers	GLE	MS–AD	—	V
Teen Parenting Skills	GLE	MS–HS	—	B
Teenage Parents	LLS	HS	—	V
Tip-Top Tots: Nutritional Pyramid for Pre-K	KSA	EL–MS	—	V
What Do You Really Want for Your Children?	LLS	—	—	V
When Mom & Dad Break Up	KSA	HS–AD	—	V
Who's Watching Your Kids? Child Care Decision Making	GLE	HS–AD	—	V
Working with Children	GLE	MS–AD	—	V
Your Baby's First Year	KSA	HS–AD	—	V

Outdoor Activities

Material	Publisher	Age Level	Reading Level	Type
101 Games for Groups	PRO	EL–AD	—	G
At the Zoo	PCI	EL	—	B
Best Friends Teaching Kit	AKC	EL–HS	—	K
Forest Animals Unit Book	PCI	EL	—	TR
Graph Master	NSP	EL–HS	—	SW
I Can	PRO	—	—	TR
Insects Unit Book	PCI	EL	—	TR
Math VIP	NSP	MS–JH	—	SW
Math Word Problems: Sports	NSP	EL–JH	—	SW
Plan Your Day	NSP	EL–MS	—	SW

Outdoor Activities (*Continued*)

Material	Publisher	Age Level	Reading Level	Type
Sim Park	NSP	EL–HS	—	SW
Sim Safari	NSP	EL–HS	—	SW
Sim Theme Park	NSP	EL–HS	—	SW
Sportsmanship	NSP	EL	—	SW
Tool Factory Applications	NSP	EL–HS	—	SW
Toys, Recreation, & Sports Kit	PRO	EL–MS	—	K
Zoo Unit Book	PCI	EL	—	TR

Community/Neighborhood Activities

Material	Publisher	Age Level	Reading Level	Type
Community-Based Instruction Package	PDA	MS–HS	—	CP
Community Construction Kit	NSP	EL–MS	—	SW
Community Success	NSP	MS–HS	—	SW
Geography Workshop	NSP	EL–JH	—	SW
Let's Learn: Location & Direction	NSP	EL–MS	—	SW
The Map Detectives	NSP	EL–MS	—	SW
My Town: Language Activities for Daily Living	LLS	EL–AD	—	SW
Neighborhood Map Machine	NSP	EL–MS	—	SW
Our Century Magazines	GLF	MS–HS	3.0–4.0	B, TR
Plan Your Day	NSP	EL–MS	—	SW
SimCity 3000	NSP	JH–AD	—	SW

Travel

Material	Publisher	Age Level	Reading Level	Type
Choosing Your Way Series	SAD	MS–HS	5.0	B
Crosscountry USA	ERE	—	—	SW

Travel (*Continued*)

Material	Publisher	Age Level	Reading Level	Type
Crosscountry USA 2	NSP	MS–AD	—	SW
Daily Experiences and Activities for Living	PRO	MS–AD	3.0–5.0	K
Driving School	NSP	HS–AD	—	SW
Explore America	NSP	EL–AD	—	SW
Eye on History Series	SAD	MS–HS	—	B
Focus on Transition	PRO	HS–AD	—	WB
GeoCycle USA	NSP	EL–AD	—	SW
Geosafari USA Search	PCI	EL–MS	—	G
Going Places	PCI	EL	—	B
Government in Action	SAD	MS–AD	2.5–4.0	B, DM
I Know America Series	SAD	MS–HS	3.0	B
Instant Internet Activities Folder—CA Missions	SAD	EL–HS	—	TR
Instant Internet Activities Folder—Ellis Island	SAD	EL–HS	—	TR
Instant Internet Activities Folder—Oregon Trail	SAD	EL–HS	—	TR
Instant Internet Activities Folder—Pyramids & Mummies	SAD	EL–HS	—	TR
Instant Internet Activities Folder—Washington, DC	SAD	EL–HS	—	TR
Let's Discover States	NSP	EL–MS	—	SW
The Map Detectives	NSP	EL–MS	—	SW
Map Skills	ERE	—	—	SW
Math for Everyday Living	SAD	JH–HS	4.5–5.0	B
Math Word Problems: Travel	NSP	EL–JH	—	SW
Nigel's World	PRO	EL	—	SW
Out in the World–Second Edition	PRO	EL–MS	—	B
Portrait of America	STV	EL–MS	4.0–5.0	B
Postcards from 20 Countries	STV	EL–MS	2.0–3.0	B
Postcards from South America	ACA	MS–HS	2.0	B
Public Transportation & Travel	SAD	MS–AD	4.0	WB
State Books—Early Childhood Curriculum	PCI	EL	—	TR
States & Capitals	NSP	EL–MS	—	SW, A, B
Survival Math	SAD	JH–AD	2.0–4.0	DM, A

Travel (*Continued*)

Material	Publisher	Age Level	Reading Level	Type
The Twentieth Century Series	SAD	MS–HS	—	B
U.S. Worksheets & Games	PCI	EL–MS	—	G, WB
U.S.A. Explorer	NSP	EL	—	SW

Entertainment

Material	Publisher	Age Level	Reading Level	Type
Basic Menu Math Software	PCI	EL	—	SW
Focus on Transition	PRO	HS–AD	—	WB
Going to the Fair Unit Book	PCI	EL	—	TR
Hamburger Hut	REM	EL–HS	3.0–4.0	B
The Inside Story	CUR	EL–MS	—	B
Old-Fashioned Ice Cream Parlor	REM	EL–HS	3.0–4.0	B
On My Own with Language	LSI	MS–HS	4.5–5.5	DM
Picture This	PRO	EL–AD	—	SW
Stepping Out	ATT	—	—	K

Citizenship

Material	Publisher	Age Level	Reading Level	Type
20th Century America	STV	AD	6.0–7.0	WB
All About Elections	NSP	EL–MS	—	SW
America Rock: Can You Help Bill Become a Law?	NSP	EL–MS	—	SW
American Government	GLF	MS–HS	3.0–4.0	B, WB
American Government: Quicktests Across the Curriculum	GLF	MS–HS	4.0–5.0	TR, DM
America's Early Years	STV	AD	6.0–7.0	WB
The American Presidency	NSP	EL–AD	—	SW
Becoming an Informed Citizen	STV	AD	6.0	WB

Citizenship (*Continued*)

Material	Publisher	Age Level	Reading Level	Type
Being with Authority Figures	JMS	—	—	V
Branches of Government	NSP	JH–HS	—	SW
Character Quest Curriculum: Citizenship	PBS	EL	—	V
Choosing Your Way Series	SAD	MS–HS	5.0	B
Citizens Today	STV	AD	6.0–7.0	WB
Citizenship & the Law	JMS	—	—	SW, V, FS
Community Bingo Series	PCI	EL	—	G
Community Helpers	PCI	EL	—	B
Community Resources	SAD	MS–AD	4.0	WB
The Constitution of the United States of America	CHB	MS–HS	—	B
Eye on History Series	SAD	MS–HS	—	B
Government and Civics Series	SAD	MS–AD	2.5	B, WB
How We Got the Vote	LLS	—	—	V
I Know America Series	SAD	MS–HS	3.0	B
Instant Internet Activities Folder—Bill of Rights	SAD	EL–HS	—	TR
Know Your Government	LLS	—	—	B
Living in the U.S.A.	SAD	JH–AD	—	B, WB
Math for Everyday Living	SAD	JH–HS	4.5–5.0	B
Moving Out on Your Own	SAD	MS–AD	4.0	WB
My Country—The U.S.A.	STV	AD	2.0–3.0	WB
Our American Constitution	STV	JH–HS	7.0–8.0	WB
Our Century Magazines	GLF	MS–HS	3.0–4.0	B, TR
Our Democracy	STV	JH–HS	7.0–8.0	WB
The Roots of the Bill of Rights	LLS	—	—	B
Survival Math	SAD	JH–AD	2.0–4.0	DM, A
Teacher's Guide to the Constitution	HIN	—	—	TR
The Twentieth Century Series	SAD	MS–HS	—	B
U.S. Government Series	HIN	—	—	B
U.S. Presidents Unit Book	PCI	EL	—	TR
Vocabulary in Context—Everyday Living Words	SAD	HS–AD	4.0	WB, TR

Citizenship (*Continued*)

Material	Publisher	Age Level	Reading Level	Type
Who Am I? Community Helpers	PCI	EL	—	G
WiseLives Curriculum	NPR	EL–MS	—	TR
WiseQuotes Curriculum	NPR	EL–MS	—	TR
WiseWords Curriculum	NPR	EL	—	TR

Community Awareness

Material	Publisher	Age Level	Reading Level	Type
25 Life Skill, Math & Language Programs	PDA	EL–HS	—	SW
Around the Community	PCI	EL	—	B
Beginning Menu Math	REM	EL–HS	1.0–2.0	B
Building Character Through Service Learning	NPR	MS–HS	—	B
Catalogs: Practical Practice Reading	REM	MS–HS	3.0–4.0	WB
Choosing Your Way Series	SAD	MS–HS	5.0	B
Colorcards Color Library Food	PRO	EL–AD	—	FC
Colorcards Everyday Objects	PRO	EL–AD	—	FC
Colorcards Verbs	PRO	EL–AD	—	FC
Community-Based Instruction Package	PDA	MS–HS	—	CP
Community Construction Kit	NSP	EL–MS	—	SW
Community Construction Kit	TSP	EL–MS	—	SW, DM
Community Kit	PRO	EL–MS	—	K
Community Resources	SAD	MS–AD	4.0	WB
Community Skills	PCI	—	—	G
Community Success	NSP	MS–HS	—	SW
Community Success	PDA	MS–HS	—	B
Community Words	PCI	EL	—	SW
Day-to-Day Life Skills: Reading	ACA	MS–AD	—	B
Day-to-Day Life Skills: Speaking	ACA	MS–AD	—	B
Department Store Math	REM	EL–HS	1.0–2.0	B
Department Store Math	REM	EL–HS	3.0–4.0	B

Community Awareness (*Continued*)

Material	Publisher	Age Level	Reading Level	Type
Developing Character for Classroom Success	NPR	MS–HS	—	B
Directories & Guides: Practical Practice Reading	REM	MS–HS	3.0–4.0	WB
The Ecology Kidds Series	ACA	MS–HS	2.0	B, WB
Employment Signs	ATT	—	—	SW
Environmental Action Series	GLF	MS–HS	—	B, TR
Equipped for Life	REM	JH–HS	—	G
Essential Vocabulary: Department Store Words	REM	MS–HS	3.0–4.0	WB
Essential Vocabulary: Restaurant Words	REM	MS–HS	3.0–4.0	WB
Essential Vocabulary: Supermarket Words	REM	MS–HS	3.0–4.0	WB
Everyday Activities	PRO	EL–AD	—	FC
Eye on History Series	SAD	MS–HS	—	B
Filling out Forms: Practical Practice Reading	REM	MS–HS	3.0–4.0	WB
Fire Prevention Unit Book	PCI	EL	—	TR
Focus on Function	CSB	HS–AD	—	CP
Focus on Transition	PRO	HS–AD	—	WB
Following Directions: Around the Town	REM	EL–MS	—	B
Geography Workshop	NSP	EL–JH	—	SW
Government and Civics Series	SAD	MS–AD	2.5	B, WB
I Know America Series	SAD	MS–HS	3.0	B
Lesson Plans for Service Learning	NPR	MS–HS	—	TR
Let's Discover States	NSP	EL–MS	—	SW
Let's Learn: Location & Direction	NSP	EL–MS	—	SW
Life Coping Skills Series: Facts & Sources	STV	MS–JH	2.0–4.0	WB
Life Coping Skills Series: Signs & Labels	STV	MS–JH	2.0–4.0	WB
Local Places	PRO	EL–AD	—	FC
Looking for Words	ACA	EL–HS	—	SW
Looking for Words in All the Right Places	NSP	EL–HS	—	SW
The Map Detectives	NSP	EL–MS	—	SW
Mapmaker's Toolkit	TSP	MS–HS	—	SW, TR
Map Skills	CPR	EL–HS	—	B, TR
Map Skills	ERE	—	—	SW
Map Skills—New Edition	CPR	EL–MS	—	B, TR

Community Awareness (*Continued*)

Material	Publisher	Age Level	Reading Level	Type
Market Math	REM	EL–HS	3.0–4.0	B
Medical Words	ATT	—	—	SW
Members of the Community	PDA	MS–HS	—	B
My Town: Language Activities for Daily Living	LLS	EL–AD	—	SW
My Town, My School Series	NSP	EL–MS	—	SW
Neighborhood Map Machine	NSP	EL–MS	—	SW
Neighborhood Map Machine	TSP	EL–MS	—	CP
The Newspaper: Practical Practice Reading	REM	MS–HS	3.0–4.0	WB
The Newspaper–Revised Edition	PRO	EL–MS	—	B
Newspower Study Skills	SAD	MS–HS	4.5–5.5	WB
Opportunities Are Everywhere	PDA	EL–AD	—	V
Out in the World–Second Edition	PRO	EL–MS	—	B
Picture This (Creates Flash Cards)	PDA	EL–AD	—	SW
Plan Your Day	NSP	EL–MS	—	SW
Practical Reading 2	SAD	MS–AD	4.0	B
Problem-Solving Picture Cards	PRO	MS–AD	—	FC
Public Transportation & Travel	SAD	MS–AD	4.0	WB
Real World Learning	NSP	EL–MS	—	SW
Real World Reading	PCI	MS–HS	—	CP
Relate for Teens	NSP	MS–HS	—	SW
Shopping Around the Town	REM	EL–MS	—	WB
Shopping Mall Math	REM	EL–MS	—	WB
Skills for Better Living (Volumes I, II, and III)	NSP	MS–AD	—	SW
Survival Signs Activity Cards	PCI	EL	—	FC
Survival Signs Bingo	PCI	EL	—	G
Survival Signs Curriculum	PCI	EL	—	TR
Survival Signs Software	PCI	EL	—	SW
Survival Signs Symbols Games	PCI	EL	—	G
Survival Signs Worksheets	PCI	EL	—	WB
Teaching Character … In the Middle Grades	NPR	MS	—	B
Things to Know About Cars & Driving	WAL	MS–AD	4.0	B
Things to Know About Community Resources	WAL	MS–AD	4.0	B

Community Awareness (*Continued*)

Material	Publisher	Age Level	Reading Level	Type
Toward Independence	PDA	MS–AD	—	SW
Transportation Signs	ATT	—	—	SW
The Twentieth Century Series	SAD	MS–HS	—	B
Using the Newspaper to Teach Basic Living Skills	SAD	HS–AD	3.0	RB
Vocabulary Builders for Daily Living	ACA	MS–AD	—	B
Vocabulary in Context—Everyday Living Words	SAD	HS–AD	4.0	WB, TR
Vocabulary in Context—Media & Marketplace	SAD	HS–AD	4.0	WB, TR
Vocabulary of Community & Living	ACA	MS–HS	—	WB
What's Your Point of View on the Environment?	GLF	MS–HS	3.0	B, TR
What's Your Point of View on Your Community?	GLF	MS–HS	3.0	B, TR
Winterberry City	CSB	HS–AD	—	G
You Tell Me	PCI	—	—	G

Services/Resources

Material	Publisher	Age Level	Reading Level	Type
400 Words That Work: A Life Skills Vocabulary Program	SAD	JH–AD	4.0	CP
Best Friends Teaching Kit	AKC	EL–HS	—	K
Car and Driver	SAD	MS–AD	4.0	WB
Community Resources	SAD	MS–AD	4.0	WB
Directory for Federal Aid	LLS	—	—	B
The Ecology Kidds Series	ACA	MS–HS	2.0	B, WB
Know Your Government	LLS	—	—	B
Life Coping Skills Series: Facts & Sources	STV	MS–JH	2.0–4.0	WB
Living in the U.S.A.	SAD	JH–AD	—	B, WB
Members of the Community	PDA	MS–HS	—	B
The Newspaper–Revised Edition	PRO	EL–MS	—	B
Things to Know About Cars & Driving	WAL	MS–AD	4.0	B
Things to Know About Community Resources	WAL	MS–AD	4.0	B
Practical Reading 2	SAD	MS–AD	4.0	B

Services/Resources (*Continued*)

Material	Publisher	Age Level	Reading Level	Type
Responsible Driving	GLE	HS–AD	—	CP
Safety Around Dogs, Your Safety Begins with You!	AKC	EL–HS	—	V
Winterberry City	CSB	HS–AD	—	G
You: Living, Learning, and Caring	SAD	MS–AD	5.9	CP

Physical Health

Material	Publisher	Age Level	Reading Level	Type
AIDS: What We Need to Know	PRO	JH–HS	—	TR, WB
Arthur: Personal Care and Basic Health	PBS	EL	—	V
Be Cool Play It Safe	KSA	EL–MS	—	V
Big Chances, Big Choices	SAD	MS–AD	—	V
Body, Clothes, Grooming & Health Words	PCI	EL	—	SW
The Body Kit	PRO	EL–MS	—	K
The Body Transparent	ERE	MS–HS	—	SW
Bodywatch	LLS	—	—	V
Bodyworks	NSP	HS–AD	—	SW
The Breast Center Video	LLS	—	—	V
Child Safety at Home	KSA	HS–AD	—	V
Circles I: Intimacy & Relationships	JMS	—	—	SW
Circles III: Safer Ways	JMS	—	—	SW, V
Common Childhood Illnesses	KSA	HS–AD	—	V
Common Childhood Injuries	KSA	HS–AD	—	V
Community Nutrition Action Kit	AKC	EL–HS	—	K
Creating a Clean & Healthy Home	KSA	HS–AD	—	V
Daily Experiences and Activities for Living	PRO	MS–AD	3.0–5.0	K
"Dear Student"—Take Home Nutrition Education	AKC	MS–HS	—	DM
Developing Health Skills	WAL	MS–HS	—	DM
Diet/Nutrition	CHB	MS–HS	—	B

Physical Health (*Continued*)

Material	Publisher	Age Level	Reading Level	Type
Discovering Food & Nutrition	GLE	MS–HS	—	CP
Don't Get Hurt in the Kitchen	WAL	MS–HS	—	P
Drug Alert	ERE	MS–HS	—	SW
Drug Alert	SAD	MS–HS	—	SW
Ease Into Fitness	PDA	MS–AD	—	V
Elementary Science: The Human Body	NSP	EL–HS	—	SW
Emergency Family Preparedness	KSA	HS–AD	—	V
Everyday Health: Exercise	GLF	MS–HS	3.0–4.0	B, TR
Everyday Health: Family Living	GLF	MS–HS	3.0–4.0	B, TR
Everyday Health: Insurance Basics	GLF	MS–HS	3.0–4.0	B, TR
Everyday Health: Nutrition	GLF	MS–HS	3.0–4.0	B, TR
Everyday Health: Safety	GLF	MS–HS	3.0–4.0	B, TR
Everyday Health: Wellness	GLF	MS–HS	3.0–4.0	B, TR
Exercise: Personal Care	REM	JH–HS	3.0–4.0	B
Fire Prevention Unit Book	PCI	EL	—	TR
Fire Safety	PDA	MS–AD	—	V
Fire Safety for Kids	KSA	EL–MS	—	V
Food, Family, & Fun	AKC	MS–HS	—	RB
Food for Thought	SUN	MS–AD	—	SW
Food for Today	GLE	HS–AD	—	CP
Fun Tips: Using the Dietary Guidelines at Home	AKC	EL–MS	—	WB
Globe Health Program: AIDS & Other STDs	GLF	MS–HS	6.0	B, TR
Globe Health Program: Alcohol & Other Drugs	GLF	MS–HS	6.0	B, TR
Globe Health Program: Family Living & Sex Education	GLF	MS–HS	6.0	B, TR
Globe Health Program: Nutrition & Dieting	GLF	MS–HS	6.0	B, TR
Globe Health Program: Self-Esteem	GLF	MS–HS	6.0	B, TR
Go, Glow, Grow Foods for You	AKC	EL		PH
Good Enough to Eat	KSA	HS–AD	—	B
Great Nutrition Adventure Action Kit	AKC	EL–MS	—	K
Grooming Curriculum	REM	EL–HS	—	CP

Physical Health (*Continued*)

Material	Publisher	Age Level	Reading Level	Type
Grooming for Life	NSP	EL–MS	—	SW
Grooming for Life	PDA	MS–AD	—	SW
Grooming: Personal Care	REM	JH–HS	3.0–4.0	B
Health	GLF	MS–HS	3.0–4.0	CP
Health & Safety	SAD	MS–AD	4.0	WB
Healthy Habits Book Series	KSA	EL	—	V, B
The Home Alone Video for Kids	KSA	EL–MS	—	V
How to Get Well When You're Sick or Hurt	WAL	MS–AD	3.0	B
How to Stay Healthy	WAL	MS–AD	3.0	B
The Human Body	GLF	HS	5.0–6.0	B, TR
The Human Body	NSP	HS–AD	—	SW
In Search of Character	SAD	MS–AD	—	V
Kids Health: TV Late Breaking News	AQU	EL–MS	—	V
Learn About Life: Sexuality & Social Skills	PDA	MS–AD	—	B
Life Horizons I	JMS	—	—	SW
Life Horizons II	JMS	—	—	SW
Life Science: Cells & Tissues	GAM	MS–AD	—	SW
Life Science: Classification of Living Things	GAM	MS–AD	—	SW
Life Science: Green Plants	GAM	MS–AD	—	SW
Life Science: The Human Body	GAM	MS–AD	—	SW
LifeFacts 1	JMS	—	—	K
LifeFacts 2	JMS	—	—	K
LifeFacts 3	JMS	—	—	K
Looking Good	PDA	MS–AD	—	V
Looking Good Key	PCI	—	—	G
My Body, My Buddy	KSA	EL	—	V
My Health	KSA	EL–MS	—	B
Nine Month Miracle	NSP	EL–AD	—	SW
Nutrition & Fitness	WAL	HS–AD	7.0	TR, DM
Nutrition & Health	GLE	MS–HS	—	CP

Physical Health (*Continued*)

Material	Publisher	Age Level	Reading Level	Type
Nutrition & Wellness	GLE	MS–HS	—	CP
Nutrition, Food, and Fitness	SAD	MS–HS	7.9	B, TR
Nutrition: Personal Care	REP	JH–HS	3.0–4.0	B
On Fire: A Family Guide to Fire Safety	KSA	HS–AD	—	V
Person to Person	PDA	MS–AD	—	V
Personal Care Skills	PRO	EL–AD	—	K
Personal Care Words: Life-Skill Lessons	REP	EL–HS	4.0–5.0	B
Personal Success	NSP	EL–MS	—	SW
The Power of Choice Video Series	SAD	MS–AD	—	V
Practical Reading 1	SAD	MS–AD	4.0	B
Reading Realities	ERE	EL–HS	2.0–6.0	SW
Real Life Teens	SAD	MS–AD	—	V
Safety Around Dogs, Your Safety Begins with You!	AKC	EL–HS	—	V
Safety in and Around the Home, Set One	PRO	EL–AD	—	FC
Safety in and Around the Home, Set Two	PRO	EL–AD	—	FC
Safety in the Home: How to Prevent Falls	PDA	MS–AD	—	V
Say No to Drugs	LLS	—	—	V
Science Workshop Series: Human Biology	GLF	MS–HS	4.0–5.0	B, TR
Self Defense for Women	LLS	—	—	V
Sexuality Education for Persons with Severe Developmental Disabilities	JMS	—	—	SW
Speaking of Sex	JMS	—	—	V, B, TR
Story Starters: Science	ERE	—	—	SW
Strong Kids, Safe Kids	KSA	EL–MS	—	V
Taking Care of Simple Injuries	PRO	—	—	K
Teacher's Support Handbook: Tips, Tools, & Jewels for Busy Educators	AKC	EL	—	B
Team Up at Home: Team Nutrition Activity Booklet	AKC	EL–MS	—	PH
Teen Awareness Videos	SAD	MS–AD	—	V
Things to Know About Medicine & Health	WAL	MS–AD	4.0	B
Tobacco	CHB	MS–AD	—	B

Physical Health (*Continued*)

Material	Publisher	Age Level	Reading Level	Type
Toiletries & Medical Supplies Kit	PRO	EL–MS	—	K
The Ultimate Human Body	NSP	EL–AD	—	SW
Vocabulary in Context—Everyday Living Words	SAD	HS–AD	4.0	WB, TR
Water Safety for Kids	KSA	EL–MS	—	V
Wellness—Taking Charge of Your Health	CHB	MS–HS	—	B
Yourself Nutrition Education Kit	AKC	MS–HS	—	K

Emotional Health

Material	Publisher	Age Level	Reading Level	Type
All About You	PCI	—	—	G
Behavior Skills	PCI	—	—	G
Big Chances, Big Choices	SAD	MS–AD	—	V
Building Self-Esteem in the Classroom: The Experts Speak	LLS	—	—	A, TR
Circles I: Intimacy & Relationships	JMS	—	—	SW
Circles II: Stop Abuse	JMS	—	—	SW, FS, V
Coping with Books	AGS	JH–HS	—	K
Coping with Crisis	SOW	EL–HS	—	TR
Developing Health Skills	WAL	MS–HS	—	DM
Fire Prevention Unit Book	PCI	EL	—	TR
Focus on Transition	PRO	HS–AD	—	WB
Hope & Help for Depression	CHB	MS–AD	—	B
How to Look Out for Yourself	WAL	MS–AD	3.0	B
Improving Your Self Esteem	CHB	HS–AD	—	B
In Search of Character	SAD	MS–AD	—	V
Let's Share Our Feelings	ACA	EL	—	B
Life Horizons I	JMS	—	—	SW
LifeFacts 1	JMS	—	—	K
LifeFacts 2	JMS	—	—	K

Emotional Health (*Continued*)

Material	Publisher	Age Level	Reading Level	Type
Managing Anger—Keeping Your Cool	CHB	HS–AD	—	PH
Managing Anger: A Self-Care Handbook	CHB	HS–AD	—	B
Many Moods & Feelings	ACA	EL–MS	—	B
My Friends, My Family, & Me	PCI	EL	—	B
On Managing Anger	CHB	HS–AD	—	WB
Personal Power	PRO	MS–HS	—	TR
Pouvant I	PRO	MS–HS	—	TR, B
The Power of Choice Video Series	SAD	MS–AD	—	V
Prepare Curriculum	REP	JH–HS	—	TR
Real Life Teens	SAD	MS–AD	—	V
Refusal Skill Video	REP	JH–HS	—	B, V
Refusal Skills	REP	JH–HS	—	TR
Seeds of Self-Esteem	AGS	EL–JH	—	K
Self-Esteem in the Classroom: A Curriculum Guide	LLS	—	—	TR, B
Sexuality Education for Persons with Severe Developmental Disabilities	JMS	—	—	SW
Skills for Living	REP	—	—	B
Skills for Managing Anger	CHB	MS–HS	—	V, CP
Social Skills for Daily Living	AGS	JH–HS	—	B
Stress—Don't Let It Get You Down	CHB	HS–AD	—	PH
Teen Awareness Videos	SAD	MS–AD	—	V
Teenage Stress	LLS	MS–HS	—	V
What's Up with Peer Pressure	CHB	MS–HS	—	WB
What's Up with Self-Esteem	CHB	MS–HS	—	WB
When Anger Heats Up—Keep Your Cool	CHB	HS–AD	—	B
You Tell Me	PCI	—	—	G

Personal Confidence/Understanding

Material	Publisher	Age Level	Reading Level	Type
All About You	PCI	—	—	G
Appearances Count	PDA	MS–AD	—	V
Arthur: Personal Responsibility	PBS	EL	—	V
Arthur: Trials and Tribulations of Growing Up	PBS	EL	—	V
Asset: Social Skills Program for Adolescents	REP	JH–HS	—	K
Behavior Skills	PCI	—	—	G
Being with a Date, Parts I & 2	JMS	—	—	V
Being with Acquaintances & Strangers	JMS	—	—	V
Being with Authority Figures	JMS	—	—	V
Being with Friends, Parts 1 & 2	JMS	—	—	V
Bridges: Making the Transition from School to Work	SAD	MS–AD	—	WB, TR
Building a Positive Self-Concept	SAD	MS–AD	—	RB
Building Self-Esteem in the Classroom	SOW	EL–MS	—	B
Building Self-Esteem in the Classroom: The Experts Speak	LLS	—	—	A, TR
Character Quest Curriculum: Charity	PBS	EL	—	V
Character Quest Curriculum: Compassion	PBS	EL	—	V
Character Quest Curriculum: Courage	PBS	EL	—	V
Character Quest Curriculum: Determination	PBS	EL	—	V
Character Quest Curriculum: Diligence	PBS	EL	—	V
Character Quest Curriculum: Friendship	PBS	EL	—	V
Character Quest Curriculum: Generosity	PBS	EL	—	V
Character Quest Curriculum: Gratitude	PBS	EL	—	V
Character Quest Curriculum: Honor	PBS	EL	—	V
Character Quest Curriculum: Humility	PBS	EL	—	V
Character Quest Curriculum: Integrity	PBS	EL	—	V
Character Quest Curriculum: Loyalty	PBS	EL	—	V
Character Quest Curriculum: Patience	PBS	EL	—	V
Character Quest Curriculum: Perseverance	PBS	EL	—	G
Character Quest Curriculum: Respect	PBS	EL	—	V
Character Quest Curriculum: Responsibility	PBS	EL	—	V

Personal Confidence/Understanding (*Continued*)

Material	Publisher	Age Level	Reading Level	Type
Character Quest Curriculum: Self-Discipline	PBS	EL	—	V
Character Quest Curriculum: Trustworthiness	PBS	EL	—	V
Character Quest Curriculum: Work	PBS	EL	—	V
Choices, Choices	TSP	EL–MS	—	SW, TR, FC
Community Success	PDA	MS–HS	—	B
Conflict Resolution Quiz Show	NSP	EL–JH	—	SW
The Coolien Challenge: Youth Violence Prevention	NSP	MS–HS	—	SW
Decisions, Decisions	TSP	MS–HS	—	CP
Dilemma: Making Choices in Difficult Real-Life Situations	NSP	EL–AD	—	SW
Double Trouble (Peer Pressure)	NSP	EL	—	SW
From Mad to Worse	NSP	EL	—	SW
Get on Top of It!	SOW	EL–HS	—	B
Glad to Be Me	NSP	EL	—	SW
Grooming for Life	PDA	MS–AD	—	SW
Helping Kids Find Their Strengths	SOW	EL–MS	—	B
Helping Kids Handle Anger	SOW	EL–MS	—	B
Helping Kids Handle Conflict	SOW	EL–MS	—	B
Helping Kids Handle Put-Downs	SOW	EL–MS	—	B
Helping Kids Make Wise Choices and Reduce Risky Behavior	PRO	EL–MS	—	B
I Belong Out There!	PDA	MS–AD	—	V
Impact!	PRO	MS–HS	—	CP
Improving Your Self-Esteem	NSP	JH–HS	—	SW
Job Readiness Skills CD-ROM Series	GLE	MS–HS	—	SW
Learn About Life: Sexuality & Social Skills	PDA	MS–AD	—	B
Life Lessons for Young Adolescents	REM	MS–HS	—	TR
Life Skills for Teens	PRO	MS–HS	—	K
Looking Good	PDA	MS–AD	—	V
Marathon	JMS	—	—	K
Mind Your Manners—Self-Confidence	JMS	—	—	V

162   Appendix A

Personal Confidence/Understanding (Continued)

Material	Publisher	Age Level	Reading Level	Type
Mind Your Manners—Social Success	JMS	—	—	V
More Power to You: Building Confidence and Self-Esteem	WAL	MS–AD	4.0	B
Moving to Middle School	PRO	EL–MS	—	WB
Multimedia Dropout Prevention	NSP	MS–HS	—	SW
My Life	NSP	MS–HS	—	SW
My Life Book	PDA	MS–HS	—	WB
Person to Person	PDA	MS–AD	—	V
Person-Centered Planning	PDA	HS–AD	—	B
Personal Development	NSP	MS–AD	—	SW
Pouvant I	PRO	MS–HS	—	TR, B
Preparing for Career Success	GLE	MS–HS	—	B, WB, TR
Problem-Solving Picture Cards	PRO	MS–AD	—	FC
Problem-Solving Situations for Adolescents	ACA	MS–HS	—	WB
Problem-Solving Situations for Children	ACA	EL	—	WB
Problem Solving Skills for Children	PRO	EL	—	WB
Push and Shove	NSP	EL	—	SW
Resource of Activities for Peer Pragmatics	LSI	MS–HS	0–4.5	DM
Responsible Assertion	REP	—	—	V
Right Choices	SOW	MS–HS	—	CP
Safe and Strong: Strategies for Personal Safety for Persons with Developmental Disabilities	PDA	MS–AD	—	V
Seeds of Self-Esteem	AGS	EL–JH	—	K
Self-Advocacy for Persons with Developmental Disabilities	JMS	—	—	V
Self-Determination	PDA	MS–AD	—	V
Self-Esteem	GLE	HS	—	V
Self-Esteem in the Classroom: A Curriculum Guide	LLS	—	—	TR, B
Skills for Better Living	GLE	HS–AD	—	SW
Skills for Better Living (Volumes I, II, or III)	NSP	MS–AD	—	SW
Skillstreaming the Adolescent	REP	MS–HS	—	B
Skillstreaming Video	REP	MS–HS	—	B, V

Personal Confidence/Understanding (*Continued*)

Material	Publisher	Age Level	Reading Level	Type
Social Skills Activities for the Elementary Grades	PRO	EL–MS	—	B
Stepping Out	ATT	—	—	K
Straight Talk	NSP	MS–AD	—	SW
Stress Management for Adolescents	REM	MS–HS	—	CP
Supporting Self-Determination	PDA	MS–AD	—	V
Teaching Cooperation Skills	SOW	EL–MS	—	B
The Teen Success Handbook	PRO	MS–HS	—	B
Thinking It Through: Challenges	GLF	MS–JH	4.0–5.0	B, TR
Thinking It Through: Changes	GLF	HS	7.0–8.0	B, TR
Thinking It Through: Community	GLF	JH–HS	5.0–6.0	B, TR
Tips	JMS	—	—	V, S
Tough Decisions	SAD	MS–AD	7.0	RB
Transitions to High School	PDA	EL–MS	—	V, PH
Unlocking Your Potential	LLS	—	—	A, TR
Viewpoints	REM	MS–HS	—	TR
The Waksman Social Skills Curriculum	PRO	MS–HS	—	B, WB
The Walker Social Skills Program	PRO	MS–HS	—	B, WB
What Could I Say?	REP	JH–HS	—	V
What Do I Do Now?	PRO	EL–MS	—	B
What Is Self-Determination & How to Make It Work!	PDA	MS–AD	—	V
What's Your Point of View on Careers?	GLF	MS–HS	3.0	B, TR
What's Your Point of View on the Environment?	GLF	MS–HS	3.0	B, TR
What's Your Point of View on School Issues?	GLF	MS–HS	3.0	B, TR
What's Your Point of View on Your Community?	GLF	MS–HS	3.0	B, TR
Who I Am & Who I Want To Be	SAD	MS–AD	4.0	WB
WiseLives Curriculum	NPR	EL–MS	—	TR
WiseQuotes Curriculum	NPR	EL–MS	—	TR
WiseWords Curriculum	NPR	EL	—	TR
You Are ... Series	HIN	MS–HS	4.0–5.0	B, WB
You Tell Me	PCI	—	—	G
You're In Charge!	GLF	MS–HS	1.0–2.0	B, TR

Goal Setting

Material	Publisher	Age Level	Reading Level	Type
Analogies	SAD	MS–HS	—	WB
Asset: Social Skills Program for Adolescents	REP	JH–HS	—	K
Attending a Two-Year College	CHB	HS	—	B
Choices, Choices	TSP	EL–MS	—	SW, TR, FC
Choose and Take Action	SOW	MS–HS	—	SW
Choosing Education Goals	SOW	MS–HS	—	K
Choosing Employment Goals	SOW	MS–HS	—	K
Choosing Personal Goals	SOW	MS–HS	—	K
Counseling Activities for Life Skills and Career Development	PRO	MS–HS	—	B
Crosscountry U.S.A.	ERE	—	—	SW
Decisions, Decisions	TSP	MS–HS	—	CP
Dilemma: Making Choices in Difficult Real-Life Situations	NSP	EL–AD	—	SW
Drug Alert	ERE	MS–HS	—	SW
Financing a College Education	CHB	HS	—	B
First Step to Success	SOW	EL	—	K
First Step to Success, Preschool Edition	SOW	EL	—	K
Goal Setting Skills–Second Edition	PRO	MS–HS	—	WB
Helping Kids Make Wise Choices and Reduce Risky Behavior	PRO	EL–MS	—	B
How to Live in the World	LLS	—	—	A, TR
Job Interview Skills	CHB	HS–AD	—	B
Learning to Manage Anger	REM	MS–HS	—	V
Life Lessons for Young Adolescents	REM	MS–HS	—	TR
Life Skills for Teens	PRO	MS–HS	—	K
Making the Grade	SAD	JH–HS	—	WB
Mind Games: Puzzles in Logic	SAD	MS–HS	—	WB
Moving Out on Your Own	SAD	MS–AD	4.0	WB
Moving to Middle School	PRO	EL–MS	—	WB
Multimedia Dropout Prevention	NSP	MS–HS	—	SW

Goal Setting (*Continued*)

Material	Publisher	Age Level	Reading Level	Type
Newspower Study Skills	SAD	MS–HS	4.5–5.5	WB
Next S.T.E.P.–Second Edition	PRO	HS–AD	—	CP
On Academic Integrity	CHB	HS	—	WB
On Building Study Skills	CHB	HS	—	WB
On Your Career	CHB	HS–AD	—	WB
On Your Senior Year	CHB	HS	—	WB
Person-Centered Planning	PDA	HS–AD	—	B
Personal Development	NSP	MS–AD	—	SW
Planning Your Career—Find the Work That's Right for You	CHB	MS–HS	—	B
Prepare Curriculum	REP	JH–HS	—	TR
Preparing Teens for the World of Work	PRO	MS–HS	—	B, DM
Problem Solving for Teens	LSI	MS–HS	2.5–3.5	WB
Reading Between the Lines	SAD	HS	—	WB
Reading Realities	ERE	EL or HS	2.0–6.0	SW
Resource of Activities for Peer Pragmatics	LSI	MS–HS	4.5	DM
Right Choices	SOW	MS–HS	—	CP
Starting College—A Guide for First-Year Students	CHB	HS	—	B
Steps to Self-Determination	PRO	MS–AD	—	CP
Straight Talk	NSP	MS–AD	—	SW
Stress Management for Adolescents	REM	MS–HS	—	CP
Study Skills Series	SAD	MS–AD	4.5–7.5	WB
Take Action	SOW	MS–HS	—	K
Teaching Behavioral Self-Control to Students	PRO	—	—	TR
The Teen Success Handbook	PRO	MS–HS	—	B
Tough Choices	SOW	MS–HS	—	K
Transition Planning Inventory	PRO	HS–AD	—	K
Unlocking Your Potential	LLS	—	—	A, TR
Viewpoints	REM	MS–HS	—	TR
The Waksman Social Skills Curriculum	PRO	MS–HS	—	B, WB
Walker Social Skills Curriculum: Access Program	PRO	JH–HS	—	TR

Goal Setting (*Continued*)

Material	Publisher	Age Level	Reading Level	Type
Way to Go! Solving Problems & Making Decisions	WAL	MS–AD	4.0	B
What Do I Do Now?	PRO	EL–MS	—	B
What's Up with Your Future	CHB	MS–HS	—	WB
Why Is It Always Me?	REP	JH–HS	—	V
Work Adjustment Inventory	PRO	HS–AD	—	K
You Are … Series	HIN	MS–HS	4.0–5.0	B, WB
You Can Survive Your Freshman Year	CHB	HS	—	B
Your Child's First Year of College—A Guide for Parents	CHB	HS	—	B
Your First Year in College	CHB	HS	—	B

Self-Improvement

Material	Publisher	Age Level	Reading Level	Type
125 Ways to Be a Better Student	LSI	MS–HS	Intermediate	DM
Academic Survival Tips for Student Athletes	LLS	—	—	A
Activities for Dictionary Practice	CUR	MS–JH	—	DM
All About You	PCI	—	—	G
Appearances Count	PDA	MS–AD	—	V
Arthur: Working Through Problems	PBS	EL	—	V
Attending a Two-Year College	CHB	HS	—	B
Basic Skills/Study Techniques Program	LLS	—	—	K
Behavior Skills	PCI	EL–MS	—	G
Being with a Date: Parts 1 & 2	JMS	—	—	V
Being with Friends: Parts 1 & 2	JMS	—	—	V
Building Character Through Service Learning	NPR	MS–HS	—	B
Building Self-Esteem in the Classroom	SOW	EL–MS	—	B
Bully-Proofing Your School	PRO	EL–MS	—	B
Bully-Proofing Your School	PRO	MS–HS	—	B
Character-Ed & Responsibility Bingo	PCI	EL–MS	—	G

Self-Improvement (*Continued*)

Material	Publisher	Age Level	Reading Level	Type
Character Way	NPR	EL–JH	—	CP, V
Choose and Take Action	SOW	MS–HS	—	SW
Choosing Education Goals	SOW	MS–HS	—	K
Choosing Employment Goals	SOW	MS–HS	—	K
Choosing Personal Goals	SOW	MS–HS	—	K
Classification & Organization Skills—Developmental	CUR	HS–AD	6.0	WB
Computer Test Preparation	LLS	HS–AD	—	SW
Core Home and School Vocabulary	PRO	—	3–11 yrs.	K
Counseling Activities for Life Skills and Career Development	PRO	MS–HS	—	B
Developing Character for Classroom Success	NPR	MS–HS	—	B
Dictionary Skills Practice	CUR	MS–AD	4.0	WB
The Dropout Prevention Program	LLS	—	—	K, TR
Educators Encouraging Self-Determination	PDA	MS–AD	—	V, WB
Effective Reading	LLS	—	—	A, WB
Elementary Study Skills	PCI	EL	—	TR
English for Everyday Living	SAD	MS–HS	4.5–5.5	B
English Survival Series	SAD	MS–AD	2.0–5.0	WB
Everyday English	SAD	JH–AD	—	WB
Financing a College Education	CHB	HS	—	B
Foundation of Library Skills Series	ERE	—	—	SW
Glad to Be Me	NSP	EL	—	SW
Helping Kids Find Their Strengths	SOW	EL–MS	—	B
Helping Kids Handle Put-Downs	SOW	EL–MS	—	B
Helping Kids Make Wise Choices and Reduce Risky Behavior	PRO	EL–MS	—	B
HomeWork Coach	AGS	JH–HS	—	K
How to Succeed in College	LLS	—	—	V
I Belong Out There!	PDA	MS–AD	—	V
Improving Your Self-Esteem	NSP	JH–HS	—	SW
In Control	REM	MS–AD	—	TR

Self-Improvement (*Continued*)

Material	Publisher	Age Level	Reading Level	Type
Insights	PRO	EL–MS	—	B
It's Up to Me (behavior program)	PCI	EL–MS	—	TR
Learning to Manage Anger	REM	MS–HS	—	V
Lesson Plans for Service Learning	NPR	MS–HS	—	TR
Life Skills for Teens	PRO	MS–HS	—	K
Making the Grade	LLS	—	—	SW
Making the Grade	SAD	JH–HS	—	WB
Mind Your Manners—Self-Confidence	JMS	—	—	V
Newspower Study Skills	SAD	MS–HS	4.5–5.5	WB
On Academic Integrity	CHB	HS	—	WB
On Building Study Skills	CHB	HS	—	WB
On Your Senior Year	CHB	HS	—	WB
The Outlining Kit	CUR	MS	—	K
Parents Promoting Self-Determination	PDA	MS–AD	—	V, WB
Personal Care Skills	PRO	—	—	K
Personal Power	PRO	MS–HS	—	TR
Problem-Solving Situations for Adolescents	ACA	MS–HS	—	WB
Problem-Solving Situations for Children	ACA	EL	—	WB
Problem Solving Skills for Children	PRO	EL	—	WB
Research Reports	CUR	MS	—	WB
Responsible Assertion	REP	—	—	V
Right Choices	SOW	MS–HS	—	CP
Roller Coaster of Life	PRO	JH–HS	—	G
Safe and Strong: Strategies for Personal Safety for Persons with Developmental Disabilities	PDA	MS–AD	—	V
Self-Advocacy for Persons with Developmental Disabilities	JMS	—	—	V
Self-Determination	PDA	MS–AD	—	V
Service Providers Supporting Self-Determination	PDA	MS–AD	—	V, WB
Simply English	HIN	EL–AD	—	B, WB
Skills for Better Living	GLE	HS–AD	—	SW

Self-Improvement (*Continued*)

Material	Publisher	Age Level	Reading Level	Type
Skills for Living	REP	—	—	B
Skills for School Success	CUR	EL	—	WB
Skillstreaming the Adolescent	REP	MS–HS	—	B
Skillstreaming Video	REP	MS–HS	—	B, V
Social Skills Activities for the Elementary Grades	PRO	EL–MS	—	B
Social Skills at Work	NSP	MS–HS	—	SW
Starting College—A Guide for First-Year Students	CHB	HS	—	B
Story Starters: Science	ERE	NS	—	SW
Story Starters: Social Studies	ERE	NS	—	SW
Strategies for Study	SAD	JH–HS	—	WB
Stress Management for Adolescents	REM	MS–HS	—	CP
Study Skills Series	SAD	MS–AD	4.5–7.5	WB
Study Skills: Strategies & Practice	CUR	HS–AD	1.0–7.0	DM
Success in the Classroom	LLS	—	—	V
Supporting Self-Determination	PDA	MS–AD	—	V
Survival Vocabulary	SAD	JH–AD	2.0–4.0	B, WB
Take Action	SOW	MS–HS	—	K
Teaching Behavioral Self-Control to Students	PRO	—	—	TR
Teaching Character ... In the Middle Grades	NPR	MS	—	B
Teaching Friendship Skills	SOW	EL–MS	—	B
Technology and Self-Advocacy	PDA	HS–AD	—	V
Test Ready Mathematics	CUR	HS–AD	gr 1.0–8.0	WB
Test Ready Practice with Cloze	CUR	HS–AD	gr 3.0–6.0	WB
Test Ready Reading & Vocabulary	CUR	HS–AD	1.0–8.0	WB
The Test Taker's Edge	SUN	MS–AD	—	SW
Thirty Lessons in Note-Taking	CUR	MS	—	WB
Thirty Lessons in Outlining	CUR	JH–HS	—	WB
Tips	JMS	—	—	V, SW
Tough Choices	SOW	MS–HS	—	K
Tough Decisions	SAD	MS–AD	7.0	RB

Self-Improvement (*Continued*)

Material	Publisher	Age Level	Reading Level	Type
Unlocking Your Potential	LLS	—	—	A, TR
Verbal Problem-Solving in Social Situations	ACA	MS–HS	—	B
The Video Test Preparation Review Series	LLS	HS–AD	—	V
Viewpoints	REM	MS–HS	—	TR
Vocabulary Building	SAD	MS–HS	—	DM
Vocabulary in Context	PRO	—	1.5–6.0	TR
Walker Social Skills Curriculum: ACCEPTS Program	PRO	EL	—	B, TR
Walker Social Skills Curriculum: ACCESS Program	PRO	MS–HS	—	B, TR
What Could I Say?	REP	JH–HS	—	V
What Do I Do Now?	PRO	EL–MS	—	B
What Is Self-Determination & How to Make It Work!	PDA	MS–AD	—	V
What's Up with Academic Integrity	CHB	MS–HS	—	WB
What's Up with Academic Success	CHB	MS–HS	—	WB
What's Up with Beating Test Anxiety	CHB	MS–HS	—	WB
What's Up with Study Skills	CHB	MS–HS	—	WB
Who Knew? The Study Smart Issue	CHB	EL–MS	—	WB
WiseLives Curriculum	NPR	EL–MS	—	TR
WiseQuotes Curriculum	NPR	EL–MS	—	TR
WiseWords Curriculum	NPR	EL	—	TR
You Can Survive Your Freshman Year	CHB	HS	—	B
Young Adults Working on Self-Determination	PDA	MS–AD	—	V, WB
Your Child's First Year of College—A Guide for Parents	CHB	HS	—	B
Your First Year in College	CHB	HS	—	B

Relationships

Material	Publisher	Age Level	Reading Level	Type
101 Games for Groups	PRO	EL–AD	—	G
Before You Say Good-bye	AQU	—	—	V, TR
Behavior Skills	PCI	—	—	G
Being with a Date: Parts 1 & 2	JMS	—	—	V

Relationships (*Continued*)

Material	Publisher	Age Level	Reading Level	Type
Being with Acquaintances & Strangers	JMS	—	—	V
Being with Authority Figures	JMS	—	—	V
Being with Friends: Parts 1 & 2	JMS	—	—	V
Being with Housemates: Parts 1 & 2	JMS	—	—	V
Big Chances, Big Choices	SAD	MS–AD	—	V
Bug Books (Character Ed Stories)	PCI	EL	—	B, A
Bully-Proofing Your School	PRO	EL–MS	—	B
Bully-Proofing Your School	PRO	MS–HS	—	B
Bully-Proofing Your School	SOW	EL–MS	—	B, P
Character Education Through Story	NPR	EL–MS	—	B
A Child's Grief	AQU	EL–JH	—	V
Circles I: Intimacy & Relationships	JMS	—	—	SW
Circles II: Stop Abuse	JMS	—	—	SW, FS, V
Circles III: Safer Ways	JMS	—	—	SW, V
Citizenship & the Law	JMS	—	—	SW, V, FS
Communication Skills Series	SAD	EL–MS	2.6–2.8	B, WB
Conflict Resolution	NSP	EL	—	SW
Conflict Resolution Quiz Show	NSP	EL–JH	—	SW
Cool Kids	SOW	EL–MS	—	K
The Coolien Challenge: Youth Violence Prevention	NSP	MS–HS	—	SW
Counseling Activities for Life Skills and Career Development	PRO	MS–HS	—	B
Creating a Caring Classroom	SOW	EL–MS	—	TR
Defusing Anger and Aggression	SOW	MS–HS	—	V, RB
Dilemma: Making Choices in Difficult Real-Life Situations	NSP	EL–AD	—	SW
Double Trouble (Peer Pressure)	NSP	EL	—	SW
Easy Stories for Social Skills	ACA	EL	—	WB
First Step to Success	SOW	EL	—	K
First Step to Success, Preschool Edition	SOW	EL	—	K
Friendzee—A Social Skills Game	LSI	EL–MS	—	G
From Mad to Worse	NSP	EL	—	SW

Relationships (*Continued*)

Material	Publisher	Age Level	Reading Level	Type
Get on Top of It!	SOW	EL–HS	—	B
Getting to Know You!	PRO	EL–MS	—	TR
Helping Kids Find Their Strengths	SOW	EL–MS	—	B
Helping Kids Handle Anger	SOW	EL–MS	—	B
Helping Kids Handle Conflict	SOW	EL–MS	—	B
Improving Your Self Esteem	CHB	HS–AD	—	B
In Search of Character	SAD	MS–AD	—	V
Journey Through the Shadows (How to Help Those You Care for When Suicide Occurs)	AQU	—	—	V, TR
Kids to Kids: When Someone Special Dies	AQU	EL–MS	—	V
Knowing What to Say!	ACA	EL–HS	—	WB
Learning Basic Social Skills	SAD	HS–AD	2.0–3.0	CP
Learning Basic Social Skills	WAL	HS–AD	2.0–3.0	DM
Learning Social Skills for Everyday Situations	ACA	MS–AD	—	WB
Learning to Manage Anger	REM	MS–HS	—	V
Life Horizons I	JMS	—	—	SW
Life Horizons II	JMS	—	—	SW
Life Lessons for Young Adolescents	REM	MS–HS	—	TR
LifeFacts 1	JMS	—	—	K
LifeFacts 2	JMS	—	—	K
LifeFacts 3	JMS	—	—	K
Lifetimes	GLF	HS	—	B
Light Among the Shadows: Hope for Healing (After Someone Has Committed Suicide)	AQU	—	—	V, TR
Marathon	JMS	—	—	K
Mind Your Manners—Self-Confidence	JMS	—	—	V
Mind Your Manners—Social Success	JMS	—	—	V
My Life	NSP	MS–HS	—	SW
The New Social Story Book–Illustrated Edition	LSI	EL–MS	—	B
No Easy Way (Coping with a Loved One's Suicide)	AQU	—	—	V, TR
No-Glamour Social Language/Behavior Cards	LSI	EL–MS	—	FC
Person to Person: Community	GLF	MS–HS	2.0–3.0	WB, TR

Relationships (*Continued*)

Material	Publisher	Age Level	Reading Level	Type
Person to Person: Developing Interpersonal Skills	WAL	MS–AD	4.0	B
Person to Person: Family & Friends	GLF	MS–HS	2.0–3.0	WB, TR
Person to Person: School & Work	GLF	MS–HS	2.0–3.0	WB, TR
Personal Development	NSP	MS–AD	—	SW
Personal Power	PRO	MS–HS	—	TR
Pouvant 1	PRO	MS–HS	—	TR, B
The Power of Choice Video Series	SAD	MS–AD	—	V
PREP for Effective Family Living	AGS	HS	—	K
Prepare Curriculum	REP	JH–HS	—	TR
Problem-Solving Situations for Adolescents	ACA	MS–HS	—	WB
Problem-Solving Situations for Children	ACA	EL	—	WB
Push and Shove	NSP	EL	—	SW
"Ready to Use" Social Skills Lessons & Activities	NPR	MS–HS	—	TR
Real Life Teens	SAD	MS–AD	—	V
Refusal Skill Video	REP	JH–HS	—	B, V
Refusal Skills	REP	JH–HS	—	TR
Relate for Teens	NSP	MS–HS	—	SW
Resolving Conflicts	GLF	MS–HS	5.0–6.0	B, TR
Room 14—A Social Language Program	LSI	EL–MS	—	CP
Room 28—A Social Language Program	LSI	MS–HS	—	CP
Saying Goodbye for Teens	AQU	JH–HS	—	V
Self-Advocacy for Persons with Developmental Disabilities	JMS	—	—	V
Sexuality Education for Persons with Severe Developmental Disabilities	JMS	—	—	SW
Simply English	HIN	EL–AD	—	B, WB
Skills for Better Living	GLE	HS–AD	—	SW
Skills for Living	REP	—	—	B
Skills for Negotiating & Resolving Conflict	CHB	MS–HS	—	V, CP
Skills for Resolving Conflict: Communicating in a Healthy Way	GLF	MS–HS	3.0–4.0	B, TR
Skills for Resolving Conflict: Handling Stress	GLF	MS–HS	3.0–4.0	B, TR
Skills for Resolving Conflict: Negotiating	GLF	MS–HS	3.0–4.0	B, TR

Relationships (*Continued*)

Material	Publisher	Age Level	Reading Level	Type
Skills for Resolving Conflict: Team Building	GLF	MS–HS	3.0–4.0	B, TR
Skills for Resolving Conflict: Valuing Others	GLF	MS–HS	3.0–4.0	B, TR
Skills for Resolving Conflict: Valuing Yourself	GLF	MS–HS	3.0–4.0	B, TR
Skillstreaming the Adolescent	REP	MS–HS	—	B
Skillstreaming Video	REP	MS–HS	—	B, V
Social Skill Builder Software	ACA	EL–MS	—	SW
Social Skills Activities for Secondary Students with Special Needs	ACA	MS–HS	—	B
Social Skills Activities for Secondary Students with Special Needs	PRO	EL–MS	—	B
Social Skills at Work	ATT	MS–HS	—	SW
Social Skills at Work	NSP	MS–HS	—	SW
Social Skills Curriculum	PCI	EL–HS	—	CP
Sportsmanship	NSP	EL	—	SW
The Stop & Think Social Skills Program	SOW	EL–MS	—	CP
Straight Talk	NSP	MS–AD	—	SW
Teaching Behavioral Self-Control to Students	PRO	—	—	TR
Teaching Cooperation Skills	SOW	EL–MS	—	B
Teaching Friendship Skills	SOW	EL–MS	—	B
Teaching Social Competence to Youth and Adults with Developmental Disabilities	PRO	MS–HS	—	CP
Teamwork Works!	PDA	MS–HS	—	V, TR
Teasing & Bullying: Sticks & Stones	NSP	EL	—	SW
Teen Awareness Videos	SAD	MS–AD	—	V
The Teen Success Handbook	PRO	MS–HS	—	B
Teenage Parents	LLS	HS	—	V
That's Life! Social Language	LSI	EL–MS	—	DM
Three Friends	NSP	EL–MS	—	SW
Tips	JMS	—	—	V, SW
The Tomorrows Children Face When a Parent Dies	AQU	EL–HS	—	V
The Tough Kid Social Skills Book	SOW	EL–MS	—	B
Verbal Problem-Solving in Social Situations	ACA	MS–HS	—	B
The Waksman Social Skills Curriculum	PRO	MS–HS	—	B, WB

Relationships (*Continued*)

Material	Publisher	Age Level	Reading Level	Type
Walker Social Skills Curriculum	PRO	JH–HS	—	B
What Could I Say?	REP	JH–HS	—	V
What's Up with Peer Pressure	CHB	MS–HS	—	WB
Why Don't They Like Me?	SOW	EL–MS	—	B
Working I	JMS	—	—	V
Working II	JMS	—	—	V, T
Yes I Can … Work with People	REP	—	—	K

Personal Expression

Material	Publisher	Age Level	Reading Level	Type
Better Writing for Better Jobs	SAD	HS–AD	—	WB, TR
Building a Positive Self-Concept	SAD	MS–AD	—	RB
Bully-Proofing Your School	SOW	EL–MS	—	B, P
Communicate!	NSP	MS–AD	—	SW
Community Success	NSP	MS–HS	—	SW
Conflict Resolution	NSP	EL	—	SW
Conflict Resolution Quiz Show	NSP	EL–JH	—	SW
Conversation Start-Ups	PCI	EL	—	G, DM
The Coolien Challenge: Youth Violence Prevention	NSP	MS–HS	—	SW
Defusing Anger and Aggression	SOW	MS–HS	—	V, RB
Double Trouble (Peer Pressure)	NSP	EL	—	SW
Emotions and Expressions	PRO	EL–JH	—	K
From Mad to Worse	NSP	EL	—	SW
Improving Your Self-Esteem	NSP	JH–HS	—	SW
In Control	REM	MS–AD	—	TR
Knowing What To Say!	ACA	EL–HS	—	WB
Learn About Life: Sexuality & Social Skills	PDA	MS–AD	—	B
Learning to Manage Anger	REM	MS–HS	—	V
Life Coping Skills Series: Forms & Messages	STV	MS–JH	2.0–4.0	WB

Personal Expression (*Continued*)

Material	Publisher	Age Level	Reading Level	Type
Person to Person	PDA	MS–AD	—	V
Person to Person: Community	GLF	MS–HS	2.0–3.0	WB, TR
Person to Person: Developing Interpersonal Skills	WAL	MS–AD	4.0	B
Person to Person: Family & Friends	GLF	MS–HS	2.0–3.0	WB, TR
Person to Person: School & Work	GLF	MS–HS	2.0–3.0	WB, TR
Push and Shove	NSP	EL	—	SW
Roller Coaster of Life	PRO	JH–HS	—	G
Room 14—A Social Language Program	LSI	EL–MS	—	CP
Room 28—A Social Language Program	LSI	MS–HS	—	CP
Situation Communication	ACA	EL–HS	—	B
Skills for Negotiating & Resolving Conflict	CHB	MS–HS	—	V, CP
Social Skills at Work	NSP	MS–HS	—	SW
Social Star Program	PCI	EL	—	WB
Sportsmanship	NSP	EL	—	SW
Success on the Job: Communicating Clearly	SAD	HS–AD	—	WB, TR
Talkabout	PRO	MS–AD	—	WB
Talkabout Activities	PRO	MS–AD	—	G
Talking It Out	PRO	EL–HS	—	WB
Teasing & Bullying: Sticks & Stones	NSP	EL	—	SW
Using a Telephone–Second Edition	PRO	EL–AD	—	K
The Walker Social Skills Curriculum	PRO	JH–HS	—	B

Selected Multicomponent Programs

Material	Publisher	Age Level	Reading Level	Type
400 Words that Work	WAL	MS–AD	4.0	DM
Books to Cope with Life's Challenges	SAD	MS–AD	2.3–4.0	WB, B
Building Life Skills	AGS	MS–HS	6.0	CP
Bully-Proofing Your School	SOW	EL–JH	—	CP

Selected Multicomponent Programs (*Continued*)

Material	Publisher	Age Level	Reading Level	Type
Careers & Opportunities	GLF	MS–HS	4.0–6.0	B
Coping Workbook Series	SAD	HS–AD	1.0–4.0	WB
Creative Living	GLE	HS	—	CP
Discovering Life Skills	GLE	MS–HS	—	CP
Essential Everyday Reading	WAL	HS–AD	7.0	DM
Everyday Life Skills	AGS	MS–HS	3.9	CP
The Janus Employability Skills Program	GLF	MS–HS	2.0–4.0	B, TR
Life Centered Career Education: A Competency Based Approach	CEC	—	—	TR
Life Centered Career Education: Activity Books I & II	CEC	—	—	TR
Life School 2000	GLF	HS–AD	1.0–4.0	CP
Life School Worktexts	GLF	MS–HS	3.5–5.0	CP
Life Skills for Today's World	STV	MS–AD	3.0–4.0	B
Living Now	GLE	MS–HS	—	CP
Living on Your Own	WAL	HS–AD	—	DM
On Your Own in Middleton, Central City, & Metro City	GLE	HS–AD	—	SW
Real-Life English	STV	AD	—	WB
Real-Life Reading Cards	WAL	MS–AD	2.0	B, FC
Shaping Your Future	GLE	HS–AD	—	CP
Shop Talk	REP	—	—	TR
Skills for Everyday Life	SAD	MS–AD	3.0	CP
Skills for Independent Living	GLF	MS–HS	3.0–4.0	CP
Skills for Life	GLE	MS–HS	—	CP
Success at Work	GLF	MS–HS	3.0–4.0	B, TR
Survival Guides	SAD	JH–AD	2.0–3.0	B, WB
Survival Reading Flash Cards	WAL	MS–AD	2.0	FC
Survival Signs Sampler	ATT	—	—	SW
Survival Vocabulary Set	WAL	MS–AD	3.0	B
Survival Vocabulary Stories	WAL	MS–HS	2.0	DM
Teaching Interpersonal and Community Living Skills	PRO	HS–AD	—	TR

Selected Multicomponent Programs (*Continued*)

Material	Publisher	Age Level	Reading Level	Type
Teaching the Moderate and Severely Handicapped	PRO	—	—	TR
Today's Teen	GLE	MS–HS	—	CP
Using the Newspaper to Teach Basic Living Skills	WAL	MS–AD	—	DM

PUBLISHERS' INFORMATION

Academic Communication Associates
4001 Avenida de la Plata
P.O. Box 4279
Oceanside, CA 92052-4279
888/758-9558
Fax: 760/722-1625
http://www.acadcom.com

AGS Publishing
4201 Woodland Road
P.O. Box 99
Circle Pines, MN 55014-1796
800/328-2560
Fax: 800/471-8457
http://www.agsnet.com

American Kennel Club
AKC Headquarters
260 Madison Avenue
New York, NY 10016
212/696-8200
Fax: 212/696-8299

Aquarius Health Care Videos
18 North Main Street
Sherborn, MA 01770
888/440-2963
Fax: 508/650-1665
http://www.aquariusproductions.com

Attainment Company
504 Commerce Parkway
P.O. Box 930160
Verona, WI 53593-0160
800/327-4269; 608/845-7880
Fax: 800/942-3865
http://www.attainmentcompany.com

Channing Bete
One Community Place
South Deerfield, MA 01973-0200
800/477-4776; 800/828-2827
Fax: 800/499-6464
http://www.channing-bete.com

Communication Skill Builders
3830 East Belleview
P.O. Box 42050-E93
Tucson, AZ 85733
520/323-7500
Fax: 520/325-0306

Continental Press
520 East Bainbridge Street
Elizabethtown, PA 17022
800/233-0759
Fax: 888/834-1303
http://www.continentalpress.com

Council for Exceptional Children
1110 Glebe Road, Suite 300
Arlington, VA 22201-5704
800/224-6830; 703/620-3660
Fax: 703/264-9494
http://www.cec.sped.org

Curriculum Associates
153 Rangeway Road
North Billerica, MA 01862-2589
800/225-0248; 978/667-8000
Fax: 978/667-5706; 800/366-1158
http://www.curriculumassociates.com

Educational Resources
1550 Executive Drive
P.O. Box 1900
Elgin, IL 60121-1900
800/860-7004; 708/888-8300
Fax: 708/888-8499; 800/610-5005
http://www.edresources.com

Gamco Industries
325 N. Kirkwood Road, Suite 200
St. Louis, MO 63122
800/351-1404; 888/726-8100;
   314/909-1670
Fax: 314/984-8063
http://www.orchardsoftware.com

Glencoe/McGraw-Hill
P.O. Box 543
Blacklick, OH 43004-0544
800/334-7344
Fax: 614/755-5682
http://www.glencoe.com

Globe Fearon/Pearson Learning Group
135 South Mount Zion Road
P.O. Box 2500
Lebanon, IN 46052
800/526-9907
Fax: 800/393-3156
http://www.pearsonlearning.com

**High Noon Books, A Division of
   Academic Therapy Publications**
20 Commercial Blvd
Novato, CA 94949-6191
800/422-7249
Fax: 888/287-9975
http://www.academictherapy.com

James Stanfield Publishing
P.O. Box 41058, Drawer WEB
Santa Barbara, CA 93140
800/421-6534
Fax: 805/897-1187
http://www.stanfield.com

KidSafety of America
6251 Schaefer Avenue, Suite B
Chino, CA 91710-9065
800/524-1156
Fax: 909/902-1343
www.kidsafetystore.com

Laureate Learning Systems
110 E. Spring Street
Winooski, VT 05404-1898
800/562-6801; 802/655-4755
Fax: 802/655-4757
http://www.laureatelearning.net

LinguiSystems
3100 4th Avenue
P.O. Box 747
East Moline, IL 61244
800/776-4332
Fax: 800/577-4555
http://www.linguisystems.com

McGraw-Hill/Contemporary
130 East Randolph Street
Suite 400
Chicago, IL 60601
800/621-1918; 312/233-6701
Fax: 312/233-6665
http://www.mhcontemporary.com

National Professional Resources
25 South Regent Street
Port Chester, NY 10573
800/453-7461; 914/937-8879
Fax: 914/937-9327
http://www.nprinc.com

National School Products
101 E. Broadway
Maryville, TN 37804
800/627-9393; 865/984-3960
Fax: 800/289-3960; 865/983-9355
http://www.nationalschoolproducts.com

PBS Video
P.O. Box 279
Melbourne, FL 32902
800/531-4727
Fax: 866/274-9043
http://www.shoppbs.org

PCI Educational Publishing
P.O. Box 34270
San Antonio, TX 78265-4270
800/594-4263
Fax: 888/259-8284
http://www.pcieducation.com

PRO-ED
8700 Shoal Creek Boulevard
Austin, TX 78757-6897
800/897-3202; 512/451-3246
Fax: 800/397-7633
http://www.proedinc.com

Program Development Associates
P.O. Box 2038
Syracuse, NY 13220-2038
800/543-2119; 315/452-0643
Fax: 315/452-0710
http://www.disabilitytraining.com

Remedia Publications
15887 North 76th Street, Suite 120
Scottsdale, AZ 85260
800/826-4740; 480/661-9900
Fax: 877/661-9901; 480/661-9901
http://www.rempub.com

Research Press
Department 26W
P.O. Box 9177
Champaign, IL 61826
800/519-2707; 217/352-3273
Fax: 217/352-1221
http://www.researchpress.com

RPM Press
P.O. Box 31483
Tucson, AZ 85751-1483
888/810-1990
Fax: 520/886-1990
http://www.rpmpress.com

Saddleback Educational
Three Watson
Irvine CA 92618-2767
888/735-2225; 949/860-2500
Fax: 888/734-4010; 949/860-2508
http://www.sdlback.com

Sopris West
4093 Specialty Place
Longmont, CO 80504
800/547-6747; 303/651-2829
Fax: 888/891-7767; 303/776-5934
http://www.sopriswest.com

Steck-Vaughn
6277 Sea Harbor Drive
Orlando, FL 32887
800/531-5015
Fax: 800/699-9459
http://rigby.harcourtachieve.com

Sunburst Visual Media
P.O. Box 9120
Plainview, NY 11803-9020
800/431-1934
Fax: 888/803-3908
http://www.sunburstvm.com

Tom Synder Productions
80 Coolidge Hill Road
Watertown, MA 02472-5003
800/342-0236
Fax: 800/304-1254
http://www.teachtsp.com

Walch Publishing
40 Walch Drive
P.O. Box 658
Portland, ME 04104-0658
207/772-2846
http://www.walch.com

SAMPLE PERMISSION LETTERS

The sample letters were adapted from the St. Bernard School System (Louisiana). We wish to give special acknowledgment to Deborah Lord for sharing this information.

DATE _____

Dear Parents:

Our class will be visiting the _____
on _____. The purpose of the field
experience is to _____.

We will/will not be eating lunch off campus. We will be eating lunch at _____
_____. Students will need $_____
for lunch.

We will be using _____ for transportation.
Students will need $_____ for transportation.

Please sign below, giving your permission for your son/daughter to participate in this field
experience.

Thank you for your continued support of our field experiences.

Sincerely,

Teacher

_____

My son/daughter _____ has my permission
to participate in but not be limited to the following activities:

    (activity) _____

    (activity) _____

    (activity) _____

Parent's Signature: _____

Parent's Name (Printed): _____

October 5, 2006

Dear Parents:

On Thursday, October 19, 2006, our class will be going to visit Maureen's Cleaners on Genoa St. The purpose of this trip is to identify the service(s) offered by Maureen's and explore the employment options offered by this local business.

The students will be required to wear regular school clothes. We will eat lunch while we are out. Please send at least $5.00 for lunch at Helen's Pizza Palace.

We will be taking public transportation. Bus coupons will be provided. The class will return to school before the last bell rings.

Please sign below, giving your permission for your son/daughter to attend this field experience.

Thank you for your continued support of our field experiences.

Sincerely,

Kathie A. Conwell

_____

My son/daughter _____ has my permission to participate in but not be limited to the following activities:

   —visit Maureen's Cleaners

   —have lunch at Helen's Pizza Palace

   —ride public transportation

Parent's Signature: _____

Parent's Name (Printed): _____

January 11, 2007

Dear Parents:

We will be visiting Colleen's Factory Outlet Mall on Thursday, February 1, 2007. The purpose of the trip will be to compare prices of items on the trip to those at Pat's closet.

Students will need at least $8.00 for the buffet-style lunch at John and Joe's Buffet. All students will be given ample time to shop if they bring money to do so.

Public transportation will be used. The students must bring their RTA photo ID and 20 cents for the discounted fare. If they do not bring these items they will have to pay the full adult fare of $1.10.

Please sign below, giving your permission for your son/daughter to participate in this field experience.

Thank you for your continued support of our class field experiences.

Sincerely,

Bridgid Burroughs

_____

My son/daughter _____ has my permission to participate in but not be limited to the following activities:

    —comparison shopping at Colleen's Factory Outlet Mall

    —lunch at John and Joe's Buffet

    —riding public transportation

Parent's Signature: _____

Parent's Name (Printed): _____

RESOURCES

The following resources may be helpful to you and your students as you assist them in their transition to adult life.

Print

Baker, B. L., & Brightman, A. J. (2004). *Steps to independence: Teaching everyday skills to children with special needs* (4th ed.). Baltimore: Brookes.

Bassett, D. S., & Lehmann, J. (2002). *Student-focused conferencing and planning.* Austin, TX: PRO-ED.

Beakley, B. A., Yoder, S. L., & West, L. L. (2003). *Community-based instruction: A guidebook for teachers.* Arlington, VA: Council for Exceptional Children.

Benson, P. L., Galbraith, M. A., & Espeland, P. (1998). *What teens need to succeed: Proven, practical ways to shape your own future.* Minneapolis, MN: Free Spirit.

Ciborowski, J. (1992). *Textbooks and the students who can't read them.* Cambridge, MA: Brookline.

Citro, T. A. (1999). *Lifetime management for success: Adults with learning disabilities.* Weston: Learning Disabilities Association of Massachusetts.

Cotton, E. G. (1998). *The online classroom: Teaching with the Internet.* Bloomington, IN: EDINFO Press.

Dede, C. (1998). *Learning with technology.* Alexandria, VA: Association for Supervision and Curriculum Development.

Ellison, S., & Gray, J. (1995). *365 afterschool activities.* Naperville, IL: Sourcebooks.

Fein, J. (1996). *Moving on: How to make the transition from college to the real world.* New York: Plume/Penguin Books.

Godin, S. (1996). *The official rules of life.* New York: Seth Godin Production.

Gregory, G. H., & Chapman, C. (2002). *Differentiated instructional strategies: One size doesn't fit all.* Thousand Oaks, CA: Corwin Press.

Guernsey, L. (2002). *College.EDU: Online resources for the cyber-savvy student.* Alexandria, VA: Octameron Associates.

Hoover, J. J., & Patton, J. R. (2007). *Teaching study skills to students with learning problems: A teacher's guide for meeting diverse needs* (2nd ed.). Austin, TX: PRO-ED.

Jist Works. (2002). *The young person's occupational outlook handbook.* Indianapolis, IN: Author.

Jorgensen, C. M. (1998). *Restructuring high schools for all students.* Baltimore: Brookes.

Kaye, C. B. (2004). *The complete guide to service learning: Proven practical ways to engage students in civic responsibility, academic curriculum, and social action.* Alexandria, VA: Association for Supervision and Curriculum Development.

Kinsley, C. W., & McPherson, K. (1995). *Enriching the curriculum through service learning.* Alexandria, VA: Association for Supervision and Curriculum Development.

Lake, J. (1997). *Lifelong learning skills: How to teach today's children for tomorrow's challenges.* Markham, Ontario, Canada: Pembrooke.

Leebow, K. (1998a). *300 incredible things to do on the Internet.* Marietta, GA: VIP Publishing.

Lewis, B. A. (1998b). *The kid's guide to service projects.* Minneapolis, MN: Free Spirit.

Lewis, B. A. (1998c). *The kid's guide to social action.* Minneapolis, MN: Free Spirit.

Lewis, B. A. (1998d). *What do you stand for? A kid's guide to building character.* Minneapolis, MN: Free Spirit.

Lieberman, S. A. (1997). *The real high school handbook.* Boston: Houghton Mifflin.

Male, M. (2003). *Technology for inclusion: Meeting the needs of all students.* Boston: Allyn & Bacon.

Mannix, D. (1995a). *Life skills activities for secondary students with special needs.* West Nyack, NY: Center for Applied Research in Education.

Mannix, D. (1995b). *Life skills for special children.* West Nyack, NY: Center for Applied Research in Education.

Meltzer, L. J., Roditi, B. N., Haynes, D. P., Biddle, K. R., Paster, M., & Taber, S. E. (1996). *Strategies for success: Classroom teaching techniques for students with learning problems.* Austin, TX: PRO-ED.

Mosatche, H. S., & Unger, K. (2000). *Too old for this, too young for that! Your survival guide for the middle-school years.* Minneapolis, MN: Free Spirit.

Nolet, V., & McLaughlin, M. J. (2000). *Accessing the general curriculum: Including students with disabilities in standards-based reform.* Thousand Oaks, CA: Corwin Press.

Otfinoski, S. (1996). *The kid's guide to money: Earning it, saving it, spending it, growing it, sharing it.* New York: Scholastic.

Packer, A. J. (1992). *Bringing up parents: The teenager's handbook.* Minneapolis: Free Spirit.

Pratt, D. (1997). *Terrific teaching: 100 great teachers share their best ideas.* Markham, Ontario, Canada: Pembrooke.

Radencich, M. C., & Schumm, J. S. (1997). *How to help your child with homework.* Minneapolis, MN: Free Spirit.

Rich, J. (1997). *The everything college survival book.* Holbrook, MA: Adams Media.

Rose, D. H., & Meyer, A. (2002). *Teaching every student in the digital age: Universal design for learning.* Alexandria, VA: Association for Supervision and Curriculum Development.

Scheiber, B., & Talpers, J. (2001). *Unlocking potential: College and other choices for learning disabled people: A step-by-step guide.* Bethesda, MD: Adler and Adler.

Snyder, C. (1984). *Teaching your child about money.* Reading, MA: Addison-Wesley.

Tomlinson, C. A., & Cunningham Eidson, C. (2003). *Differentiation in practice: A resource guide for differentiating curriculum, grades 5–9.* Alexandria, VA: Association for Supervision and Curriculum Development.

Valletutti, P. J., Bender, M., & Hoffnung, A. (2005). *Functional curriculum for teaching students with disabilities: Nonverbal and oral communication* (Vol. 2, 3rd ed.). Austin, TX: PRO-ED.

Valletutti, P. J., Bender, M., & Sims-Tucker, B. (2005). *Functional curriculum for teaching students with disabilities: Functional academics* (Vol. 3, 2nd ed.). Austin, TX: PRO-ED.

Vaughn, S., Bos, C. S., & Schumm, J. S. (2006). *Teaching students who are exceptional, diverse, and at-risk in the general education classroom* (4th ed.). Boston: Allyn & Bacon.

Worthington, J. F., & Farrar, R. (1998). *The ultimate college survival guide.* Princeton, NJ: Peterson's.

Wenz-Gross, M., Anderson, K., Parker, R., O'Meara, A., & King, I. (2002). *Moving to middle school: Life skills and coping skills for successful student transition.* Austin, TX: PRO-ED.

Web Sites

Ask for Kids. This site has links to various study tools (dictionary, thesaurus, almanac, clip art, science, biography, math help, history), fun and games (classic games, video games, family learning games, and word games), and news resources (e.g., Weekly Reader, National Geographic for Kids, Kids News Room, BBC for Kids, and Scholastic News Zone). http://www.askforkids.com

Assess Your School. How accessible is your school for everyone? This site provides ways to assess a school building for its accessibility. http://www.dx.org/ud2004/education/assess.html

Center for Youth as Resources. Youth as Resources (YAR) is a philosophy and a program that recognizes youth as valuable community resources and engages them as partners with adults in bringing about positive community change. http://www.yar.org

CHARACTER COUNTS! (CC!). CC! is a nonprofit, nonpartisan, nonsectarian character education framework that teaches the Six Pillars of Character: trustworthiness, respect, responsibility, fairness, caring, and citizenship. The CHARACTER COUNTS! Coalition includes thousands of schools, communities, and nonprofit organizations. http://www.charactercounts.org

Character Education Partnership (CEP). CEP is a nonpartisan coalition of organizations and individuals dedicated to developing moral character and civic virtue in our nation's youth as one means of creating a more compassionate and responsible society. http://www.character.org

Columbia Education Center (CEC) Lesson Plans. This site makes available more than 600 lesson plans, all submitted by teachers. http://www.col-ed.org/lessons_page.html

The Family Involvement Network of Educators (FINE). Launched by Harvard's Family Research Project, FINE is a national network of more than 2,000 people who are interested in promoting strong partnerships among educators, families, and communities. FINE believes that engaging families is essential to achieve high-performing schools and successful students. The Web site features monthly announcements, current ideas, new resources, training tools, and a member insight and opinion section. http://www.gse.harvard.edu/hfrp/projects/fine.html

KidsClick. This Web site includes links to facts and reference materials, science and math, the environment, several arts sites, health and family, home and household, machines and transportation, society and government, computers and the Internet, plus history and biographies. This site has student-safe and child-friendly search tools. http://www.kidsclick.org

Minnesota Governor's Council on Developmental Disabilities. Making Your Case. (2002). [On line Training]. This self-study course is designed to help people with developmental disabilities and their families create positive change through advocacy. This course seeks to enhance an individual's advocacy skills. http://www.partnersinpolicymaking.com/makingyourcase

National Business and Disability Council (NBDC). This site is a resource for employers seeking to integrate persons with disabilities into the workforce. http://www.business-disability.com

National Centre for Work Based Learning Partnerships (NCWBLP). NCWBLP is a program of Middlesex University in the U.K. It works in close partnership with employers to create university-level learning in the workplace. http://www.mdx.ac.uk/www/ncwblp/index.html

The National Council on Independent Living (NCIL). NCIL is a membership organization that advances the independent living philosophy and advocates for the human rights of, and services for, people with disabilities to further their full integration and participation in society. http://www.ncil.org

National Institute for Urban School Improvement. This Web site contains resources and publications about ways to promote positive linkages among schools, families, and communities. http://urbanschools.org

National Rehabilitation Information Center (NARIC). NARIC is committed to providing direct, personal, and high-quality information services to anyone interested in disability and rehabilitation issues. It serves consumers, researchers, family members, health professionals, educators, counselors, students, librarians, and administrators throughout the country. http://www.naric.com

National Service-Learning Clearinghouse (NSLC). NSLC provides a user-friendly site for teachers. It offers several resources on service learning including a Community-Based Service-Learning Starter Kit, available on CD-ROM; links to other sites on service learning; funding sources; lesson plans; conferences; and books and other literature on service learning. http://www.servicelearning.org

NLTS2 Reports. The National Longitudinal Transition Study–2 (NLTS2) reports include information about the characteristics and experiences of youth with disabilities in secondary school. The first four reports from parent interviews and school surveys include findings related to individual and household characteristics of youth, their activities in nonschool hours, their achievements, and experiences in school. http://www.nlts2.org/reports/reports_collapsed.html

PACER Center. The mission of the Parent Advocacy Coalition for Educational Rights (PACER) Center is to expand opportunities and enhance the quality of life of children and young adults with disabilities and their families, based on the concept of parents helping parents. http://www.pacer.org

Research Information for Independent Living (RIIL). RIIL is a joint effort of the Research and Training Center on Independent Living (RTCIL) at the University of Kansas and the Independent Living Research Utilization (ILRU) program of The Institute for Rehabilitation and Research (TIRR). http://www.getriil.org

Southwest Educational Laboratory (SEDL). SEDL is a nonprofit educational research and development corporation. It creates and provides research-based products and services to improve teaching and learning. http://www.sedl.org

Teachers.Net Lesson Bank. This is a Web site with lesson plans searchable by curriculum area. It also provides opportunity to submit and request plans. http://www.teachers .net/lessons

Universal Design—Digital Content in the Classroom: Toolkits. Software with universal design for learning (UDL) features facilitates individualization of learning materials and experiences for maximum inclusion and teaching effectiveness. http://www.cast .org/teachingeverystudent

U.S. Department of Education Office of Civil Rights. (2005, May). Students with disabilities preparing for postsecondary education: Know your rights and responsibilities. This online article provides practical advice for students with disabilities concerning their rights and responsibilities as they enter into postsecondary education. It also contains links to forms and resources. http://www.ed.gov/about/offices/list/ocr/ transition.html

REFERENCES

Affleck, J., Edgar, E., Levine, P., & Kortering, L. (1990). Post school status of students classified as mentally retarded: Does it get better with time? *Education and Training in Mental Retardation, 25,* 315–324.

Agran, M., Snow, K., & Swaner, J. (1999). A survey of secondary level teachers' opinions on community-based instruction and inclusive education. *Journal of the Association for Persons with Severe Handicaps, 24,* 58–62.

Baker, A., & Soden, L. M. (1998). *The challenges of parent involvement research.* ERIC Clearinghouse on Urban Education, Institute for Urban and Minority Education, Teacher College, Columbia University, New York. (ERIC Document Reproduction Service No. ED419030)

Bassett, D. S., & Kochhar-Bryant, C. (2003). Future directions for transition and standards-based education. In C. Kochhar-Bryant & D. S. Bassett (Eds.), *Aligning transition and standards-based education: Issues and strategies* (pp. 187–202). Arlington, VA: Council for Exceptional Children.

Beakley, B. A., Yoder, S. L., & West, L. L. (2003). *Community-based instruction: A guidebook for teachers.* Alexandria, VA: Council for Exceptional Children.

Beck, J., Broers, J., Hogue, E., Shipstead, J., & Knowlton, E. (1994). Strategies for functional community-based instruction and inclusion for children with mental retardation. *Teaching Exceptional Children, 26*(2), 44–48.

Beirne-Smith, M., Patton, J., & Kim, S. (2006). *Mental retardation: An introduction to intellectual disabilities* (7th ed.). Upper Saddle River, NJ: Prentice Hall.

Bergstrom, J. M., & O'Brien, L. A. (2001). Themes of discovery. *Educational Leadership, 58*(7), 29–33.

Bessier, S. (1998). Service learning: Developing a curriculum for caring. *Delta Kappa Bulletin, 62*(2), 15–19.

Billingsley, F. F., & Albertson, L. R. (1999). Finding a future for functional skills. *Journal of the Association for Persons with Severe Handicaps, 24,* 298–302.

Blackorby, J., Edgar, E., & Kortering, L. (1991). A third of our youth? A look at the problems of high school dropout among students with mild handicaps. *Journal of Special Education, 25,* 102–113.

Blankenship, C. S. (1985). Using curriculum-based assessment data to make instructional decisions. *Exceptional Children, 52,* 233–243.

Blankenship, C. S., & Lily, M. S. (1981). *Mainstreaming students with learning and behavior problems: Techniques for the classroom teacher.* New York: Holt, Reinhart & Winston.

Brigance, A. H. (1995). *Life Skills Inventory.* North Billerica, MA: Curriculum Associates.

Brinckerhoff, L. C., McGuire, J. M., & Shaw, S. F. (2002). *Postsecondary education and transition for students with learning disabilities* (2nd ed.). Austin, TX: PRO-ED.

Brolin, D. E. (1992). *Life Centered Career Education (LCCE) Knowledge and Performance Batteries.* Reston, VA: Council for Exceptional Children.

Brolin, D. E. (1993). *Life centered career education: A competency-based approach* (4th ed.). Reston, VA: Council for Exceptional Children.

Brolin, D. E. (1997). *Life centered career education: A competency-based approach* (5th ed.). Arlington, VA: Council for Exceptional Children.

Brolin, D. E., & Loyd, R. J. (2004). *Career development and transition services.* Upper Saddle River, NJ: Prentice Hall.

Browder, D. M., & Grasso E. (1999). Teaching money skills to individuals with mental retardation: A research review with practical applications. *Remedial and Special Education 20*(5), 297–308.

Brown, L., & Leigh, J. E. (1986). *Adaptive Behavior Inventory.* Austin, TX: PRO-ED.

Brown, P. (2000). Linking transition services to student outcomes for students with moderate/severe mental retardation. *Career Development for Exceptional Individuals, 23*(1), 39–55.

Bruininks, R. H., Woodcock, R. W., Weatherman, R. F., & Hill, B. K. (1996). *Scales of Independent Behavior–Revised.* Itasca, IL: Riverside.

Burgess, B., & Wood, S. J. (2004). Home/school/community partnerships: Continuum of opportunities for family engagement. Unpublished figure.

Champlin, J. (1991). A powerful tool for school transformation. *School Administrator, 48*(9), 34.

Ciampa Stoller, L. (1998). *Low-tech assistive devices: A handbook for the school setting.* Framingham, MA: Therapro.

Clark, G. M. (1996). Transition planning assessment for secondary-level students with learning disabilities. *Journal of Learning Disabilities, 29,* 79–92.

Clark, G. M. (1998). *Assessment for transition planning.* Austin, TX: PRO-ED.

Clark, G. M., Carlson, B., Fisher, S., Cook, I. D., & D'Alonzo, B. J. (1991). Career development for students with disabilities in elementary schools: A position statement of the Division on Career Development. *Career Development for Exceptional Individuals, 14,* 109–120.

Clark, G. M., & Patton, J. R. (2006). *Transition Planning Inventory–Updated Version.* Austin, TX: PRO-ED.

Coleman, M. R. (2001). Middle schools: New trends and issues. *Gifted Child Magazine, 24*(4), 20–21.

Collins, B. C. (2003). Meeting the challenge of conducting community-based instruction in rural settings. *Rural Special Education Quarterly, 22*(1), 31–35.

Cronin, M. E. (1996a). Life skills curricula for students with learning disabilities: A review of the literature. In J. R. Patton & G. Blalock (Eds.), *Transition and students with learning disabilities* (p. 88). Austin, TX: PRO-ED.

Cronin, M. E. (1996b). Life skills curriculum for students with learning disabilities: A review of the literature. *Journal for Learning Disabilities, 29*(1), 53–68.

Cronin, M. E. (2000). Instructional strategies. In P. L. Sitlington, G. M. Clark, & O. P. Kolstoe (Eds.), *Transition education and services for adolescents with disabilities* (pp. 255–283). Boston: Allyn & Bacon.

Cronin, M. E., Wendling, K., Lord, D., & Palmisano, D. (1991). Community vocational training: Transition to employment. *Intervention in School and Clinic, 27*(1), 52–55, 59.

Decker, L. E. (2001). Allies in education. *Principal Leadership, 2*(1), 42–46.

Deno, S. L. (1985). Curriculum-based assessment: The emergency alternative. *Exceptional Children, 52,* 219–232.

Dever, R. B. (1988). *Community living skills: A taxonomy.* Washington, DC: American Association on Mental Retardation.

DuFur, S. H., Getzel, E. E., & Trossi, K. (1996). Making the post-secondary match: A role for transition planning. *Journal of Vocational Education, 6,* 231–240.

Durkin, D. (1984). Is there a match between what elementary teachers do and what basal reader manuals recommend? *The Reading Teacher, 37,* 734–745.

Dymond, S. K. (2004). Community participation. In P. Wehman & J. Kregel (Eds.), *Functional curriculum for elementary, middle, and secondary age students with special needs* (pp. 259–292). Austin, TX: PRO-ED.

Edgar, E. (1987). Secondary programs in special education: Are many of them justifiable? *Exceptional Children, 53*(6), 555–561.

Edgar, E. (1990). Education's role in improving the quality of life: Is it time to change our view of the world? *Beyond Behavior, 1*(1), 9–13.

Edgar, E. (1991). Providing ongoing support and making appropriate placements: An alternative to transition planning for mildly handicapped students. *Preventing School Failure, 35*(2), 36–39.

Elias, M. J., Bryan, K., Patrikakou, E. N., & Weissberg, R. P. (2003). Challenges in creating effective home-school partnerships in adolescence: Promising paths for collaboration. *School Community Journal, 13*(1), 133–153.

Enderle, J., & Severson, S. (2003a). *Enderle–Severson Transition Rating Scale-J–Revised.* Moorehead, MN: ETRS.

Enderle, J., & Severson, S. (2003b). *Enderle–Severson Transition Rating Scale–III.* Moorehead, MN: ETRS.

Esposito, J. F., & Curcio-Cole, C. (2002). What works and what doesn't work in five teacher advisory programs. *Middle School Journal, 34*(1), 27–35.

Falvey, M. A. (1989). *Community-based curriculum: Instructional strategies for students with severe disabilities* (2nd ed.). Baltimore: Brookes.

Flexer, R. W., Simmons, T. J., Luft, P., & Baer, R. M. (2005). *Transition planning for secondary students with disabilities.* Upper Saddle River, NJ: Prentice Hall.

Friedland, S. (1992). Building student self-esteem for school improvement. *NASSP Bulletin, 76*(540), 96–102.

Gajar, A. (1992). Adults with learning disabilities: Current and future research priorities. *Journal of Learning Disabilities, 25,* 507–519.

Galvin, J. C., & Scherer, M. J. (1996). *Evaluating, selecting, and using appropriate assistive technology.* Gaithersburg, MD: Aspen.

Garland, T. (1999). *Life skills education: Perceived effectiveness of a 4-H out-of-school program.* (ERIC Document Reproduction Service No. ED436697)

Gibb, G. S., & Dyches, T. T. (2000). *Guide to writing quality individualized education programs: What is best for students with disabilities?* Boston: Allyn & Bacon.

Greenspan, S., & Driscoll, J. (1997). The role of intelligence in a broad model of personal competence. In D. P. Flanagan, J. L. Genshaft, & P. L. Harrison (Eds.), *Contemporary intellectual assessment: Theories, tests, and issues* (pp. 131–150). New York: Guilford.

Greenspan, S., Switzky, H. N., & Granfield, J. M. (1996). Everyday intelligence and adaptive behavior: A theoretical framework. In J. W. Jacobson & J. A Mulick (Eds.), *Manual of diagnostic and professional practice in mental retardation* (pp. 127–135). Washington, DC: American Psychological Association.

Grubbs, K. (2003). Tracing a place: A collaboration that brings students closer to home. *Orion, 22*(3), 18–19.

Hall, T., Strangeman, N., & Meyer, A. (2003). *Differentiated instruction and implications for UDL implementation.* National Center on Accessing the General Curriculum. Washington, DC: Office of Special Education Programs, Office of Special Education and Rehabilitative Services.

Halpern, A., Benz, M. R., & Lindstrom, L. E. (1992). A system change approach to improving secondary special education and transition programs at the community level. *Career Development for Exceptional Individuals, 15,* 109–120.

Halpern, A. S., Irvin, L., & Landman, J. J. (1979). *Tests for Everyday Living.* Monterey, CA: CTB/McGraw-Hill.

Hammill, D. D. (1987). Assessing students in the schools. In J. L. Wiederholt & B. R. Bryant (Eds.), *Assessing the abilities and instructional needs of students* (pp. 1–32). Austin, TX: PRO-ED.

Hammill, D. D., & Bartel, N. R. (2004). *Teaching students with learning and behavior problems.* Austin, TX: PRO-ED.

Handal, G. A., Leiner, M. A., Gonzalez, C., & Rogel, E. (1999). *Linear multimedia benefits to enhance students' ability to comprehend complex subjects.* (ERIC Document Reproduction Service No. ED432221)

Harrison, P., & Oakland, T. (2003). *Adaptive Behavior Assessment System–Second Edition.* San Antonio, TX: Psychological Corp.

Hasazi, S. B., Gordon, L. B., & Roe, C. A. (1985). Factors associated with the employment status of handicapped youth exiting from high school from 1979 to 1983. *Exceptional Children, 51,* 455–469.

Hawaii Transition Project. (1987). Honolulu: Department of Special Education, University of Hawaii.

Heber, R. A. (1961). A manual on terminology and classification in mental retardation (Rev. ed.). *Monograph Supplement to the American Journal of Mental Deficiency, 64.*

Hinojosa, J., & Blount, M. L. (2000). *The texture of life: Purposeful activities in occupational therapy.* Washington, DC: American Occupational Therapy Association.

Individuals with Disabilities Education Act Amendments of 1997, 20 U.S.C. § 1401 *et seq.*

Individuals with Disabilities Education Improvement Act of 2004, 20 U.S.C. § 1400 *et seq.*

Karge, B. D., Patton, P. L., & de la Garza, B. (1992). Transition services for youth with mild disabilities: Do they exist, are they needed? *Career Development for Exceptional Individuals, 15,* 47–68.

Kaye, C. B. (2004). *The complete guide to service learning: Proven practical ways to engage students in civic responsibility, academic curriculum, and social action.* Minneapolis: Free Spirit.

Keith, K. D., & Schalock, R. L. (1995). *Quality of Student Life Questionnaire.* Worthington, OH: IDS.

King, J. A., & Evans, K. M. (1991). Can we achieve outcome based education? *Educational Leadership, 49*(2), 73–75.

Kinsley, C. W., & McPherson, K. (1995). *Enriching the curriculum through service learning.* Alexandria, VA: Association for Supervision and Curriculum Development.

Knowles, M. (1990). *The adult learner: A neglected species* (4th ed.). Houston, TX: Gulf.

Knowles, M., Holton, E. F., & Swanson, R. A. (1998). *The adult learner: The definitive classic in adult and human resource development* (5th ed.). Houston, TX: Gulf.

Kochhar-Bryant, C., & Bassett, D. (2003). *Aligning transition and standards-based education: Issues and strategies.* Arlington, VA: Council for Exceptional Children.

Kohler, P. D., & Hood, L. K. (2000). *Improving student outcomes: Promising practices and programs for 1999–2000. A directory of innovative approaches for providing transition services for youth with disabilities.* Champaign, IL: Transition Research Institute.

Kolstoe, O. P. (1976). *Teaching educable mentally retarded children* (2nd ed.). New York: Holt, Reinhart & Winston.

Kortering, L. J., & Elrod, G. F. (1991). Programs for mildly handicapped adolescents: Evaluating where we are contemplating change. *Career Development for Exceptional Individuals, 14,* 145–157.

Kucher, M., Smith-Rockhold, G., Bemis, D., & Wiese, V. (1998). *Parents as partners in career education.* Pierre: South Dakota Curriculum Center.

Lambert, N., Nihira, K., & Leland, H. (1993). *AAMR Adaptive Behavior Scales–School* (2nd ed.). Austin, TX: PRO-ED.

Lee, B., & Small, R. V. (1999). Web-based resources for K–12 instructional planning. *Educational Media and Technology Yearbook, 24,* 58–63.

Lewis, B. (1991). *The kid's guide to social action.* Minneapolis, MN: Free Spirit.

Lewis, B. (1995). *The kid's guide to service project.* Minneapolis, MN: Free Spirit.

Lindsey, J. D. (2000). *Technology and exceptional individuals.* Austin, TX: PRO-ED.

McCarney, S. B. (1995). *Adaptive Behavior Evaluation Scale–Revised.* Columbia, MO: Hawthorne Educational Service.

McCarney, S. B., & Anderson, P. D. (2000). *Transition Behavior Scale–Second Edition.* Columbia, MO: Hawthorne Educational Services.

McDonnel, J., Wilcox, B., & Hardman, M. (1991). *Secondary programs for students with developmental disabilities.* Boston: Allyn & Bacon.

McLaughlin, J. A, & Lewis, R. L. (2005). *Assessing students with special needs* (6th ed.). Upper Saddle River, NJ: Prentice Hall.

McLaughlin, M. W. (2001). Community counts. *Educational Leadership, 58*(7), 14–18.

Meyer-Meinbach, A., Fredericks, A., & Rothlein, L. (2000). *The complete guide to thematic units: Creating the integrated curriculum.* Norwood, MA: Christopher-Gordon.

Minner, D. D. (2002). *Environmental educational materials evaluation questionnaire (EEMEQ): Using interdisciplinary theory to assess quality.* (ERIC Document Reproduction Service No. ED466407)

Mithaug, D., Horiuchi, C., & Fanning, P. (1985). A report on the Colorado statewide follow-up survey of special education students. *Exceptional Children, 51*(5), 397–404.

Mohler, J. L. (2001). *The implication of well-formedness on web-based educational resources.* Charlottesville, VA: Association for the Advancement of Computing in Education.

Moore, S., Agran, M., & McSweyn, C. (1990). Career education: Are we starting early enough? *Career Development for Exceptional Individuals, 13,* 129–134.

Mosatche, H. S., & Unger, K. (2000). *Too old for this, too young for that!* Minneapolis, MN: Free Spirit.

National and Community Service Act of 1990, 42 U.S.C. 12572.

National and Community Service Trust Act of 1993, 107 Stat. 785.

National Center on Accessing the General Curriculum. (2003). *Research to practice FAQs: Meeting the need for access.* Washington, DC: Office of Special Education Programs, Office of Special Education and Rehabilitative Services.

Neubert, D. A., & Moon, M. S. (2000). How a transition profile helps students prepare for life in the community. *Teaching Exceptional Children, 33*(2), 20–25.

Neugebauer, R. (2000). Purchasing educational materials—Questions from the field. *Child Care Information Exchange, 133,* 88.

Nihira, K., Leland, H., & Lambert, N. (1993). *AAMR Adaptive Behavior Scales–Residential and Community* (2nd ed.). Austin, TX: PRO-ED.

No Child Left Behind Act of 2001, 20 U.S.C. 70 § 6301 *et seq.*

Norris, D., & Schumacker, R. E. (2000, January). *Texas effectiveness study: Adult outcome follow-up.* Paper presented at the annual meeting of the Southwest Educational Research Association, Dallas, TX.

Patton, J. R. (1986). *Transition: Curricular implications at the secondary level.* Honolulu: Project Ho'Okoho, Department of Special Education, University of Hawaii.

Patton, J. R., & Browder, P. (1988). Transitions into the future. In B. Ludlow, R. Luckasson, & A. Turnbull (Eds.), *Transition to adult life for persons with mental retardation: Principles and practices* (pp. 293–311). Baltimore: Brookes.

Patton, J. R., Cronin, M. E., & Wood, S. J. (1999). *Infusing real-life topics into existing curricula.* Austin, TX: PRO-ED.

Patton, J. R., & Trainor, A. (2002). Using applied academics to enhance curricular reform in secondary education. In C. Kochhar-Bryant & D. S. Bassett (Eds.), *Aligning transition and standards-based education: Issues and strategies* (pp. 55–76). Arlington, VA: Council for Exceptional Children.

Pettig, K. L. (2000). On the road to differentiated practice. *Educational Leadership, 8*(1), 14–18.

Pisha, B., & Coyne, P. (2001). Smart from the start: The promise of universal design for learning. *Remedial and Special Education, 22*(4), 197–203.

Polloway, E. A., Patton, J. R., Epstein, M. H., & Smith, T. (1989). Comprehensive curriculum for students with mild handicaps. *Focus on Exceptional Children, 21*(8), 1–12.

Polloway, E. A., Patton, J. R., & Serna, L. (2005). *Strategies for teaching learners with special needs* (8th ed). Upper Saddle River, NJ: Prentice Hall.

Polloway, E. A., Patton, J. R., Smith, J. D., & Roderique, T. (1991). Issues in program design for elementary students with mild retardation: Emphasis on curriculum development. *Education and Training in Mental Retardation, 26,* 142–150.

Potter, K. D. (2003). *Using open courseware in curriculum development. Fastback 508.* Bloomington, IN: Phi Delta Kappa Educational Foundation.

Raskind, M. H., Goldberg, R. J., Higgins E. L., & Herman, K. L. (2002). Teaching "life success" to students with LD: Lessons learned from a 20-year study. *Intervention in School and Clinic, 37*(4), 201–208.

Reschly, D. J., Myers, T. G., & Hartel, C. R. (2002). *Mental retardation: Determining eligibility for Social Security benefits.* Washington, DC: National Academies Press.

Roessler, R. (1991). A problem-solving approach to implementing career education. *Career Development for Exceptional Individuals, 14,* 59–66.

Rose, D. (2001). Universal design for learning: Deriving guiding principles from networks that learn. *Journal of Special Education Technology, 16*(2), 66–67.

Rose, D., & Meyer, A. (2002). *Teaching every student in the digital age: Universal design for learning.* Alexandria, VA: Association for Supervision and Curriculum Development.

Sabornie, E. J., & de Bettencourt, L. U. (2004). *Teaching students with mild and high-incidence disabilities at the secondary level.* Upper Saddle River, NJ: Prentice Hall.

Samuels, S. J. (1984). Basic academic skills. In J. E. Ysseldyke (Ed.), *School psychology: The state of the art.* Minneapolis: National School Psychology Inservice Training Network, University of Minnesota.

Salvia, J., & Ysseldyke, J. E. (2000). *Assessment in special education and inclusive education* (8th ed.). Boston: Houghton Mifflin.

Sattler, J. M. (2002). *Assessment of children: Behavioral and clinical applications* (4th ed.). San Diego, CA: Author.

Schmitz, C., Staab, S., Studer, R., Stumme, G., & Tane, J. (2002). *Accessing distributed learning repositories through a courseware watchdog.* Norfolk, VA: Association of the Advancement of Computing in Education.

Schneider, R. M., & Krajcik, J. (1999). *The role of educative curriculum materials in reforming science education.* (ERIC Document Reproduction Service No. ED445889)

Schoenlein, J. (2001). Making a huge school feel smaller. *Educational Leadership, 58*(6), 28–30.

Scott-Stein, M., & Thorkildsen, R. J. (1999). *Parent involvement in education: Insights and applications from research.* Bloomington, IN: Phi Delta Kappa.

Sitlington, P. L., & Clark, G. M. (2005). *Transition education and services for adolescents with disabilities.* Boston: Allyn & Bacon.

Sitlington, P., Frank, A., & Carson, R. (1993). Adult adjustment among graduates with mild disabilities. *Exceptional Children, 59,* 221–233.

Smith, M. A., & Schloss, P. J. (1988). Teaching to transition. In P. J. Schloss, C. A. Hughes, & M. A. Smith (Eds.), *Community integration for persons with mental retardation* (pp. 1–16). Austin, TX: PRO-ED.

Smith, S. W. (1990). Individualized Education Programs (IEPs) in special education: From intent to acquiescence. *Exceptional Children, 57,* 6–14.

Spady, W. G. (1986). The emerging paradigm of organizational excellence: Success through planned adaptability. *Peabody Journal of Education, 63*(3), 67–72.

Spady, W. G., & Marshall, K. J. (1991). Beyond traditional outcome-based education. *Educational Leadership, 49*(2), 67–72.

Sparrow, S. S., Cicchetti, D. V., & Balla, D. A. (2005). *Vineland–II Adaptive Behavior Scales.* Circle Pines, MN: American Guidance Service.

Spinelli, C. G. (2002). *Classroom assessment for students with special needs in inclusive settings.* Upper Saddle River, NJ: Prentice Hall.

Strickland, B. B., & Turnbull, A. P. (1990). *Developing and implementing individualized educational programs* (3rd ed.). New York: Macmillan.

Synatschk, K., Clark, G. M., Patton, J. R., & Copeland, R. (2007). *Informal assessments for transition: Career planning and employment.* Austin, TX: PRO-ED.

Taylor, G. (2000). *Parental involvement: A practical guide for collaboration and teamwork for students with disabilities.* Springfield, IL: Charles C. Thomas.

Taylor, L., & Adelman, H. S. (2000). Connecting schools, families, and communities. *Professional School Counseling, 2*(5), 298–307.

Taylor, R. (2003). *Assessment of exceptional students: Educational and psychological procedures* (6th ed.). Boston: Allyn & Bacon.

Thier, H. D. (2001). *Developing inquiry-based science materials: A guide for educators.* Williston, VT: Teachers College Press.

Tomlinson, C. A. (2000). Reconcilable difference? Standards-based teaching and differentiation. *Educational Leadership, 58*(1), 6–11.

Tomlinson, C. A. (2001a). *At work in the differentiated classroom: Facilitator's guide.* Alexandria, VA: Association for Supervision and Curriculum Development.

Tomlinson, C. A. (2001b). *How to differentiate instruction in mixed-ability classrooms* (2nd ed.). Alexandria, VA: Association for Supervision and Curriculum Development.

U.S. Department of Education. (1994). *Sixteenth annual report to Congress on the implementation of the Individuals with Disabilities Education Act.* Washington, DC: Office of Special Education Programs, Office of Special Education and Rehabilitative Services.

U.S. Department of Education. (2004). *Twenty-sixth annual report to Congress on the implementation of the Individuals with Disabilities Education Act.* Washington, DC: Office of Special Education Programs, Office of Special Education and Rehabilitative Services.

Wagner, J. O. (1999). *Locating vocational educational materials.* Office of Educational Research and Improvement. (ERIC Document Reproduction Service No. ED435837)

Wagner, M. (1991). *Dropouts with disabilities: What do we know? What can we do?* Menlo Park, CA: SRI International.

Wagner, M., Blackorby, J., Cameto, R., Hebbeler, K., & Newman, L. (1993). *The transition experiences of young people with disabilities: A summary of findings from the National Longitudinal Transition Study of special education students.* Menlo Park, CA: SRI International.

Wehman, P. (2001). *Life beyond the classroom: Transition strategies for young people with disabilities.* Baltimore: Brookes.

Wehman, P., & Kregel, J. (2004). *Functional curriculum for elementary, middle, and secondary age students with special needs.* Austin, TX: PRO-ED.

Wenz-Gross, M., Anderson, K. L., Parker, R. C., O'Meara, A., & Carreiro King, I. (2002). *Moving to middle school: Life skills and coping skills for successful student transition.* Austin, TX: PRO-ED.

White, W., Alley, G., Deshler, D., Schumaker, J., Warner, M., & Clark, F. (1982). Are there learning disabilities after high school? *Exceptional Children, 49,* 273–274.

Wilcox, B. (1988). Identifying programming goals for community participation. In B. Ludlow, A. Turnbull, & R. Luckasson (Eds.), *Transitions to adult life for people with mental retardation* (pp. 119–135). Baltimore: Brookes.

Williams, J., & Deal-Reynolds, T. (1993). Courting controversy: How to build interdisciplinary units. *Educational Leadership 50*(7), 13–15.

Willis, S. (1995). Refocusing the curriculum: making interdisciplinary efforts work. *Education Update, 37*(1), 1, 3, 8.

Wittreich, Y. M., Jacobi, E. F., & Hogue, I. E. (2000). *Getting parents involved: A handbook of ideas for teachers, schools, and communities.* Norwood, MA: Christopher-Gordon.

Wolk, S. (2001). The benefits of exploratory time. *Educational Leadership, 59*(2), 56–59.

Wood, J. (1992). *Adapting instruction for mainstreamed and at-risk students.* New York: Macmillan.

Ziegler, W. (2000). Venturing beyond the schoolyard to bring parents in. *High School Magazine, 7*(5), 22–25.

ABOUT THE AUTHORS

Mary E. Cronin is a professor of Special Education and Habilitative Services at the University of New Orleans. She has experience in teaching students at the preschool, elementary, middle, and secondary special needs levels. Her current interests include teacher training, inclusive education, life skills program development, and transition issues for students with mild disabilities. Dr. Cronin received her BA from Avila College, her MEd from the University of Kansas, and PhD from the University of Texas at Austin.

James R. Patton is currently an independent consultant and adjunct associate professor in the Department of Special Education at the University of Texas at Austin. He formerly was a special education teacher, having taught students with special needs at the elementary, secondary, and postsecondary levels of schooling. He has written books, chapters, articles, and tests in the area of special education. Dr. Patton's current areas of professional interest are the assessment of transition strengths and needs of students, the infusion of real-life content into existing curricula, life skills instruction, study skills instruction, behavioral intervention planning, and the accommodation of students with special needs in inclusive settings.

Susan J. Wood is with the Rhode Island Department of Education, Office of Special Populations. She directs Rhode Island's focused monitoring system for special education programs and services. She has both extensive teaching and administrative experience. Her research interests include positive behavioral supports, self-management techniques, program assessment and evaluation, life skills instruction, and transition issues. Dr. Wood earned a BS in elementary education, a BA in psychology and an MEd in special education from Boston University. She has an MEd in educational administration and a PhD from the University of New Orleans.